IMAGES
of America

WILLCOX

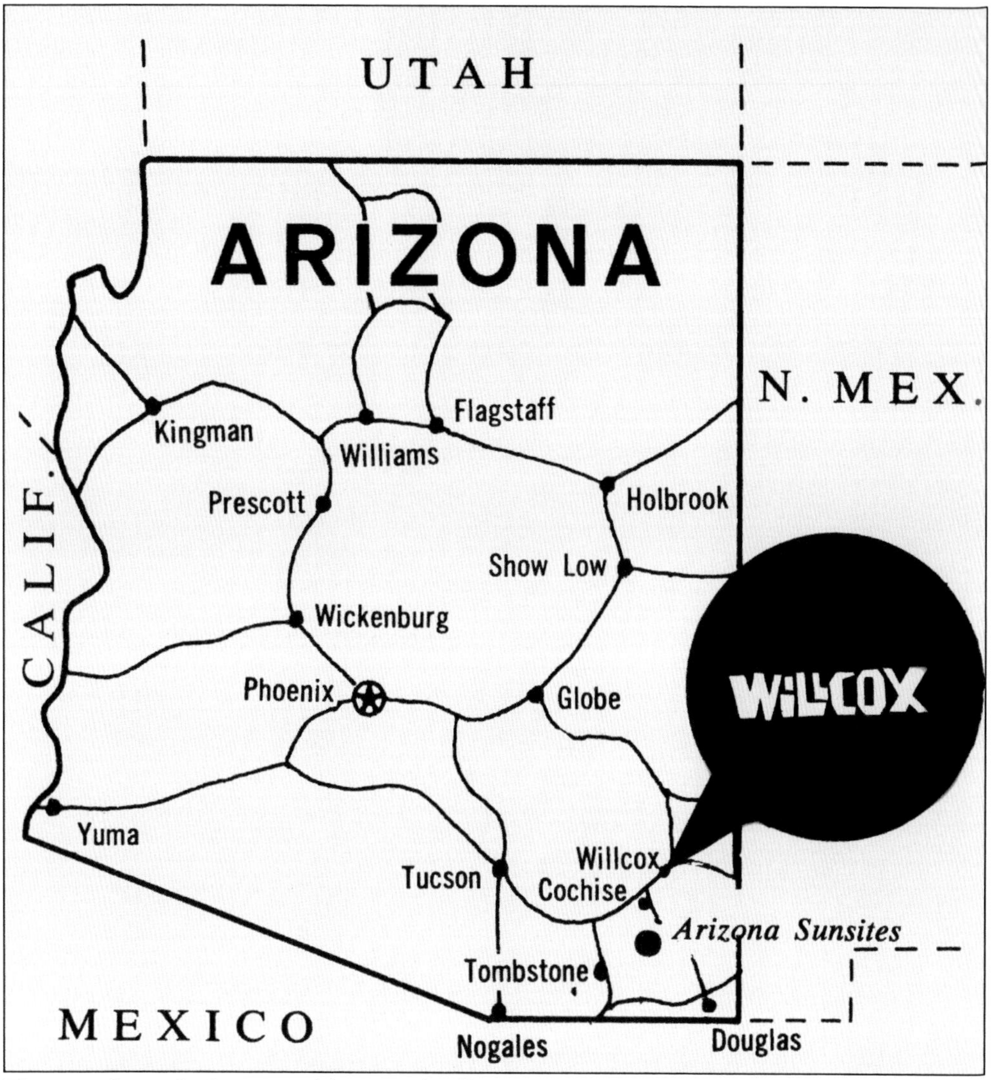

This map shows the location of the city of Willcox, Arizona, just off Interstate 10, in the southeast corner of the state. At an elevation of 4,167 feet, it is surrounded by beautiful mountain ranges (Sulphur Springs Valley Historical Society.)

On the Cover: Frank Rottman's store, as seen from the interior about 1918, was located at 107 East Maley Street. Frank Rottman, first man on the left, came to Willcox in 1909. He operated Frank's Court Motel, started in 1957 on Haskell Avenue, and was a partner in the Reilly-Rottman Funeral Home on Maley Street behind the drugstore. (Sulphur Springs Valley Historical Society.)

IMAGES
of America

WILLCOX

Kathy Klump and Peta-Anne Tenney for the
Sulphur Springs Valley Historical Society

ARCADIA
PUBLISHING

ISBN 978-0-7385-7177-5

Published by Arcadia Publishing
Charleston, South Carolina

Printed in the United States of America

Library of Congress Control Number: 2009923819

For all general information contact Arcadia Publishing at:
Telephone 843-853-2070
Fax 843-853-0044
E-mail sales@arcadiapublishing.com
For customer service and orders:
Toll-Free 1-888-313-2665

Visit us on the Internet at www.arcadiapublishing.com

To Mark Simmons, whose contagious enthusiasm for local history, amazing memory for names and dates, plus years of research made this book possible.

Contents

ACKNOWLEDGMENTS

We are indebted to the founding members of the Sulphur Springs Valley Historical Society, including Mary Leighton and Dorman Brown. Through their efforts, the artifacts and archives began to be collected, a historic district was formed, and the buildings were restored. We appreciate the volunteers over the years who have helped in our mission to collect, preserve, and exhibit the history of Willcox and the surrounding area. To our current members and to all those who have made donations to us over the years, we thank you. Coresearchers Mark Simmons and Brad Smith make local history exciting and have added a tremendous amount of materials for the research library.

We wish to thank Denise Lundin and staff of the Cochise County Superior Court, Christine Rhodes and staff of the County Recorder's Office, Carrie Gustavson and Annie Larkin of the Bisbee Mining and Historical Museum, the Arizona Historical Society, and the University of Arizona Special Collections Library for always being gracious in helping us with our research.

Unless otherwise noted, all images appearing in this book were provided from the collections of the Sulphur Springs Valley Historical Society.

Many wonderful photographs were brought to us by families with ties to Willcox. Thanks to Linda Torres for the Lundquist family photographs, Betty Kowalczyk and Wanda Linam Perry for the Lula Briscoe collection, Sandy Thomas, and many others as noted by each courtesy line.

We wish to thank our editor at Arcadia Publishing, Jared Jackson, for his expert guidance and keeping us on track for our deadlines. Also, thanks to the *Arizona Range News* for providing us with the original newspapers, which were an important asset in researching our stories. We also appreciate the use of the business directories provided by Arizona token collector Peter N. Spooner.

Finally, to our husbands, Todd Tenney and Keith Klump, thank you for all your encouragement and support.

INTRODUCTION

Before Willcox was born, the Sulphur Springs Valley was home to the Apache Indians. After years of conflict, the Chiricahua Indian Reservation, which included the Willcox area, was established with Tom Jeffords as agent. The famous Chief Cochise died in 1874. In 1876, the reservation was returned to public domain, and the Chiricahua were moved to the San Carlos Reservation. Hostilities with the Apaches continued until 1886, when Geronimo surrendered.

As the Southern Pacific Railroad made its way across the West, tent cities were put up along the route for the crews building the tracks. Willcox, Arizona, started just that way with tents for the laborers, who were mostly Chinese. W. W. Moriarity stopped here in 1877 and became part of the grading contractors. His crew called it Sour Dough Camp. It was later named Maley after Robert and James Maley, who owned the land for the railroad right-of-way. A post office was established for the town of Maley on September 13, 1880, with John F. Roll as postmaster.

The first train arrived in August 1880. On board was Gen. Orlando B. Willcox, well respected for his military operations in the Civil War and the Indian Wars. Legend has it that the people wanted the train to stop here so they could meet the general, and the crowd began shouting, "Willcox, Willcox, Willcox." The next day, a reporter of a Tucson newspaper wrote that there was a new town named Willcox. However, in the *Arizona Weekly Star* of September 9, 1880, it states: "Sulphur Spring Valley, situated between Benson and San Simion [*sic*], will probably become quite a business point. It will be the depot for Forts Grant and Bowie, and the distributing point for the entire valley in which it is situated. Large warehouses will be erected by the Government and private companies, and altogether Sulphur Spring Valley has a prosperous future in view. The S.P.R.R. Co. has named the new station Wilcox."

The post office was changed to Wilcox on October 19, 1880. The mistake in spelling was corrected to Willcox on November 23, 1889.

The first child born here was the son of Anthony and Mary Powers, who owned the Arizona Hotel, the first hotel in Willcox. General Willcox presented a silver cup with the general's initials to the boy, and he was named Willcox Powers.

The redwood depot was built in 1881. It is the last of the Southern Pacific depots built between 1879 and 1881 to remain standing. It was restored and became city hall in 1998. Following the depot, adobe and frame business buildings and houses were quickly constructed. By 1884, the population had reached 500 citizens. Willcox became the major distribution center for supplies for the military, the booming mining towns, and the huge cattle ranches. Freighters and their teams departed from here to such destinations as Fort Grant, San Carlos, Globe, Camp Thomas, Fort Bowie, and Dos Cabezas. These were very long, arduous, and sometimes dangerous sojourns, as renegade Apaches were still in the area.

Application for a town site was filed October 1, 1881. Residents could then apply for legal title to the lots on which they had built their homes and businesses. The price per lot was between $5 and $30, depending on the extent of improvement. Lots were set aside for public squares, schools, churches, and a cemetery divided into Protestant and Catholic areas. John H. Norton and Madison Stewart bought up all the lots that were not claimed. The town continued to grow and prosper as families moved in and schools and churches were built.

The merchants did extremely well in Willcox with their lumber stores and general merchandise. Many of them expanded to branch stores in surrounding towns. Oysters shipped on ice would often be served at social events. There was also the rough element that frequented the saloons and red-light district, and many a man's life was cut short by a bullet.

For many years, Willcox shipped more cattle from the open range than anywhere in the United States. In the six-month period from January to June 1896, approximately 25,000 head of cattle were shipped from here by rail. In 1893, an experimental farm was started in Willcox. Planted were 300 fruit trees, fruits and berries, 2 acres of potatoes, wheat, barley, and onions. This began an agricultural movement into the surrounding area. Barbed wire started breaking up the huge ranches as homesteaders moved in. Agriculture has since played a huge part in sustaining the Willcox economy.

As Arizona prepared for statehood, C. O. Anderson, a local attorney and newspaper editor, spearheaded the effort to form the Arizona Rangers to rid the territory of the cattle rustlers and lawless element. In 1908, the Willcox Board of Trade was organized to publicize and promote the town. The board grew to 65 members and also took up such matters as improving sanitation and developing new water supplies.

In 1915, Willcox incorporated. A mayor and city council were elected, and the first ordinances were passed. A new pride was felt in the community. Several new businesses were established up through the early 1920s. Then the Depression and a severe drought caused many businesses to file bankruptcy. In 1939, Willcox finally began to grow again. That year, about 30 new homes were built and many more were remodeled or enlarged. The paving of the highway through Stein's Pass, on the New Mexico border, brought many new people, and motor courts, hotels, and gas stations flourished. World War II brought with it a shortage of materials, though, and building came to a standstill.

Since the 1950s, the town has continued to grow and prosper. In 1969, downtown Willcox suffered a severe blow when Interstate 10 routed the traffic around the town. Not to be discouraged, the townspeople have preserved the original buildings with businesses and museums occupying this historic area. A new business center has developed near the interstate. Willcox has gone from a one-stoplight town to five stoplights, from a five-and-dime store to shopping centers and truck stops. Our town population has now reached 3,885, and our service area is 15,000.

One

A New Town on the Tracks

Willcox would not exist if the Southern Pacific Railroad had not chosen this exact spot to build their new depot in 1881. Before the first train arrived in Willcox in August 1880 carrying Gen. Orlando B. Willcox, services were needed for the work crews. Tents were set up for housing and one for a commissary owned by H. B. Cook. It was sold on January 10, 1883, to Gung Yow, the first Chinese property owner mentioned in the deed books. The Chinese shanties were located on Haskell Avenue in the middle of Block 25 and Block 30 on properties owned by Young Sick, Kwong Hing, Hom Fou, and Lay Chung. By 1894, there were four Chinese businesses in town.

The first land claims in 1880 were noted by lettered blocks A–F from a survey done by R. B. Kelley. The town site map surveyed by Theodore F. White assigned each block the number still used today. Early settlers were setting up businesses. Hotels, saloons, mercantiles, lumber companies, blacksmiths, a bakery, and forwarding agents such as J. Liberman and Company were already in place by 1883.

The first Hispanics were Estevan Ochoa of Tully and Ochoa; Juan Ochoa and Joaquin Montoya, blacksmiths; M. C. Samaniego; and Juan and Isabel Martinez. Many were freighters such as Yginio Aguirre, who contracted with the Globe smelter to haul coal from Willcox to Globe. Women who made their mark early in the business world here were Mary Powers, owner of the Arizona Hotel; Elizabeth Davis, owner of the Eureka House; Nellie Pettyjohn, property owner on Railroad Avenue; Van Ella Macy, milliner and owner of Macy's Hotel; Rosa Johnson, madam; Emma Chase, lady barber; Mrs. R. V. Jones, fashionable dressmaker; and Helen Weber, who purchased the Arizona Hotel, the Eureka House, and two blacksmith shops in town.

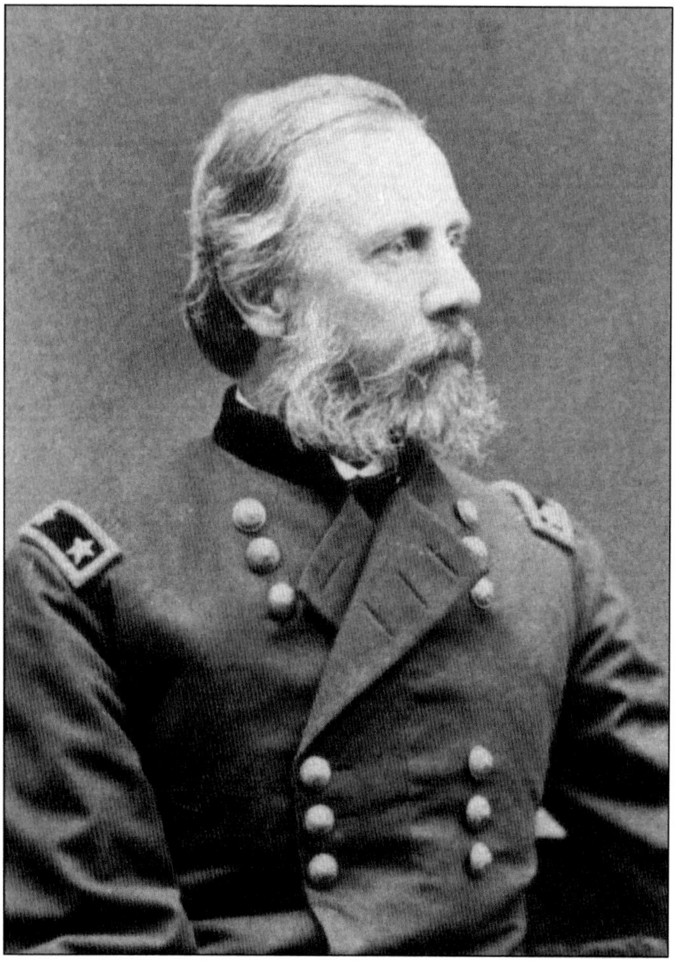

The town's namesake, Gen. Orlando B. Willcox, commander of the Department of Arizona from February 1878 to September 1882, admired the American Indian and sought a peaceful approach to problems at the reservation. The Apaches were close to starving and continuing to escape. His swift reaction to outbreaks made it possible for 576 miles of railroad to be peacefully laid and for rich mining areas to be peacefully developed.

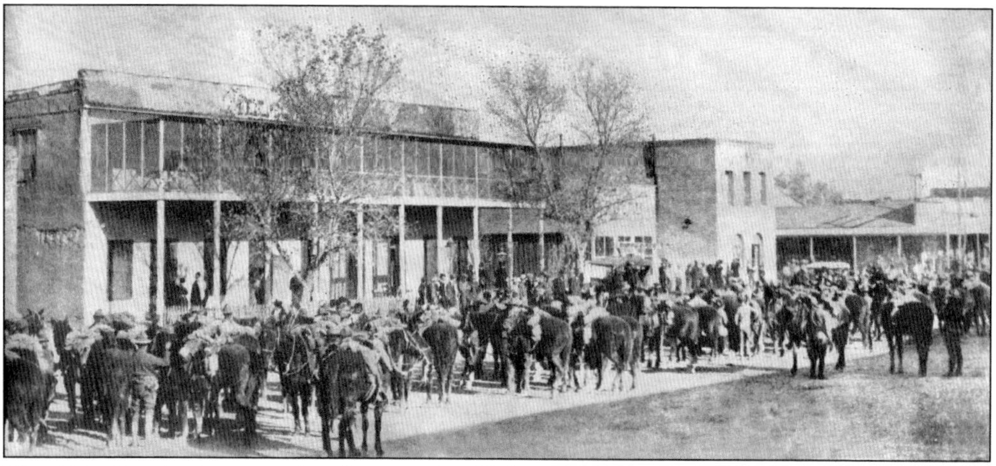

The 14th Cavalry is pictured in front of the Willcox Hotel on Railroad Avenue en route from Fort Huachuca to Fort Grant and Fort Apache. The military contributed greatly to the economy of the region and provided a very important role in protecting the settlers, allowing the area to grow and prosper during the time of the Apache.

This familiar photograph of government scout and interpreter Mickey Free was taken in Willcox in 1885. His abduction as a young boy started the Apache wars, when Chief Cochise was wrongfully accused as his captor. This led to the famous Bascom Affair, where several members of Cochise's family were killed and the tribe retaliated.

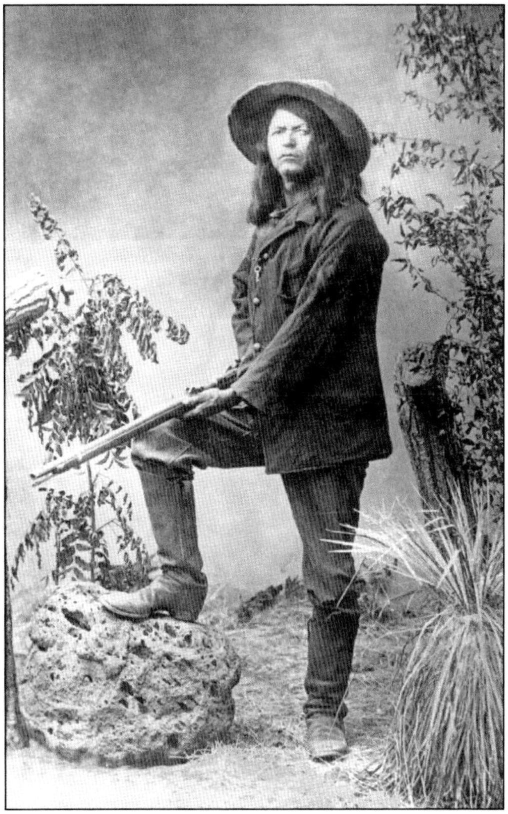

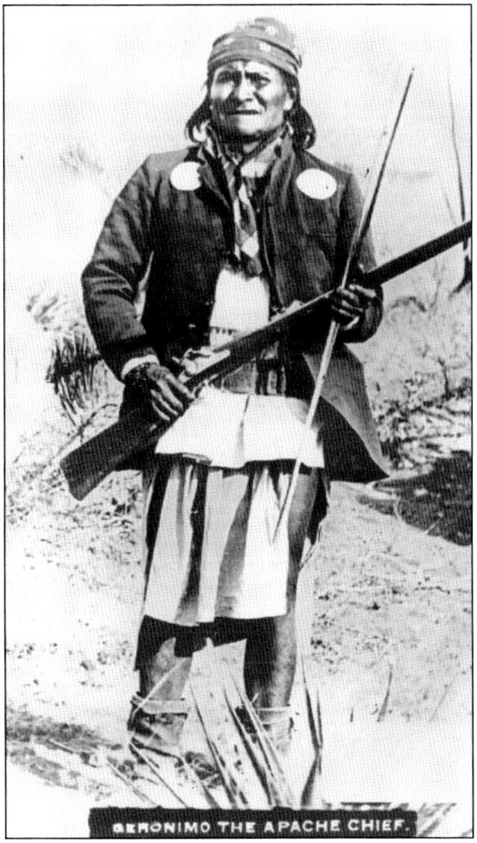

Geronimo, warrior, medicine man, and leader of the renegade Apaches, roamed and raided throughout southeast Arizona until he and his tribe surrendered in September 1886. Stories say he bought sugar in 1-pound packages at the Norton-Morgan Commercial Store. Photographer C. S. Fly took the only known photographs of American Indians in the field of war.

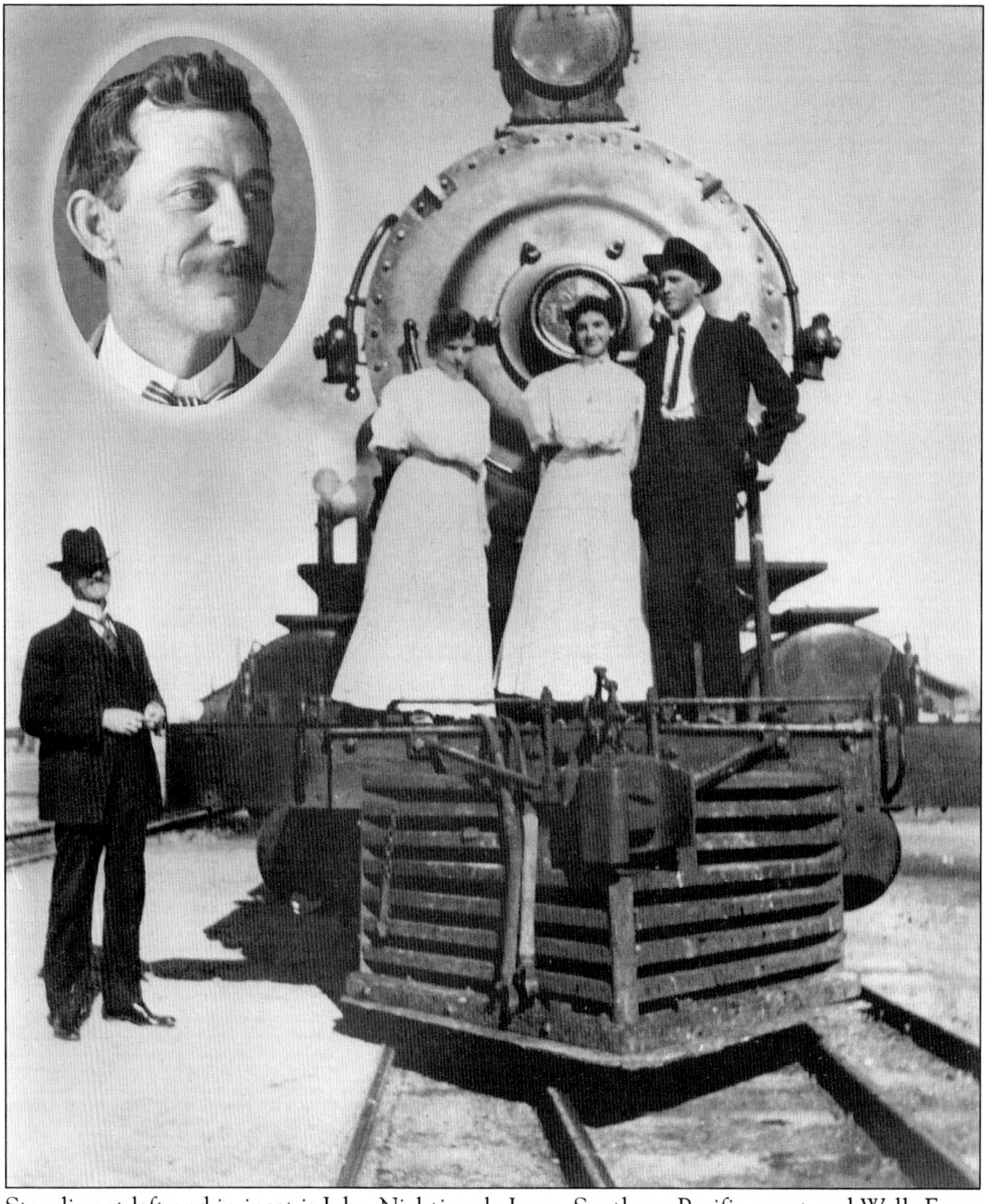

Standing at left and in inset is John Nightingale Lean, Southern Pacific agent and Wells Fargo express man from 1892 to 1904. His wife, Irene, succeeded him until 1912. From left to right, Laura Parks, Adelina Soto, and Harry Parks are standing on the train. Very few photographs of early Willcox would exist if not for Harry Parks and his camera. (Arizona Historical Society; inset photograph by Willcox Masonic Lodge.)

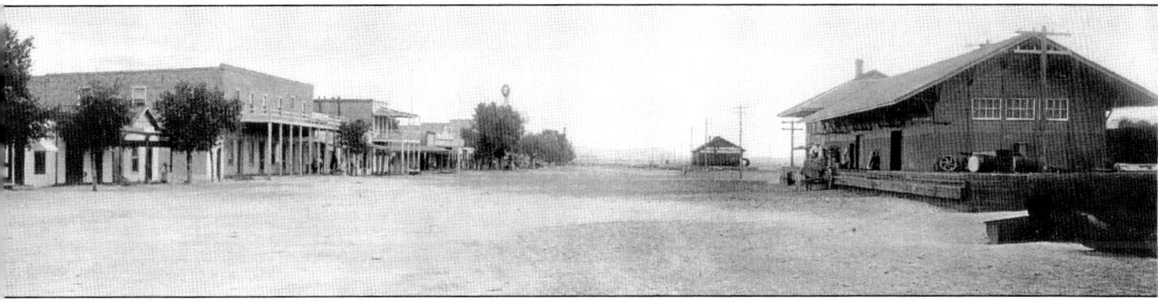

The main street of Willcox was photographed facing north on Railroad Avenue in 1890. For many years, it was called Front Street. The Willcox Hotel is on the left, and the Southern Pacific Depot is on the right. The Union Ice Company, owned by John Corbett, is in the distance on the right.

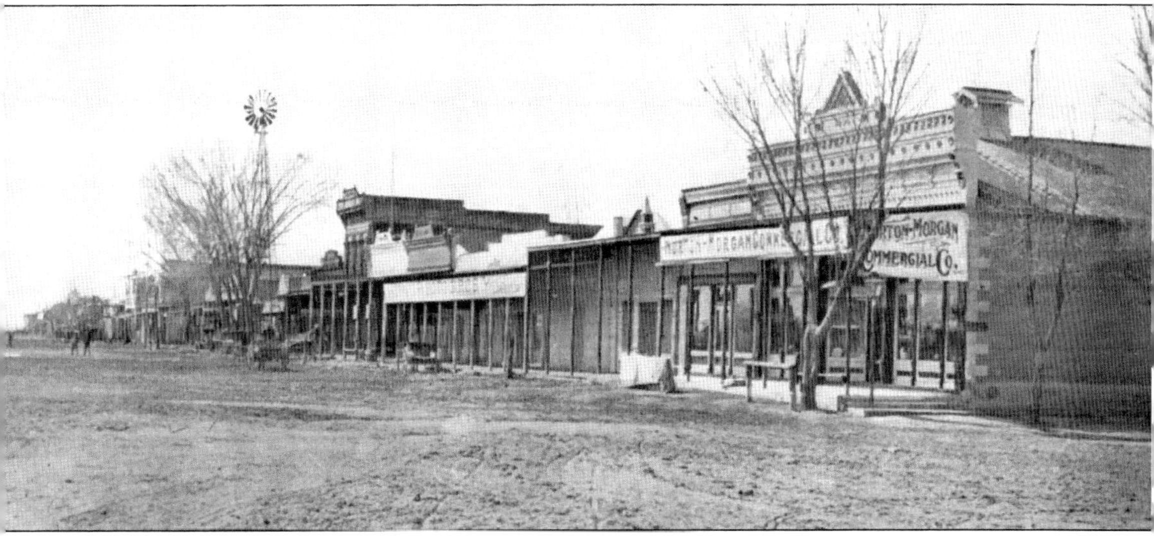

Facing south from the other end of Railroad Avenue, the Norton-Morgan Commercial Company is seen on the corner of Stewart Street. The businesses were all on the west side of the street. Looking south, other businesses included Soto Brothers, saloons, a meat market, and hotels.

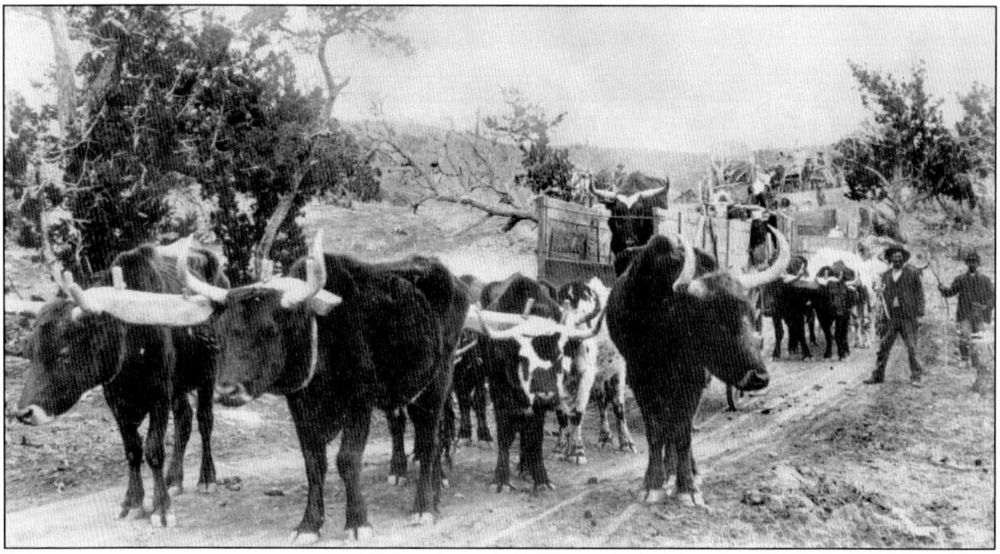

Joe Busenbark, a carpenter and teamster, and his son Charles are walking alongside the bull team used to transport supplies to the San Carlos Reservation. This photograph was taken near Fort Thomas on the return trip to Willcox in 1882. Instead of riding in a saddle, bullwhackers, as men who drove ox teams were called, trudged along on foot using an ox goad to keep the animals moving.

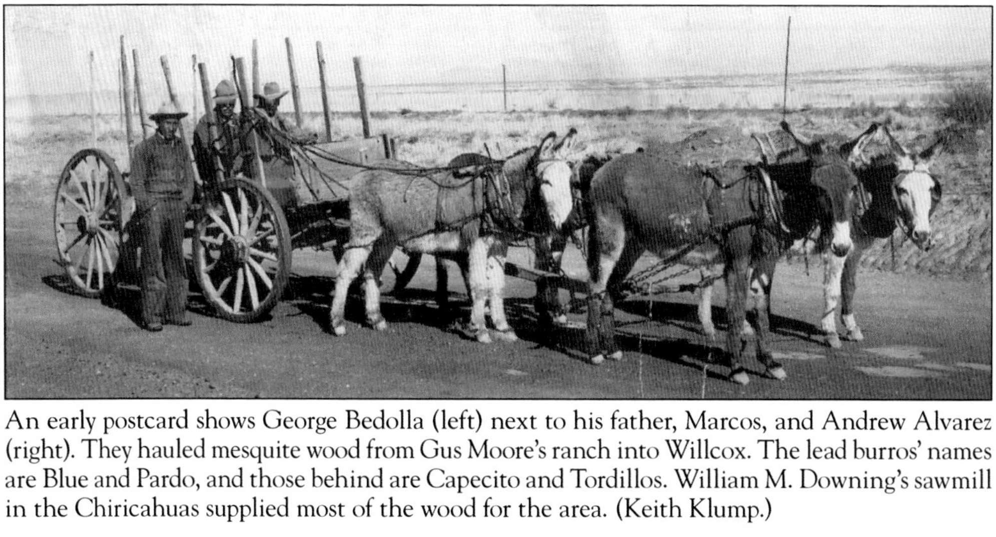

An early postcard shows George Bedolla (left) next to his father, Marcos, and Andrew Alvarez (right). They hauled mesquite wood from Gus Moore's ranch into Willcox. The lead burros' names are Blue and Pardo, and those behind are Capecito and Tordillos. William M. Downing's sawmill in the Chiricahuas supplied most of the wood for the area. (Keith Klump.)

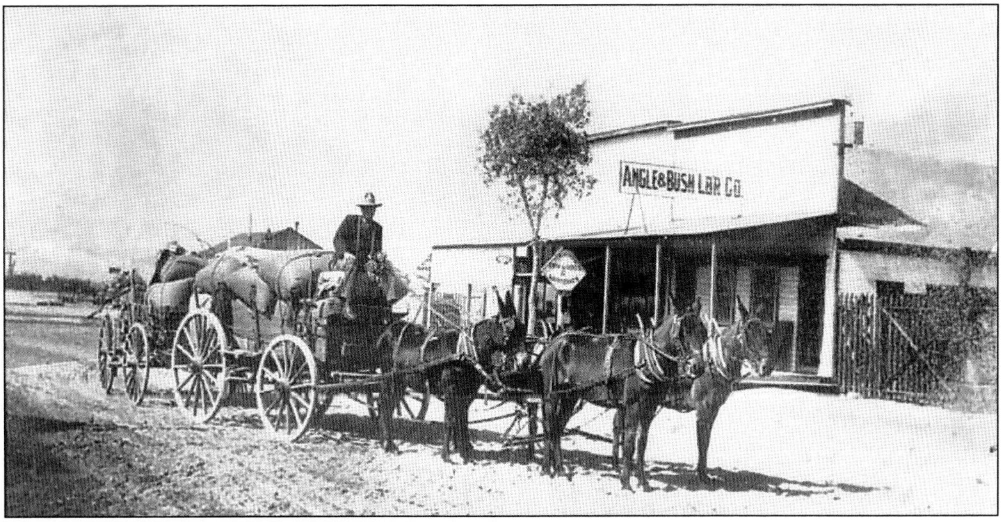

Nathan Orson Tenney brings his mule team and wagons loaded with mohair into Willcox around 1912. He married Myrtle Mary Wear and raised a family of 10 at Sunset. The Angle and Bush Lumber Company and the A. I. McAllister Dry Goods and Groceries (on sign) were on Maley Street. McAllister also ran a saloon with A. I. Rose on Railroad Avenue in the early years. (Tenney family.)

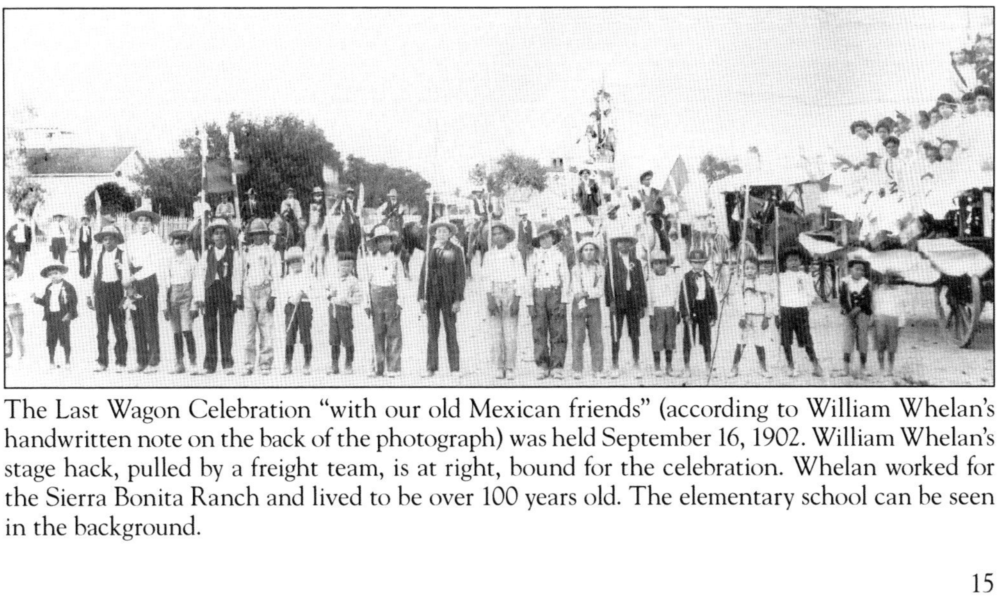

The Last Wagon Celebration "with our old Mexican friends" (according to William Whelan's handwritten note on the back of the photograph) was held September 16, 1902. William Whelan's stage hack, pulled by a freight team, is at right, bound for the celebration. Whelan worked for the Sierra Bonita Ranch and lived to be over 100 years old. The elementary school can be seen in the background.

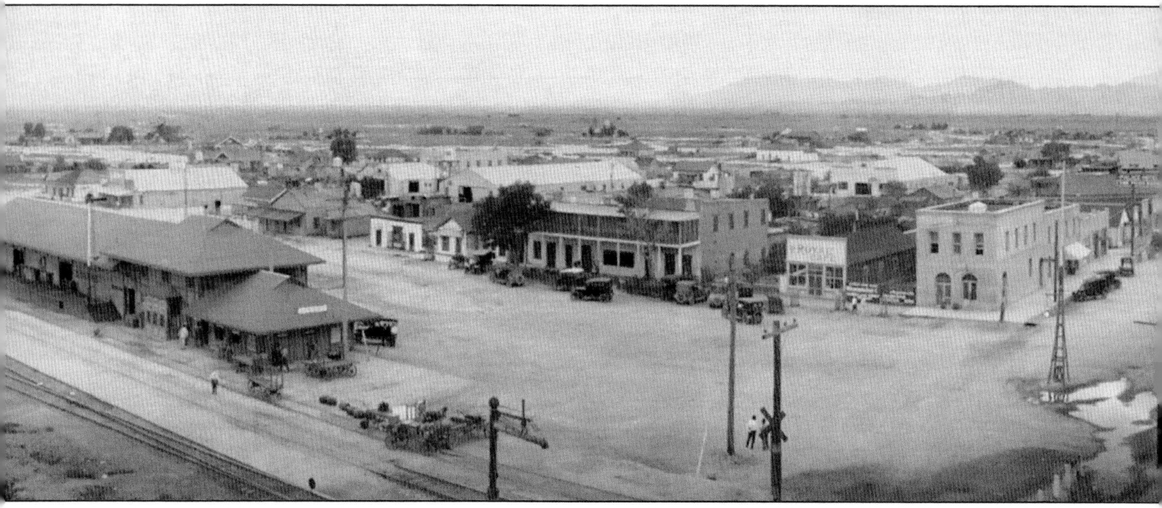

Even by 1920, the majority of businesses were located on Blocks 30 and 31 on Railroad Avenue and one block of Maley Street, which divided the two blocks. At left is the depot. Across the street are the Nicholson house, Dr. Wilson's office, the Willcox Hotel, and the Royal Café. The old Masonic building is on the corner, with the Palace Hotel down the street on Maley. On the

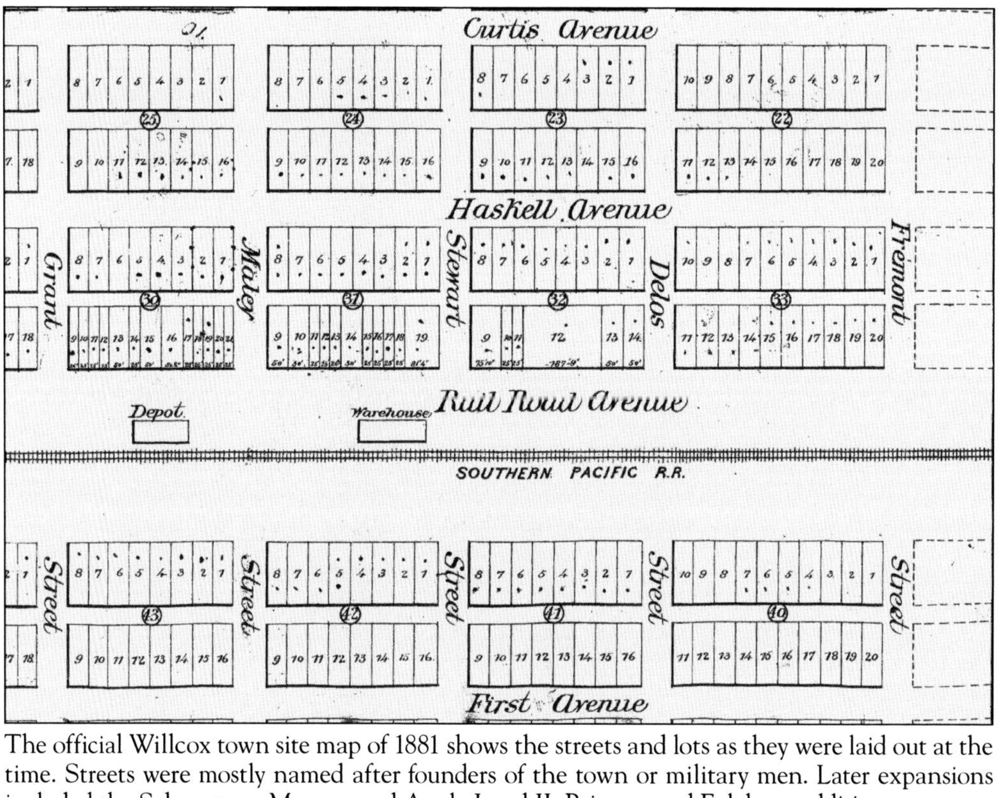

The official Willcox town site map of 1881 shows the streets and lots as they were laid out at the time. Streets were mostly named after founders of the town or military men. Later expansions included the Schwertner, Morgan and Angle I and II, Briscoe, and Fulghum additions.

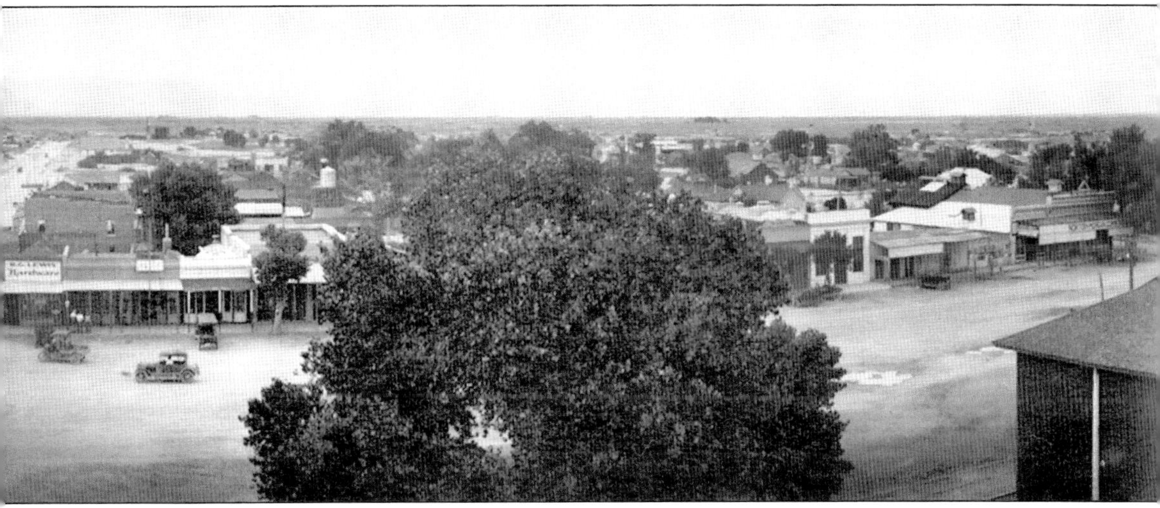

opposite corner, in the old Headquarters Saloon building, are R. G. Lewis Hardware, then the barbershop and the drugstore. The tall, white building is the Willcox Bank and Trust, and at the end is the Norton-Morgan Commercial Store. (Arizona Historical Society.)

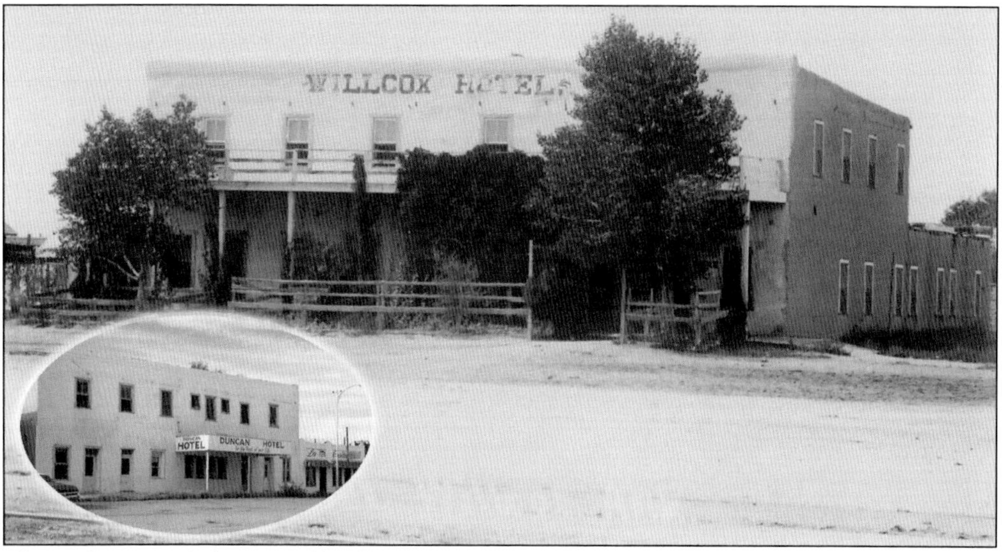

The Willcox Hotel, the second building constructed in Willcox after the depot, was located across the street from the depot. Built in 1881 by James Campbell, it burned in 1885 and was rebuilt in 1886 by Mr. and Mrs. McNulty. W. R. McComb was owner in 1900, when Johnny Boyett took two guns from behind the counter to kill Warren Earp. Renamed the Duncan Hotel in 1941, it was torn down in 1976.

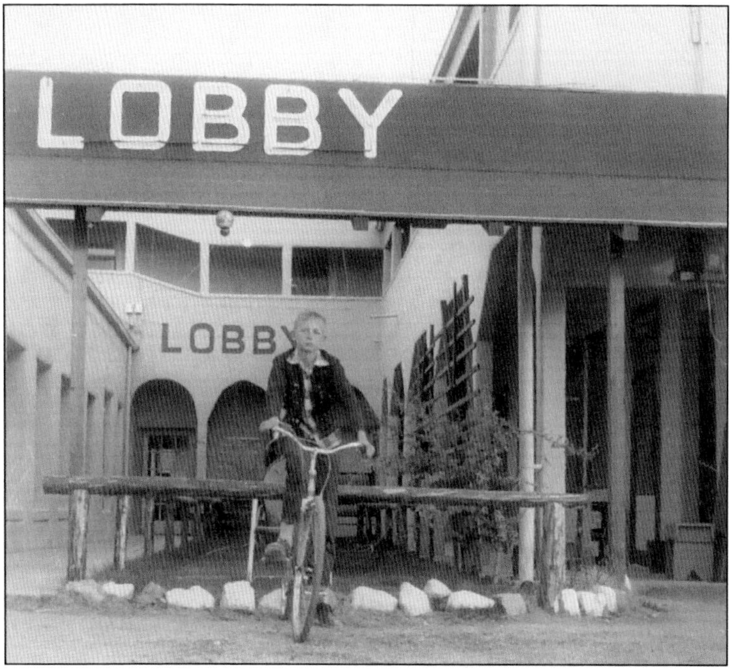

Leon Hansen rides his bike at the rear entrance to the lobby of the Duncan Hotel. Leon's mother, Lillie Hansen, began working for Paul Duncan in the 1940s, and Leon loved to hang around and listen to the old-timers tell tales. The south side of the patio was a two-story structure with hotel rooms, and the one-story north side was the manager's apartment. (Hansen family.)

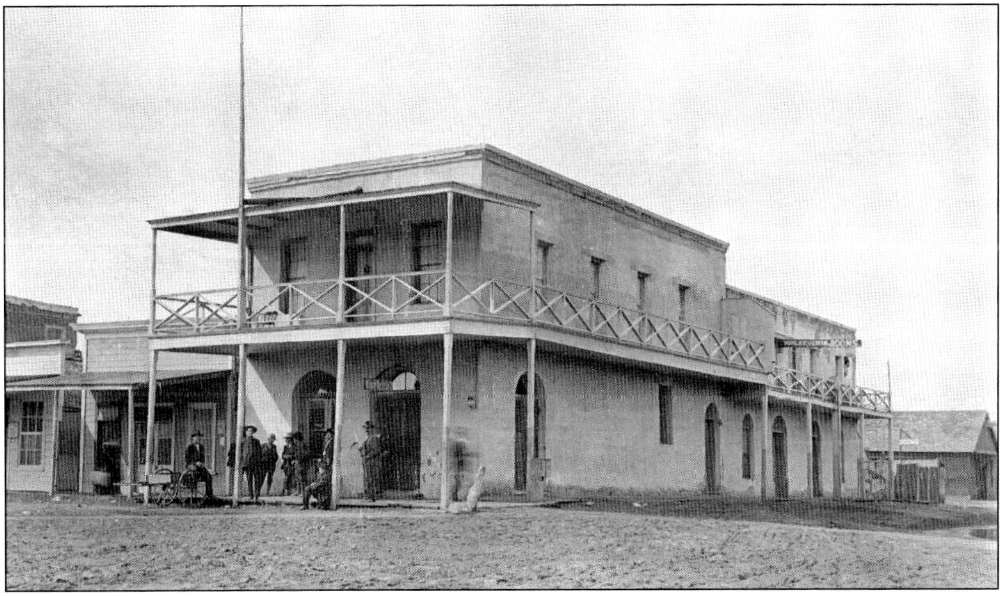

The AOUW (Ancient Order of United Workmen) Hall, known as the Willcox House, was built in 1891 by John C. Fall on the corner of Railroad Avenue and Maley Street. It was the home of Willcox Lodge No. 10 Free and Accepted Masons from June 1, 1891, to 1917. The post office was located there from 1897 to 1917, and Mrs. Severin had rooms for rent. The two-story Poindexter Building with a lodging house upstairs predated this structure. (Arizona Historical Society.)

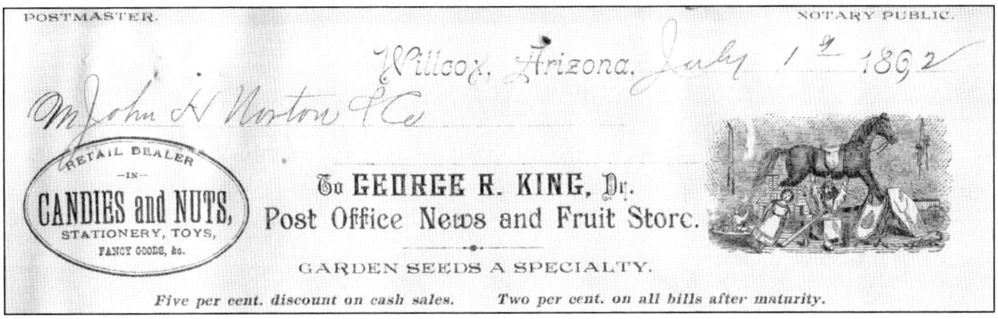

POSTMASTER. NOTARY PUBLIC.

Willcox, Arizona, July 1st 1892

M John H Norton & Co

RETAIL DEALER
—IN—
CANDIES and NUTS,
STATIONERY, TOYS,
FANCY GOODS, &c.

To GEORGE R. KING, Dr.
Post Office News and Fruit Store.

GARDEN SEEDS A SPECIALTY.

Five per cent. discount on cash sales. Two per cent. on all bills after maturity.

George R. King served as postmaster from October 2, 1883, to August 21, 1897, when the post office was located in the King Building between Maley and Stewart Streets. As indicated by this 1891 invoice, the post office was also a newsstand and fruit store. To augment to his salary, George was awarded the county contract in 1894 to bury the indigent dead at $18 each.

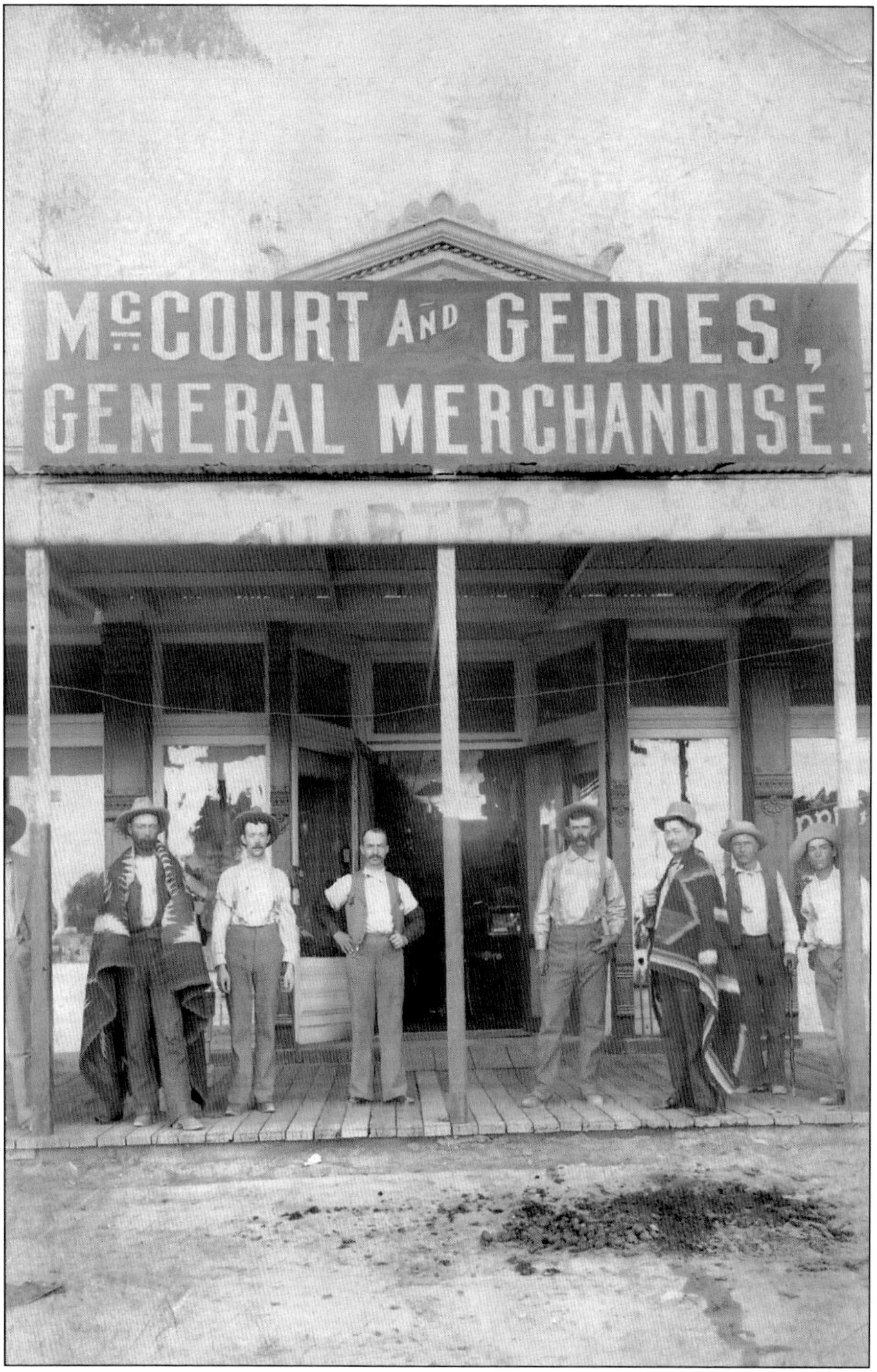

Laurence V. McCourt, after whom McCourt Street is named, and Samuel J. Geddes, postmaster from 1897 to 1903, opened their general merchandise store in March 1897 on Railroad Avenue. Fred E. Cadwell, the main builder in town, erected a new structure with an iron front in 1898. Pictured fourth from left is Dave Drew, owner of the nearby meat market. McCourt and Geddes declared bankruptcy in December 1903.

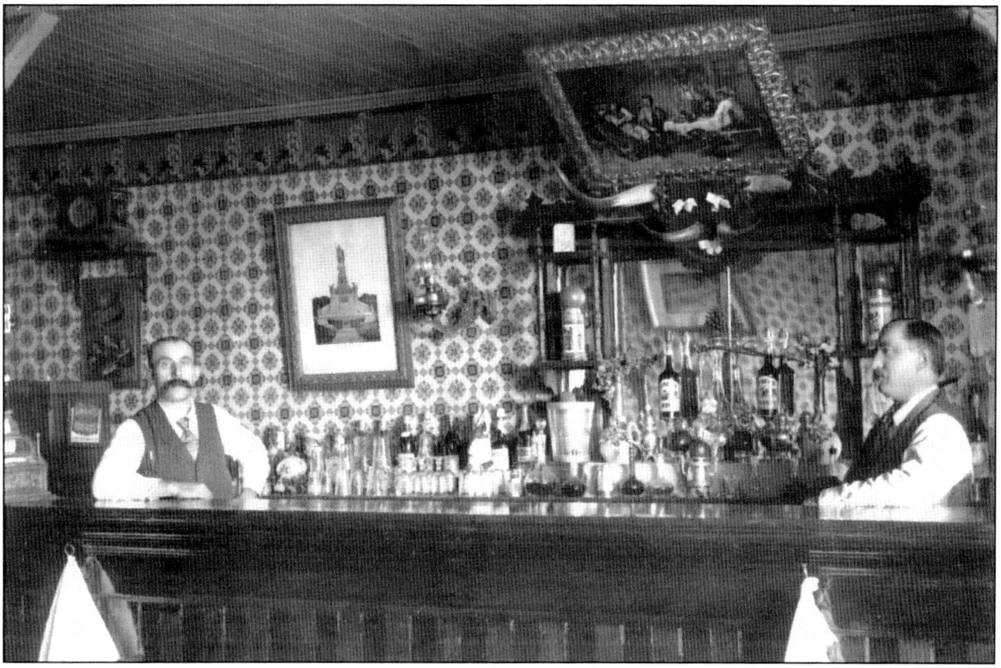

Josef Schwertner, left, tends bar in his Schley Saloon, formerly known as George Raum's Fashion Saloon. At one time, he painted it bright yellow. Prohibition forced him to turn it into a grocery store, which he ran until 1927. The first saloon known to be at this site was the Patagonia Saloon run by James Waters. The Rex Allen Museum is now at this location.

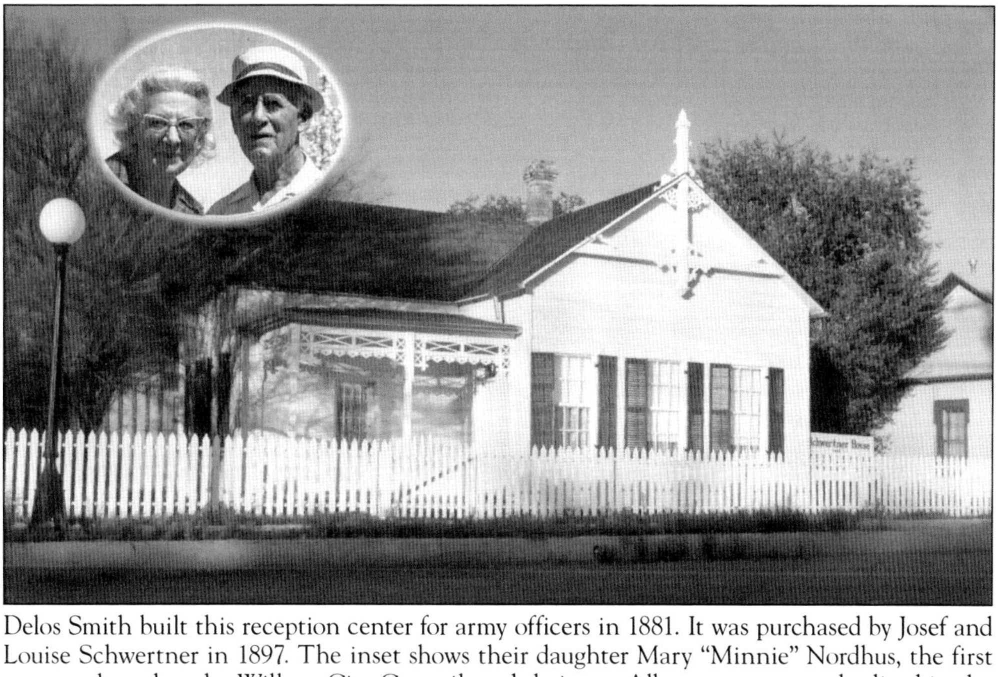

Delos Smith built this reception center for army officers in 1881. It was purchased by Josef and Louise Schwertner in 1897. The inset shows their daughter Mary "Minnie" Nordhus, the first woman elected to the Willcox City Council, and their son Albert, a surveyor who lived in the house until 1983. Deeded to the Sulphur Springs Valley Historical Society, the house and outside kitchen have been restored.

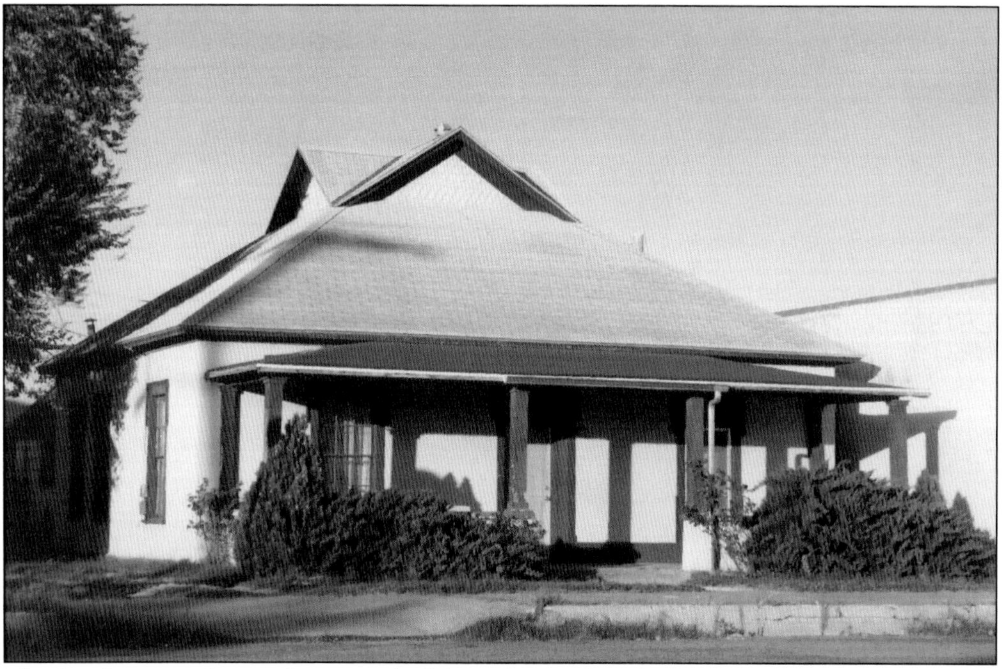

The Soto house on Stewart Street was built by Delos Smith and sold by Edward Baron and his wife to Pablo and Amelia Soto in April 1884. This adobe structure was later used as Theilan Ridge's accounting firm and Dr. Havemeyer's office. Gladys Tucker lived in the home for many years.

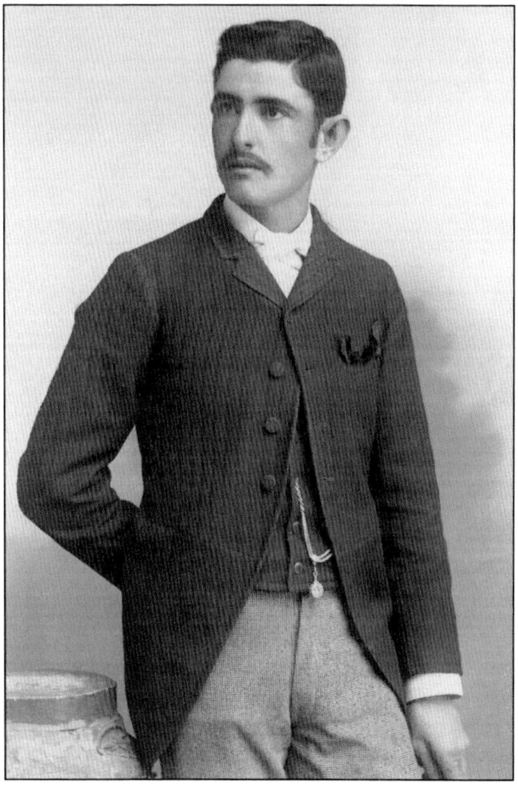

Pablo Soto first worked as a salesman for Norton and Stewart. He and his brother Mariano became partners with John C. Fall in 1888 and created a flourishing general merchandise business next door. In 1900, they sold $150,000 in merchandise in their Willcox store and $100,000 in their Pearce store. Unable to recover from the Panic of 1907, the brothers sold out and moved away in 1909. (Arizona Historical Society.)

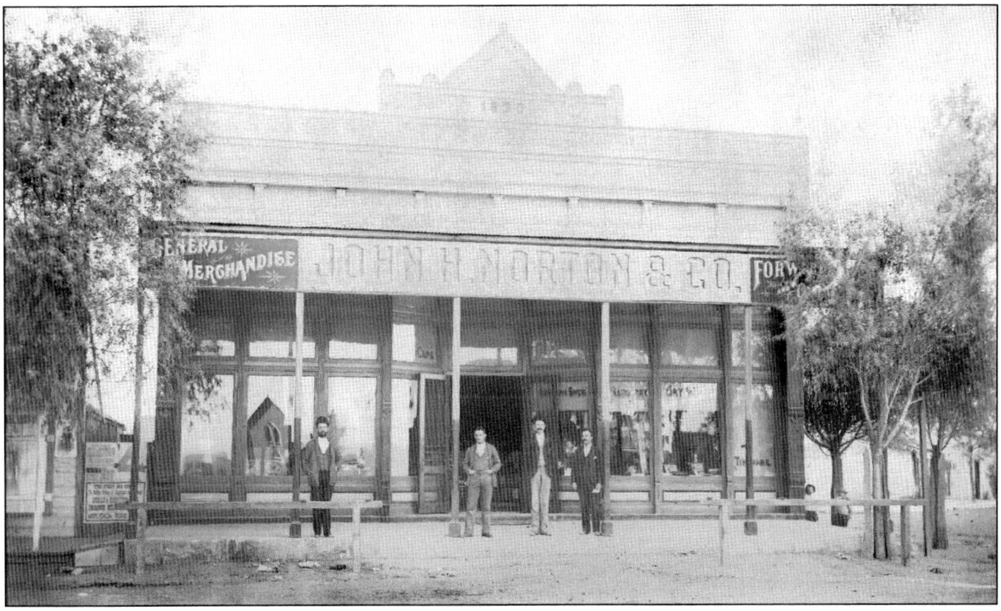

In 1880, John H. Norton built this store, pictured in 1893 when the Sells and Renfrow Circus was on its way to town. Note the reflection of the Methodist Episcopal (North) church in the window. Norton's stage line ran from Willcox to Fort Grant, where he operated a store from 1876 to 1893. Continuously operating, the store is now owned by the Seidel family. (Victor Mongeau.)

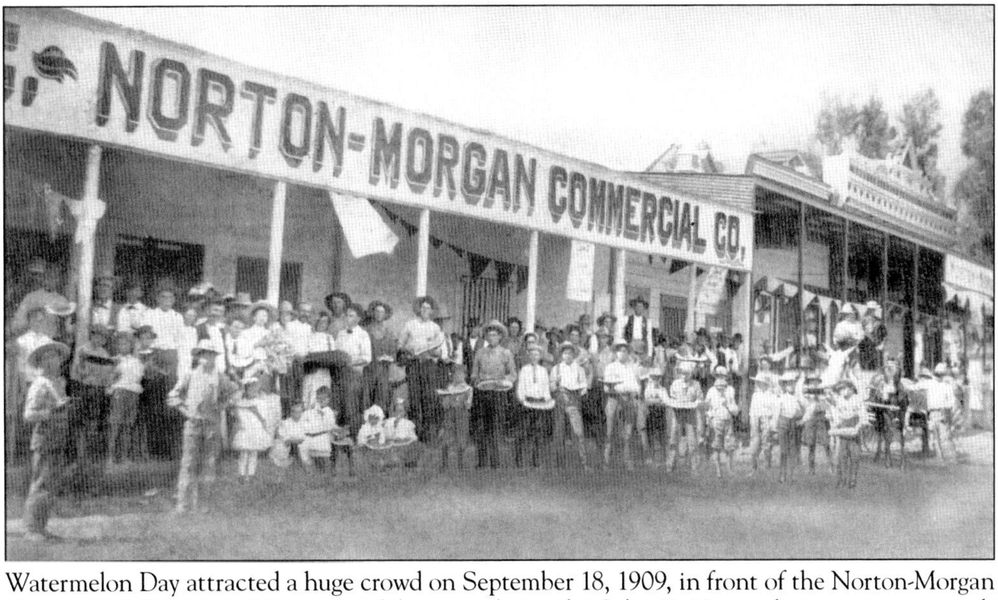

Watermelon Day attracted a huge crowd on September 18, 1909, in front of the Norton-Morgan Commercial Company. The name of the store changed as John H. Norton became partners with Madison Stewart then Henry A. Morgan. (James and Sandra Thomas.)

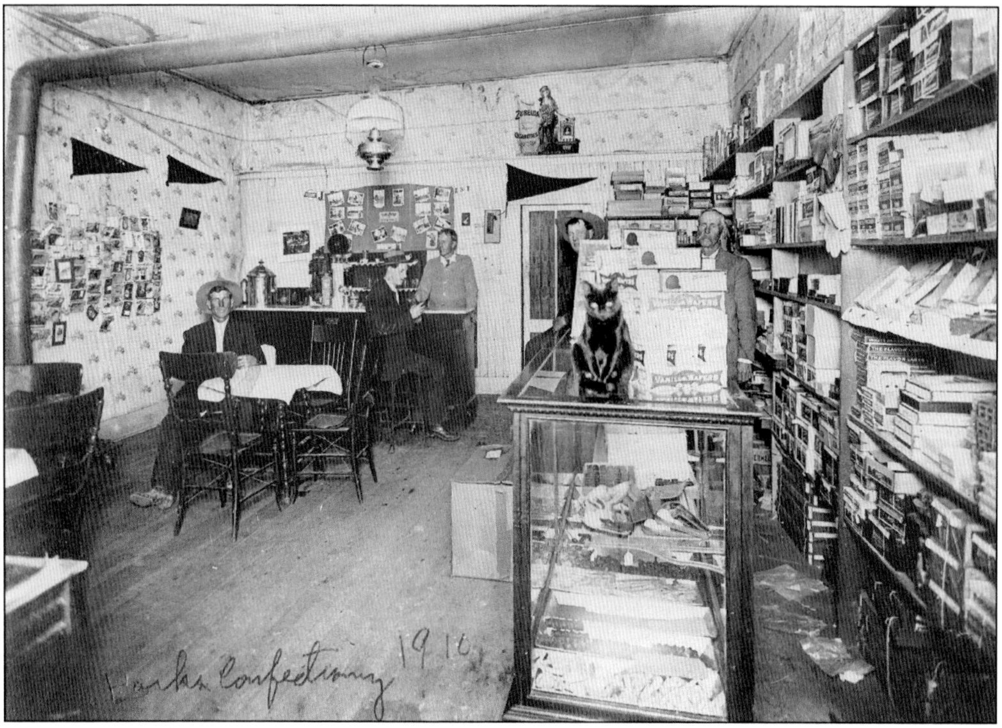

The Parks Confectionery, owned by Harry and Laura Parks, was the first place in town to sell ice cream and the first to provide a circulating library. Pictured from left to right are Charlie Busenbark, Frank Tillotson, Harry Parks, Jess Moore, and Joseph Buchanan (J. B.) Parks. Harry Parks went on to own a tobacco and stationery store, a grocery store, and a curio shop, and served as postmaster. (Arizona Historical Society.)

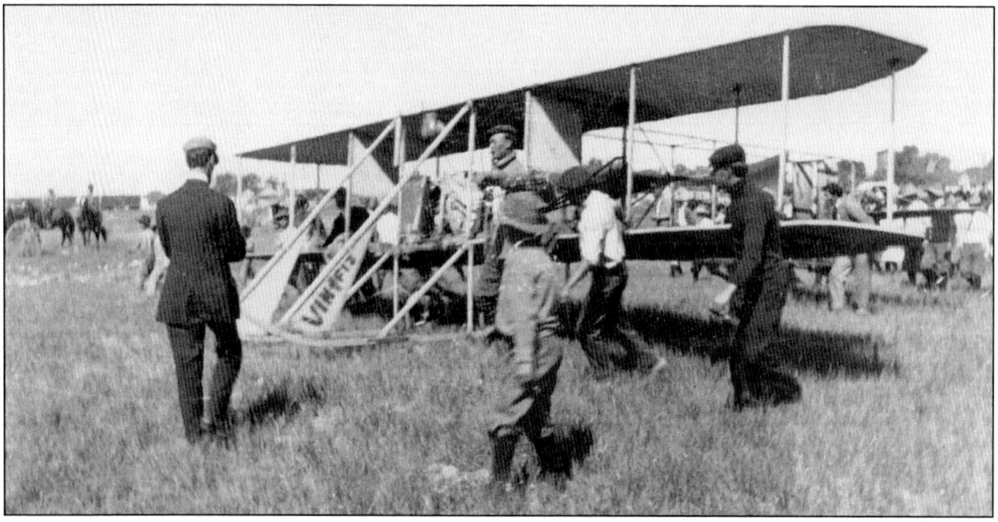

Cal Rogers, the first to complete a transcontinental flight, made his first landing in Arizona on October 31, 1911, between Maley and Stewart Streets. School was let out, and people came from miles around to see the plane as the eight mechanics that followed Rogers by special train protected it from souvenir seekers. The flight was sponsored by Vin Fiz grape drink, which was served to all at Parks Confectionery.

Two

The Law and the Lawless

While most of the townspeople were law-abiding citizens who worked hard, developed their businesses, built schools and churches, and encouraged cultural opportunities, there were still those who settled their differences with a gun. Almost every week, the local paper would report a man killed in one of the many saloons in town. Few men wanted to serve on a jury or testify. Most cases were found to be in self-defense and did not go to trial. Robbery was common, and so was rustling cattle. Even the town's own constable robbed the train. Old-timers would say, "If you are too sissy to live in Willcox, you can move to Tombstone." The red-light district was assigned to the west side of town in the blocks where the Masonic building, Methodist Episcopal (South) church, Sacred Heart Catholic Church, and post office are now. There were 43 "girls" in 1892, as testified to in court by Constable Bud Snow.

In 1881, Cochise County was newly formed and no longer a part of Pima County. Prisoners were taken to the county seat at Tombstone for trial. New county officials had to be appointed or assigned. The first constable for Willcox was J. Frendenberg, who served from January to October 1883. The county built a lockup in 1885. In 1887, jailer David Johnson, notified by the board of supervisors that a complaint had been filed stating the jail at Willcox was kept in an unclean condition, was told to clean it up or face further action. The local justice of the peace heard cases on misdemeanors, inquests, and civil suits. John A. Rockfellow, a famous surveyor and owner of the NY Ranch, served in this capacity for a short while in 1894. Ostora Gibson was a very successful lawyer in Willcox and later Tombstone, becoming mayor of that city and assistant district attorney of Cochise County.

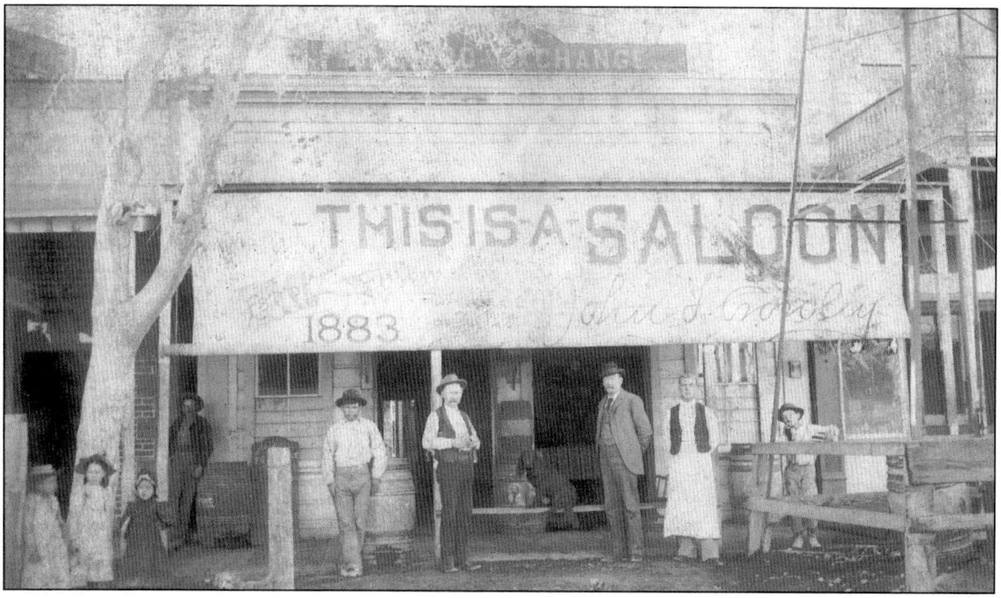

John F. Crowley partnered with Otto Johnson, Ora Phelps, and W. F. Nichols in the Elite Saloon and Billiard Exchange, where Windmill Park is now located. Crowley became deputy sheriff, deputy assessor, and deputy tax collector. He brought in Red Sample, Texas Howard, and others for robbery and murder at Castenada's store in Bisbee, the event that became known as the Bisbee Massacre. All were hanged on March 28, 1884, including Dan Kelly, alias Yorky, who was hanged by John Crowley at the robber's request. (University of Arizona Special Collections.)

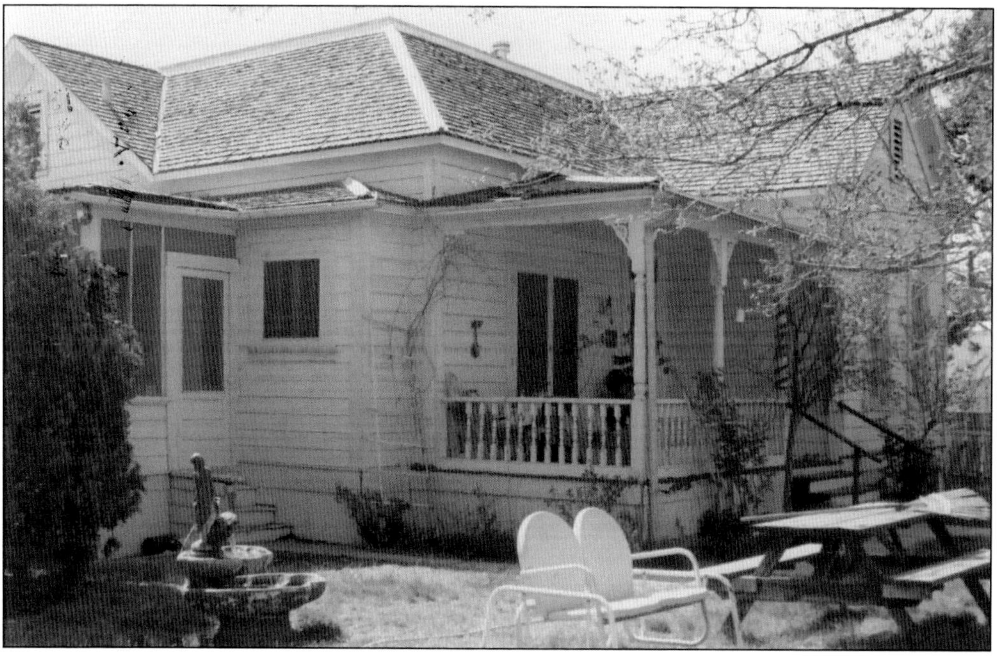

John F. Crowley built this Queen Anne–style redwood house on East Railroad Avenue in 1893, where he lived with his wife, Anastatia, son Thomas, and daughter Hope. He managed W. F. Nichols Lumber Yard, owned a transfer business, was president of the Chicago and Arizona Copper Company, dealt in diamond stocks, and held stock in the Willcox Bank and Trust. (Rose Bree.)

Important to the development of Cochise County since 1880, William Francis Nichols became the first Willcox justice of the peace in 1881 and served for over 16 years. He was secretary for the Arizona Territory from April 1904 to April 1908. He served as acting governor under Alexander Oswald Brodie but declined the governorship in 1905. He married Norah S. Seeley Butterfield in 1898.

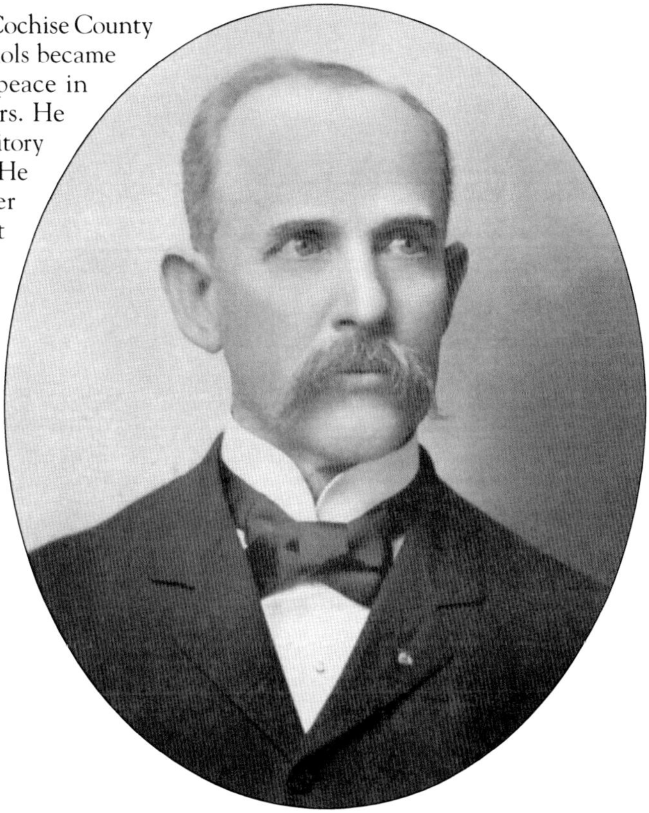

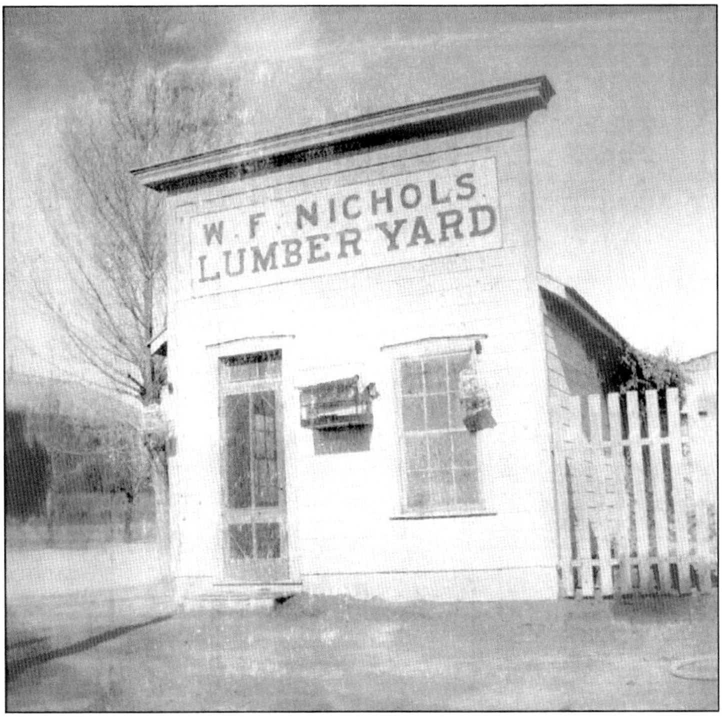

In 1888, W. F. Nichols bought out the L. W. Blinn Lumber Company on the corner of Stewart Street and Railroad Avenue for which he had been an agent. Nichols also invested in mining and cattle and was elected president of the Arizona Stock Growers Association in 1897. After John Crowley's death in 1913, his wife, Anastatia Crowley, took over as manager. (Arizona State Library.)

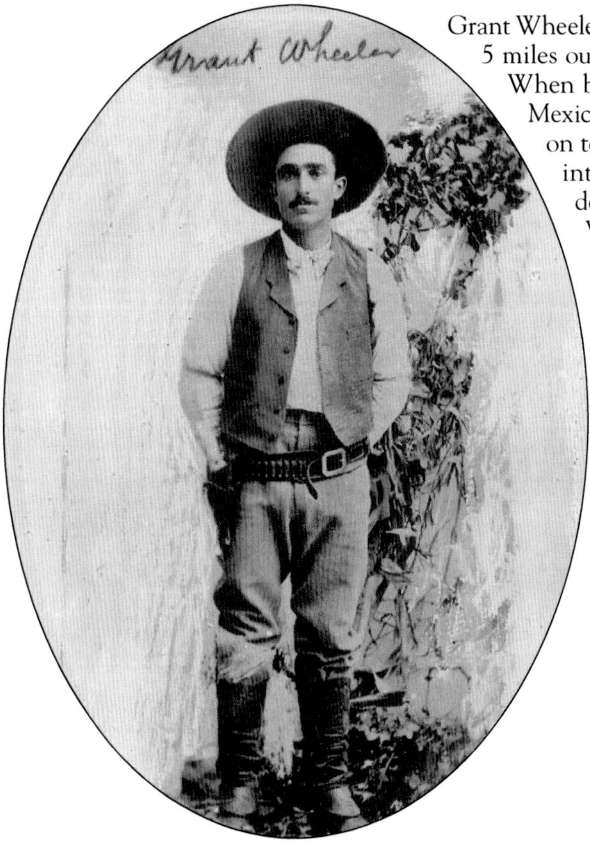

Grant Wheeler and Joe George robbed the train about 5 miles out on the dry lake on January 30, 1895. When blowing up the Wells Fargo safe, 8,000 Mexican silver dollars, in a bag they had placed on top, blew through the train car roof and into telegraph poles, scattering over the desert. Found by the law in Colorado, Wheeler shot himself to avoid capture. (Arizona Historical Society.)

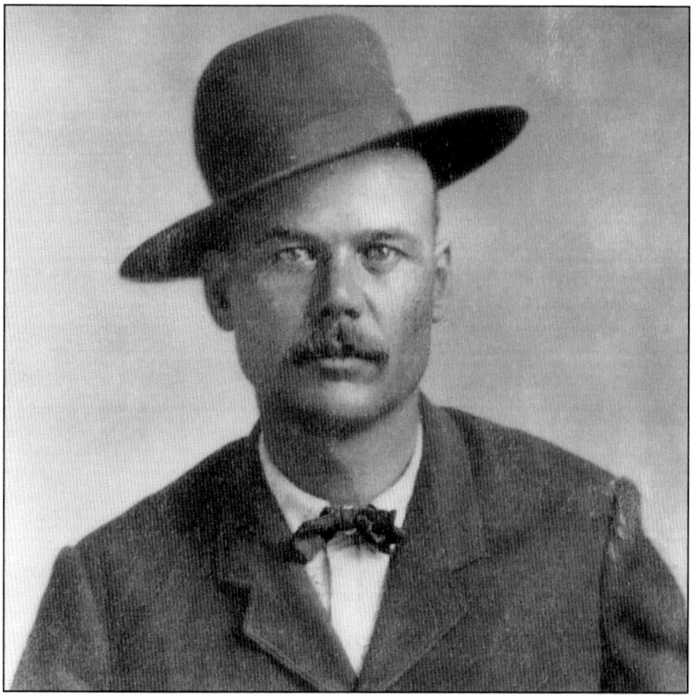

Constable Burt Alvord began as a deputy sheriff under John H. Slaughter. He was hired by the Town of Willcox to restore law and order, killing cowboy William King because of a personal grudge in 1897. In 1899, he turned from the law and robbed the train at Cochise with deputies Bill Downing, Billy Stiles, and Matt Burts. They were caught six months later while attempting to rob the train at Fairbank. (Arizona Historical Society.)

Bill Traynor (left) was shot and killed by Bill Downing in Tom Fulghum's saloon on Maley Street in May 1899. The coroner's jury ruled self defense, as Traynor had accused Downing of burning brands, and each had threatened the life of the other. Ed Brown (seated) ran a saloon in Pearce. At right is Gifford Allaire, son of early pioneer rancher Tom Allaire. (Wear family.)

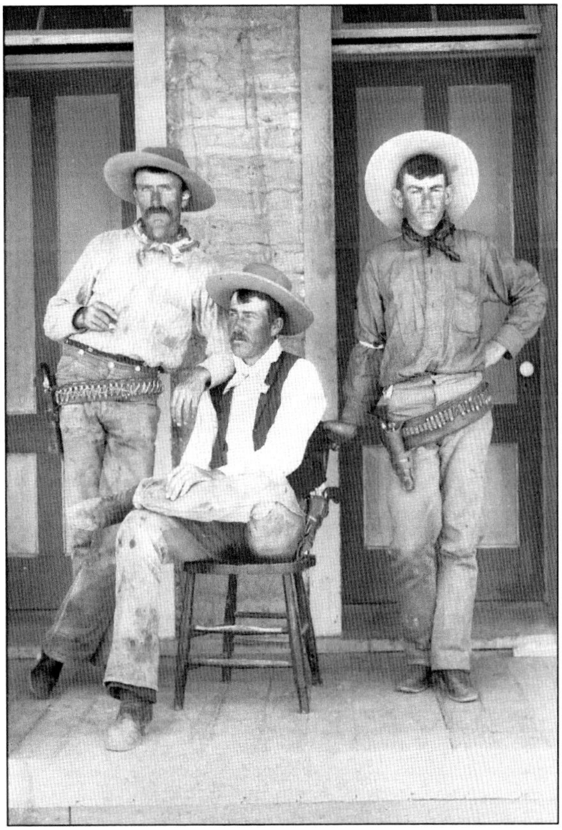

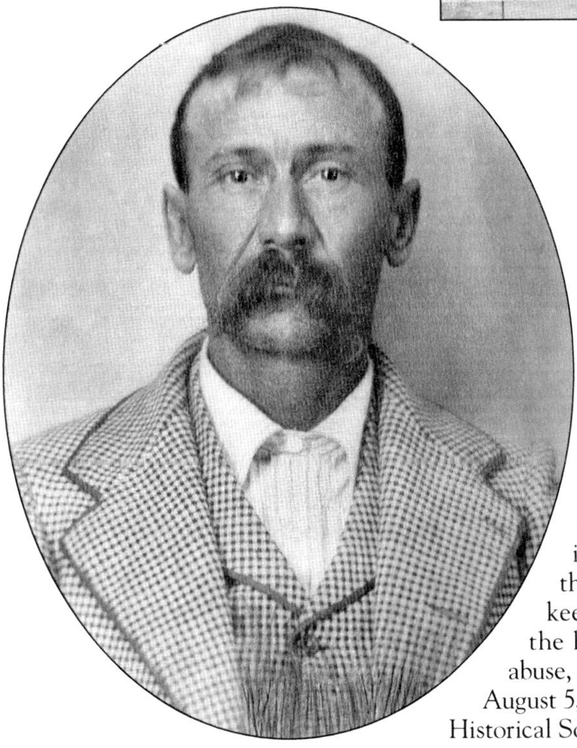

William F. Downing, rumored to be Frank Jackson of the Sam Bass Gang, was released from prison for train robbery in 1907 and returned to Willcox. He ran the Free and Easy Saloon on Maley Street, keeping women there, which was against the law. After one accused him of physical abuse, Arizona Ranger Billy Speed shot him on August 5, 1908. Downing was unarmed. (Arizona Historical Society.)

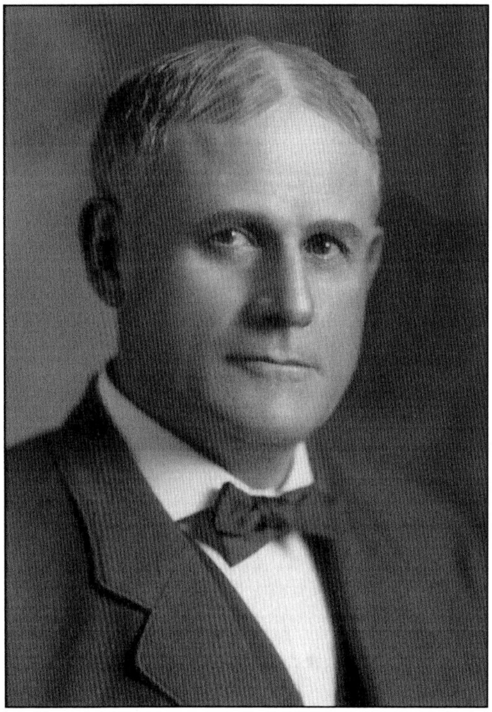

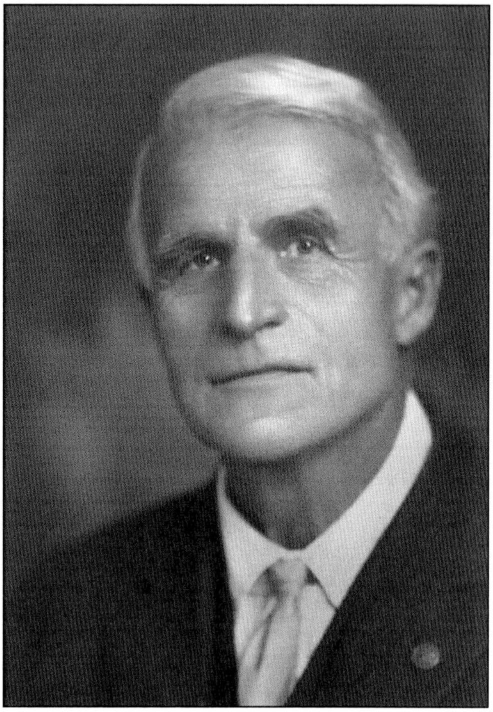

Attorney Edward R. Monk (left) was probate judge in Tombstone from 1886 to 1890. He was county superintendent of schools, on the University of Arizona Board of Regents, receiver of monies for the Federal Land Office, and first president of the Arizona Cattle Growers Association. His brother and partner, Dr. Joseph A. Munk (right), is known for his priceless library of Arizoniana, which was donated to the Southwest Museum in Los Angeles.

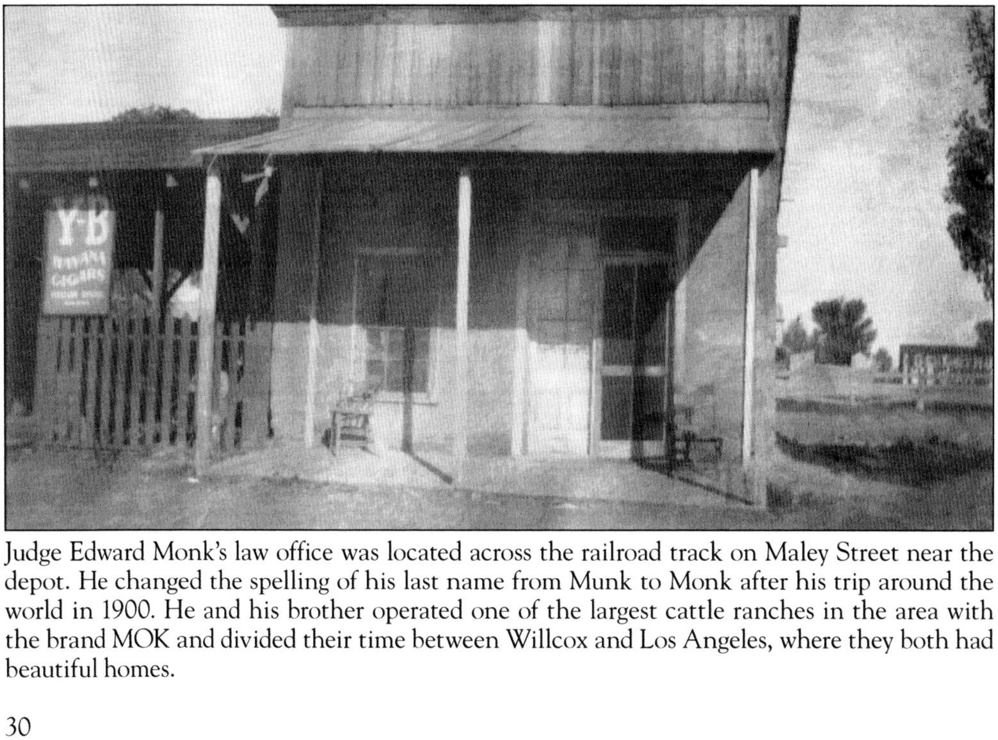

Judge Edward Monk's law office was located across the railroad track on Maley Street near the depot. He changed the spelling of his last name from Munk to Monk after his trip around the world in 1900. He and his brother operated one of the largest cattle ranches in the area with the brand MOK and divided their time between Willcox and Los Angeles, where they both had beautiful homes.

Warren Baxter Earp, the youngest of the Earp brothers, is depicted by artist Charles Perron "Chuck" Frank. Earp was shot and killed by John Boyett in Henry Brown's Headquarters Saloon at Railroad Avenue and Maley Street on July 6, 1900. No trial was deemed necessary. Warren, the only Earp buried in Arizona, was interred that afternoon. Not big news, the story was on page five of the local newspaper. (Michael M. Hickey.)

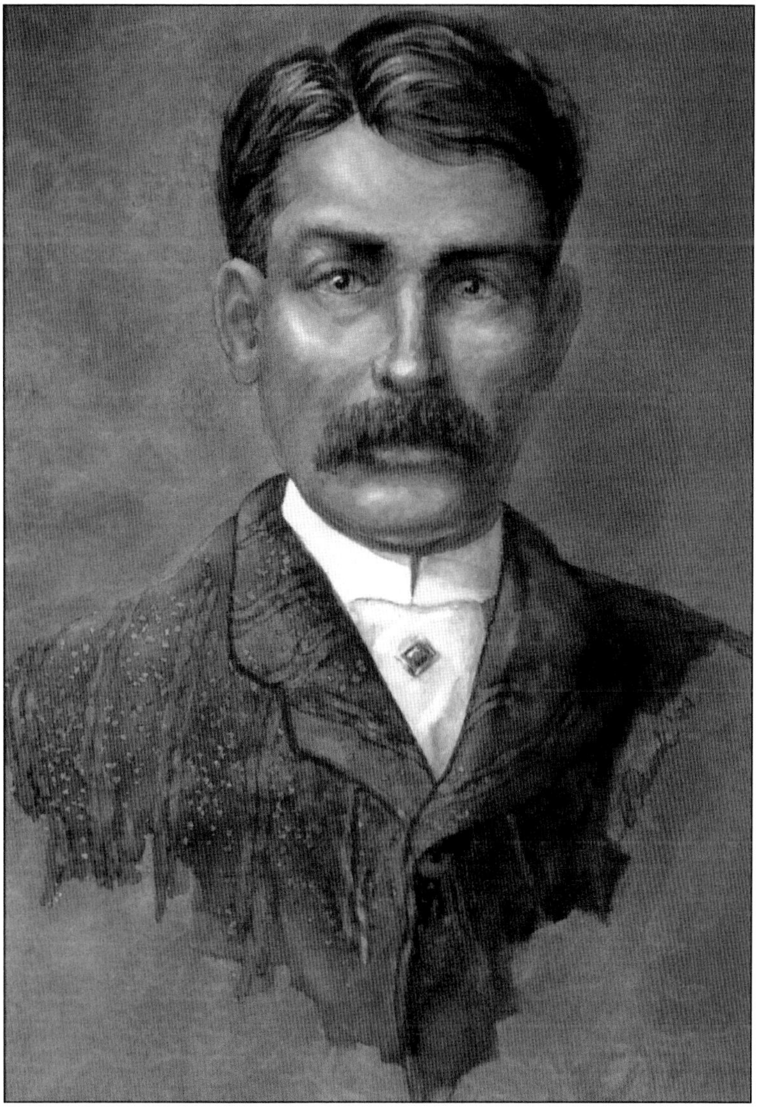

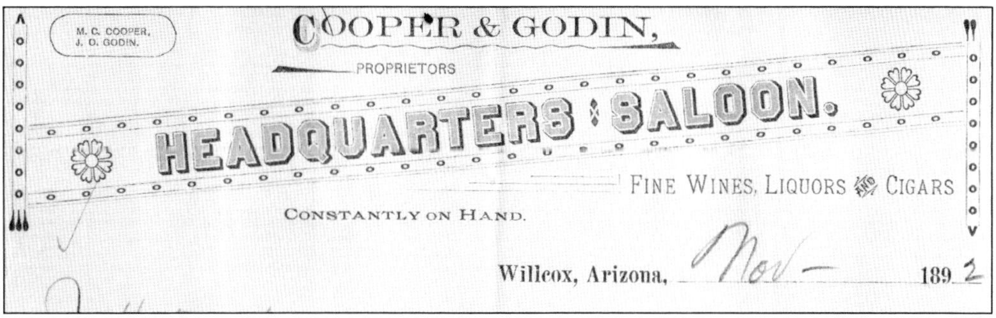

M. C. COOPER,
J. D. GODIN.

COOPER & GODIN,

PROPRIETORS

HEADQUARTERS SALOON.

FINE WINES, LIQUORS AND CIGARS

CONSTANTLY ON HAND.

Willcox, Arizona, Nov— 1892

An invoice to John H. Norton from the Headquarters Saloon in 1892 shows Merrick C. "Paddy" Cooper and Joseph Godin as proprietors, successors to Billy Wilson. Cooper was also associated with the Elite Saloon; he died on July 1, 1899. Godin died at the age of 34 on August 12, 1893, after being thrown from a horse.

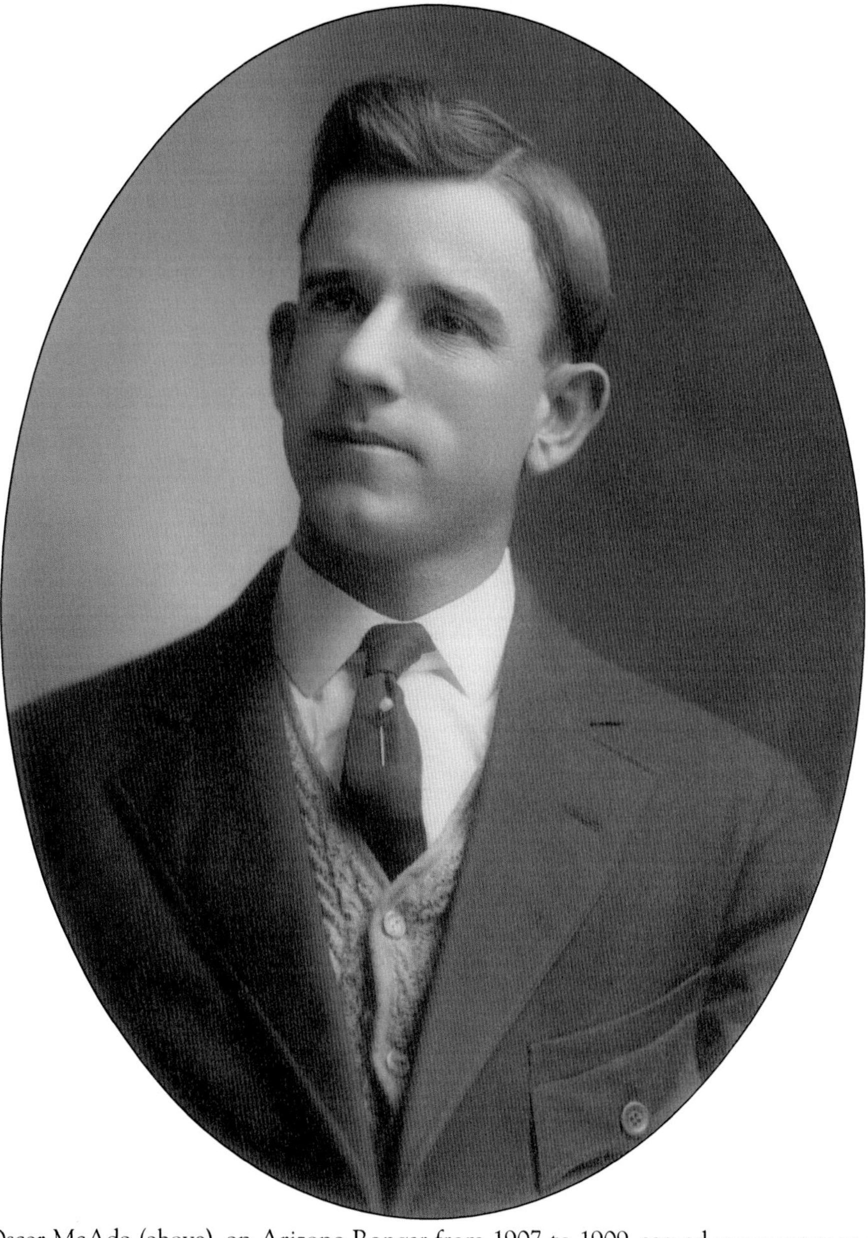

Sgt. Oscar McAda (above), an Arizona Ranger from 1907 to 1909, served many years as cattle inspector in Willcox and later in Tucson. Killed in an automobile accident in 1937, he is buried in Willcox. Pvt. John F. Greenwood, an Arizona Ranger from 1905 to 1906 and one-time owner of the Headquarters Saloon, is also buried in the local cemetery. Their graves have been marked in ceremonies by modern-day Arizona Rangers. The Arizona Rangers were established in 1901 to rid the territory of cattle rustlers and the criminal element in preparation for Arizona's statehood. During the fiscal year 1905, the Rangers reported 1,052 arrests. Capt. Harry Wheeler, his wife, Mamie, and son Allyn, moved to Willcox in 1902. He was destined to become the most outstanding ranger in the history of the force. Sgt. William Slaughter "Billy" Speed and his wife, Josephine Elizabeth Maldonado, also lived in Willcox. Having done what they set out to do, the Arizona Rangers were disbanded by the legislature in 1909. (Arizona Historical Society.)

The first city attorney from 1915 to 1928 was John C. Gung'l, who served as U.S. District Attorney for the state of Arizona until 1933. He owned the water company and married Esther Lowdermilk, daughter of one of the first city councilmen. His father, Carl S. Gung'l, was the army bandmaster at Fort Grant and wrote the official march of the Arizona National Guard. (Willcox Masonic Lodge.)

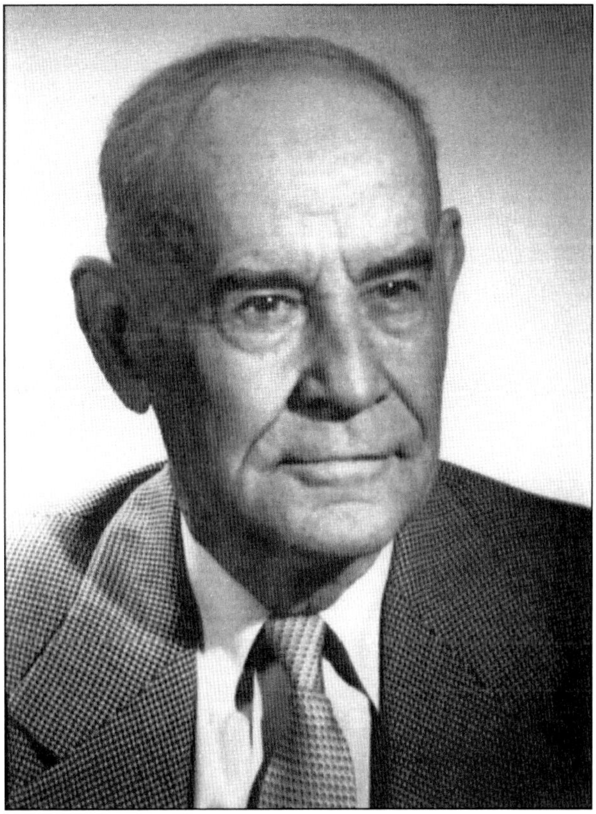

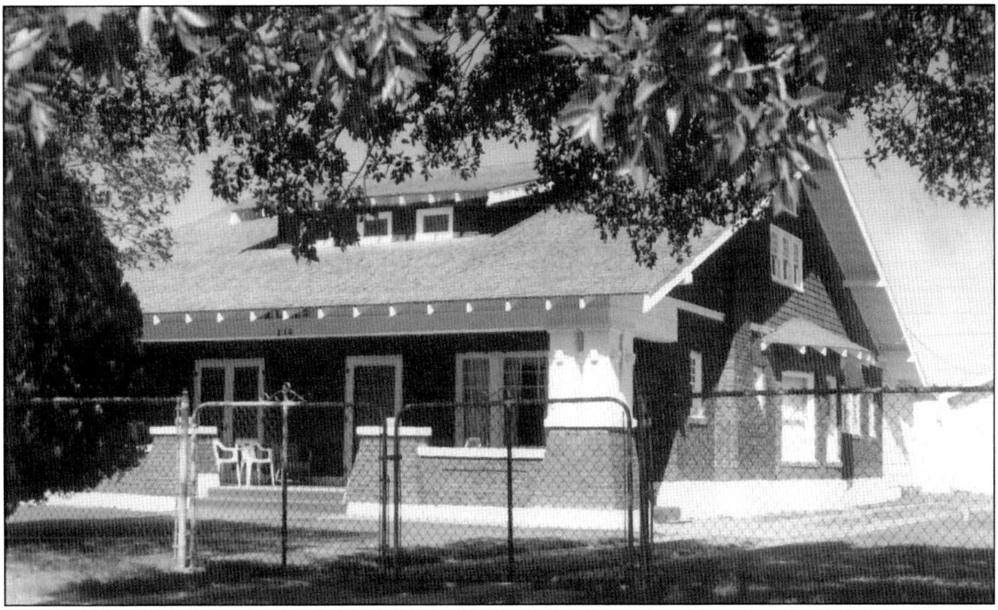

The Gung'ls' brick craftsman bungalow–style house was built in 1920 and is located on South Austin Boulevard. John C. Gung'l traveled to El Paso to obtain the design for his home and imported the bricks from El Paso. Theola Lane inherited the house in 1987 from Frank and Frances Stark. (Peta-Anne Tenney.)

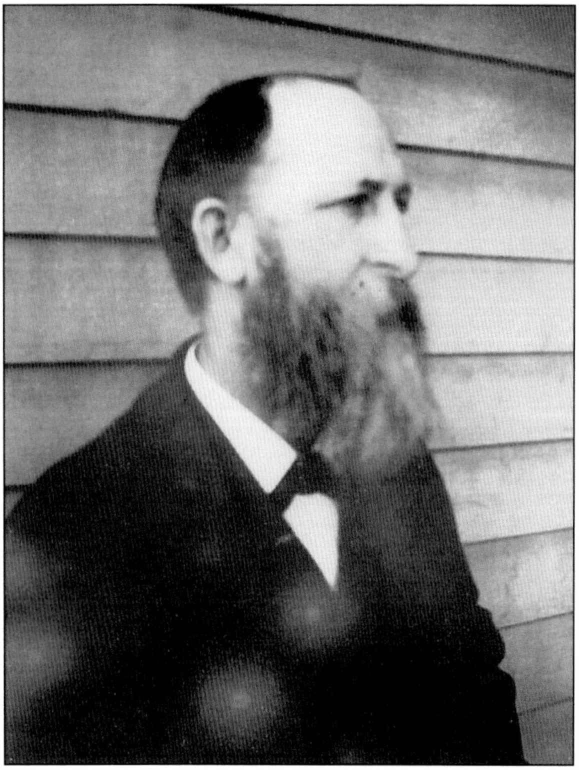

Jasper C. Page was justice of the peace from 1903 to 1915. He did a great deal towards the cause of temperance and the enactment of Prohibition. His daughter was Laura Parks. One of his six sons, Sidney Page, shot and killed S. C. Robertson of Pearce. Another son, Leonard Page, was charged with assisting a prisoner to escape from the Bisbee jail, and Gordon W. (Boozer) Page, a well-respected cattle buyer in the area, was another son.

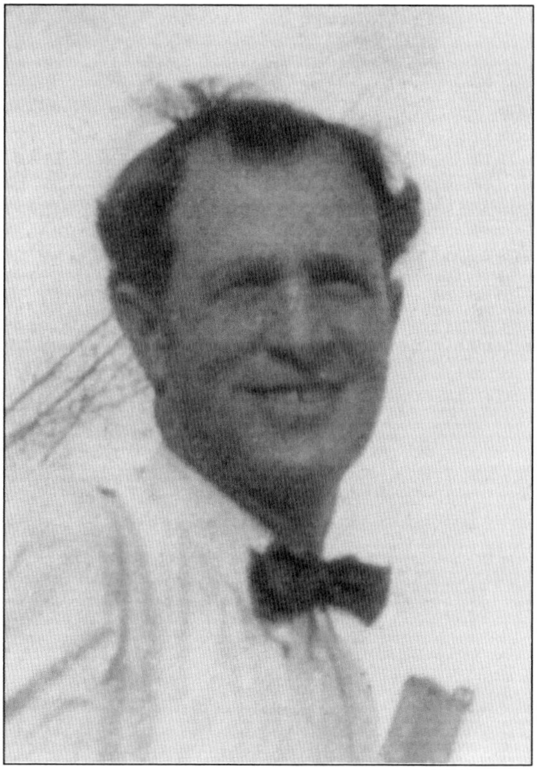

Jesse W. Moore, the first city marshal, who served until his death on November 9, 1944, was a stagecoach driver in the early days. Coming to Willcox in 1904, he became deputy sheriff in 1911 and spent his life as a peace officer. Known to be firm but true and fearless, he especially looked out for juveniles and made sure they were home by curfew. (Lee Maylen.)

Harry J. Saxon was a mounted customs inspector on the Mexican border. It was only one of his many careers. He was also mayor of Willcox in the 1930s, a member of the First State Legislature, a partner in the Three Links Cattle Company, boss of the Box Bar, chairman of the Livestock Sanitary Board, twice elected sheriff of Santa Cruz County, and was an investigator for the Mexican government under Pres. Alvaro Obregon.

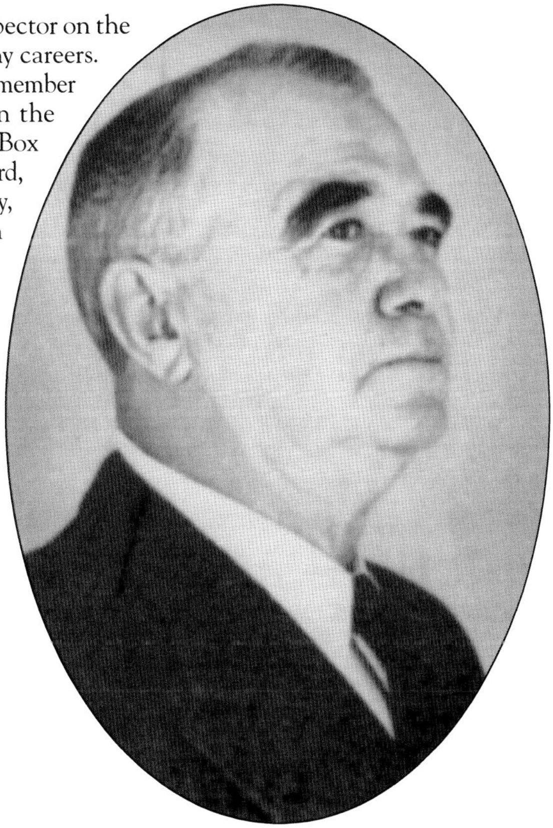

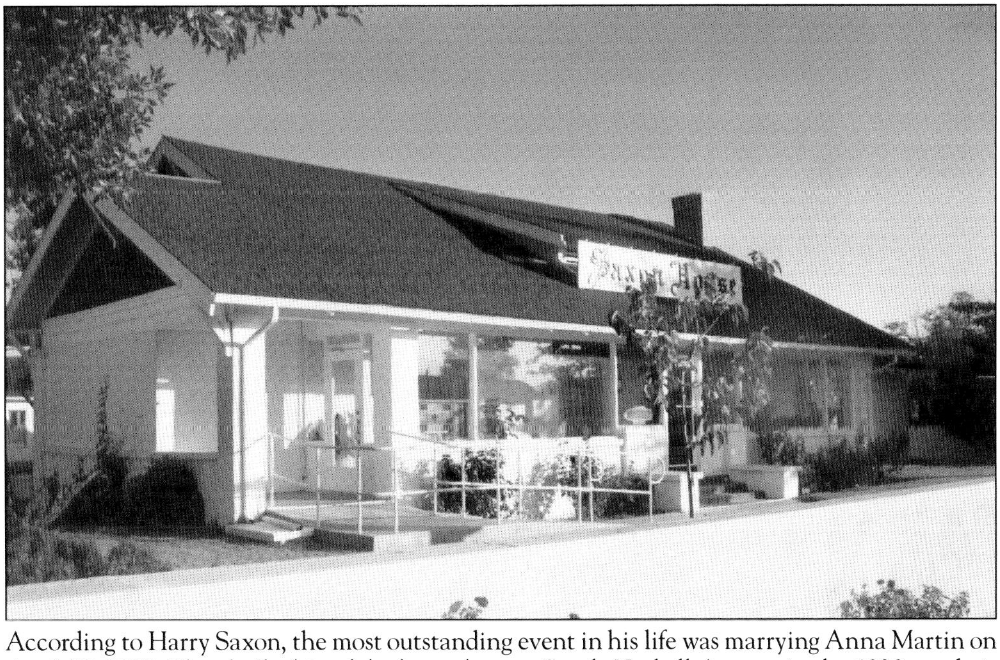

According to Harry Saxon, the most outstanding event in his life was marrying Anna Martin on April 29, 1909. They built this adobe bungalow on South Haskell Avenue in the 1920s as their town house. It is currently being used as the Saxon House restaurant. (Peta-Anne Tenney.)

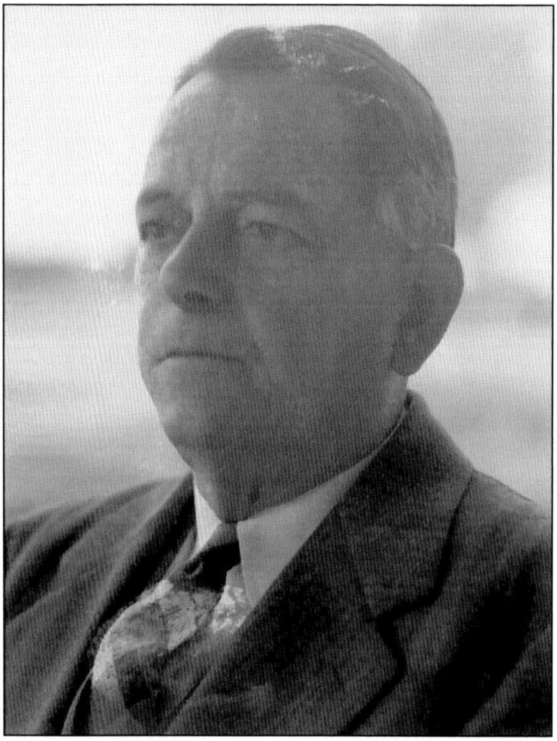

In 1909, Albert Eugene Keeth; his wife, Pearl Goodman; and their family came from Texas as homesteaders. He ran the Willcox Bakery and bought Jimmie Prine's Sanitary Bakery. Jim's Luncheonette was at this location in the 1950s. He was elected as justice of the peace in 1915 and also served from 1934 to 1944. His daughter Louise married Joe Sheehan of Sheehan's Variety Store. Judge Keeth's first wife was killed in a car accident in 1932; he married Ova Staley in 1945.

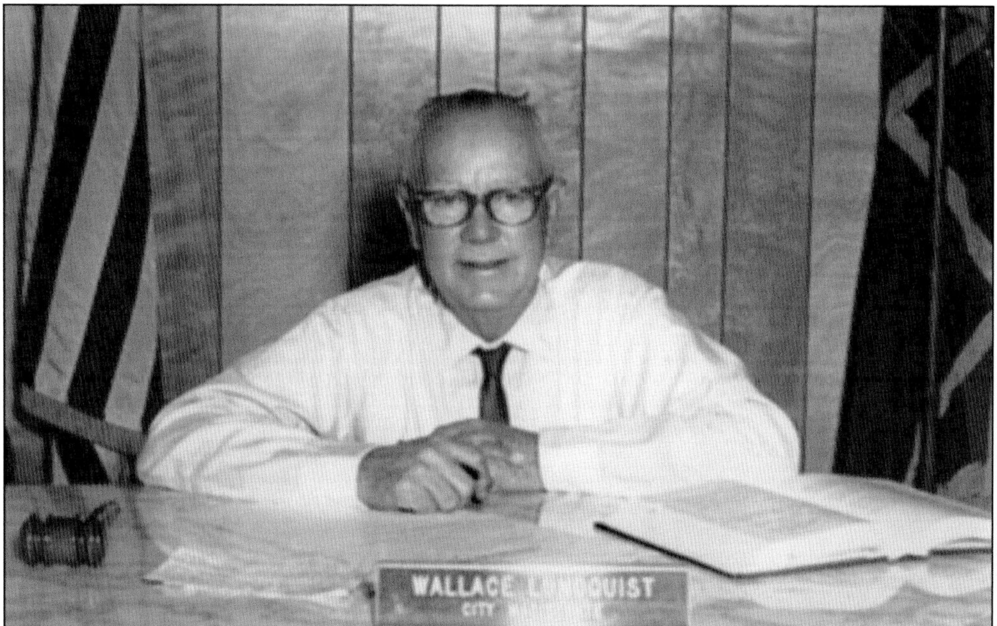

Wallace Lundquist, the first city manager in the 1950s, was also city magistrate and a 30-year veteran of the volunteer fire department. He was an award-winning newspaper boy, selling newspapers on every train that stopped in Willcox. He worked for Southern Pacific for a time, following his father's long history of employment with the railroad. He served as justice of the peace in Bowie, Arizona, from 1967 to 1974. (Lundquist family.)

Three

Cowboys and the Cattle Capital

Col. Henry Clay Hooker owned the first cattle ranch in the area, supplying the military posts and Indian agencies with beef. His brand, the "Crooked H," is the oldest Arizona brand still in use, and his Sierra Bonita Ranch is still operated by his descendants. In his time, the Sulphur Springs Valley was the finest grassland range in Arizona. Hooker; the Chiricahua, Erie, and San Simon Cattle Companies; and the Monk brothers operated the largest cattle ranches in the area.

The county was divided into roundup districts, and N. A. Gilman was appointed cattle inspector for the Willcox district in 1893. Each spring and fall, huge cattle drives would be held, bringing the cattle into Willcox to be loaded onto the trains for shipment to markets such as San Francisco and Kansas City. The name "cowpuncher" was derived from punching the cattle with prods to get them into the cars. The Southern Pacific Railroad built primitive loading facilities in 1885, and thousands of cattle would be shipped at a time. In fact, more were shipped here from the open range than anywhere in the United States, and Willcox became known as the "Cattle Capital of America." Townspeople would hear the cows bawling for their calves for days until they were taken back on the range. The open range presented problems, such as proof of livestock ownership and water rights. To discourage cattle rustling, butchers and meat markets had to submit to inspection of hides, and rewards were posted for those caught stealing cattle or horses. In order to work together for the benefit of all, local and statewide cattle growers associations were formed.

Today there are still many ranches in the area, though not producing the huge numbers of cattle as in years past. The Harris family's meat packing plant has been important in processing the beef since 1953. Every Thursday, cowboys and ranchers still gather at the Willcox Livestock Auction, the largest in Arizona, operated by the Shores family.

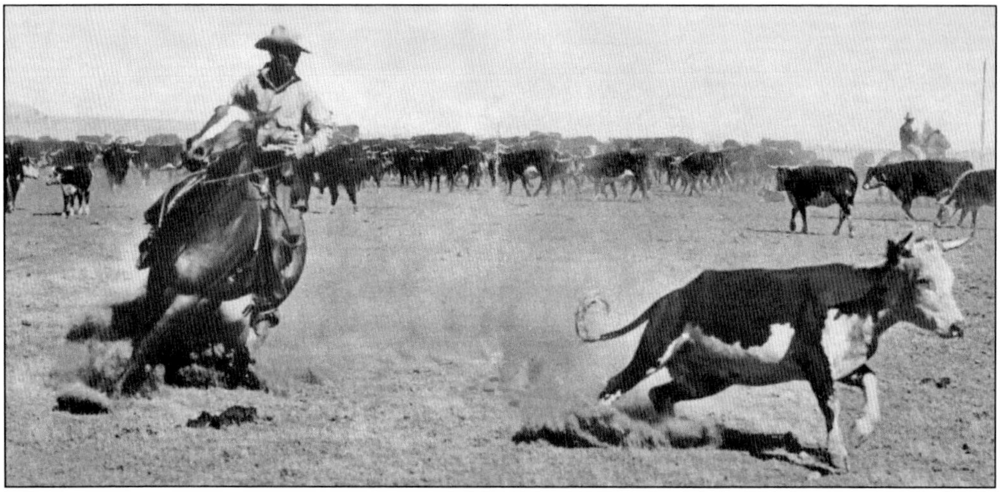

A brochure promoting Willcox, "Where the West is Still West and the Cowboys are Real," featured this picture of Mack Carter on Old Bob working cattle on the Three Links Ranch. The Three Links Ranch brand looked like three links of a chain and represented the three partners, Fred Bixby, Ted Chamberlain, and Warren Hellman. Harry Saxon was foreman.

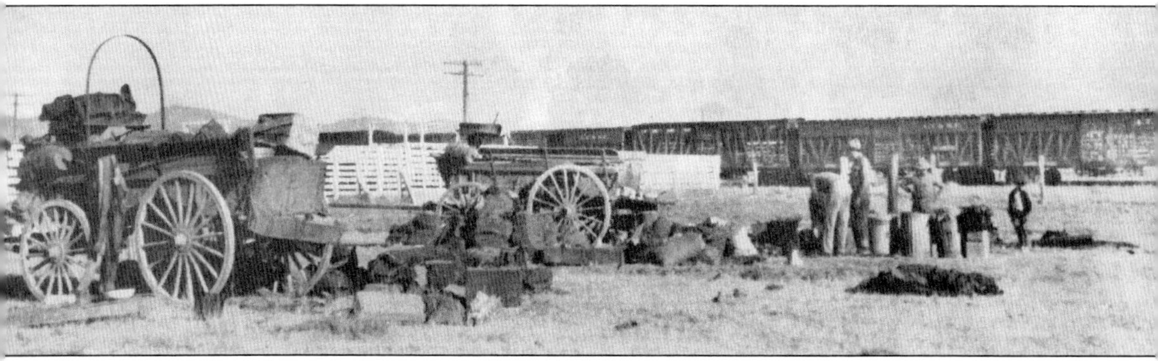

Harry Parks's photograph shows wagons with provisions for the cowboys as they wait for enough train cars to arrive to load the cattle for shipping. Advertisements in the newspaper told when and where the roundups would start. Cowboys stayed in line shacks or slept on the ground in their bedrolls. In town, they might stay at a hotel, and baths could be had at M. E. Benson's Barber Shop and Bath House.

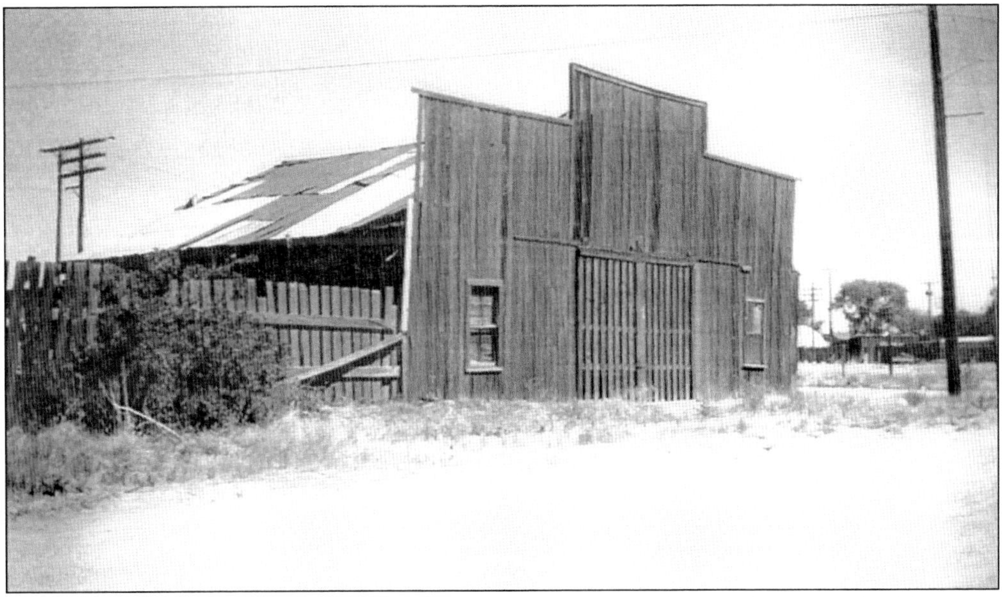

In 1910, George Kaiser purchased Gleeson's Corral and engaged in the livery and feed business. He sold it to Charles H. Grunow, and it was known as Grunow's wagon yard or stable. It was located on south Railroad Avenue across from the Standard bulk-oil plant. The building was torn down in 1964. The Cowboy Corral, another early livery stable, was located where the Chiricahua Regional Museum is today.

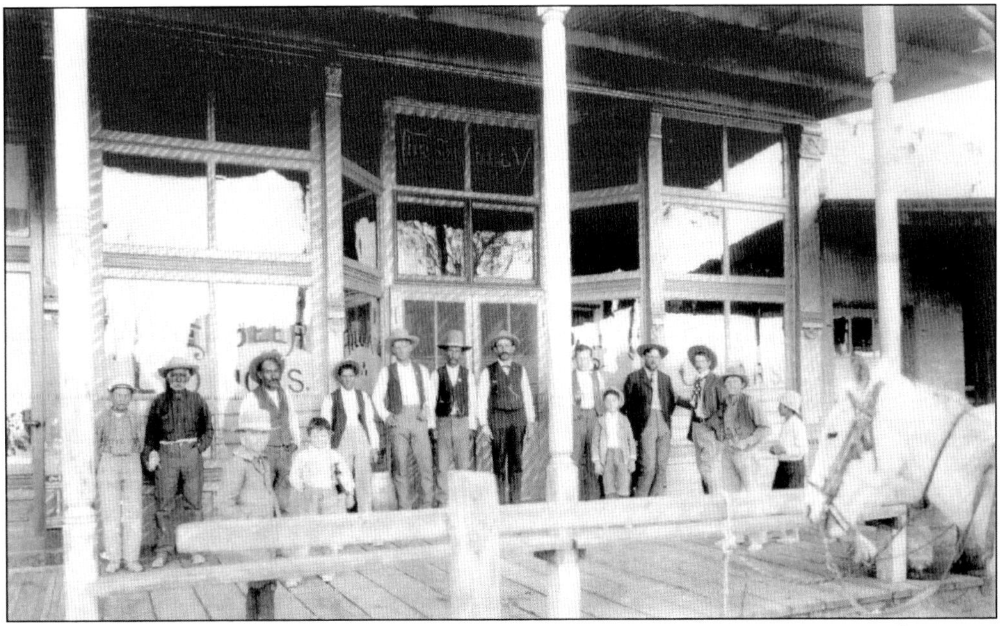

Cowboys, dressed up for town, pose in front of the Schley Saloon, owned by Josef Schwertner. This building is now the Rex Allen Arizona Cowboy Museum and Cowboy Hall of Fame.

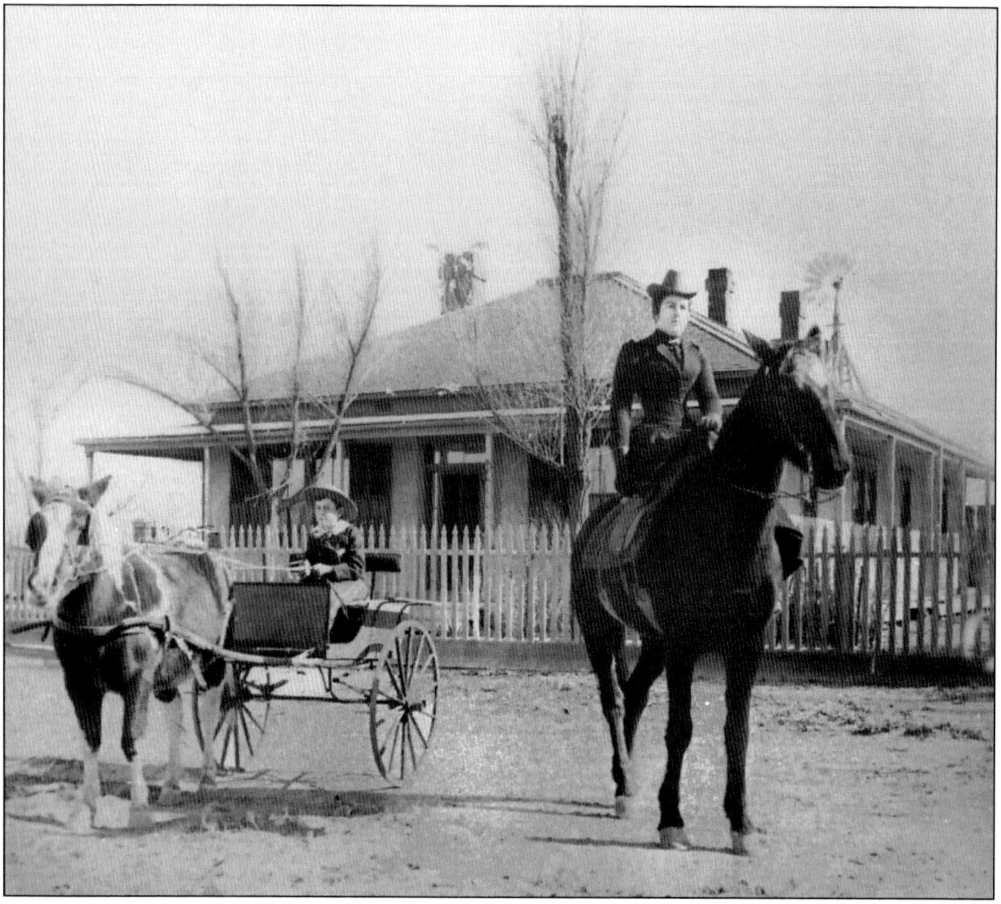

Harry Hooker's little cart is being pulled by Daisy the pony. His mother, Forrestine Hooker, rides her horse, Chinati, in front of the Hooker family town house on east Stewart Street in December 1898. Forrestine, the daughter-in-law of Col. Henry Hooker of the Sierra Bonita Ranch, wrote several children's books. Madison and Ida Hooker Stewart had previously lived in this 1880s home. (Bisbee Mining and Historical Museum.)

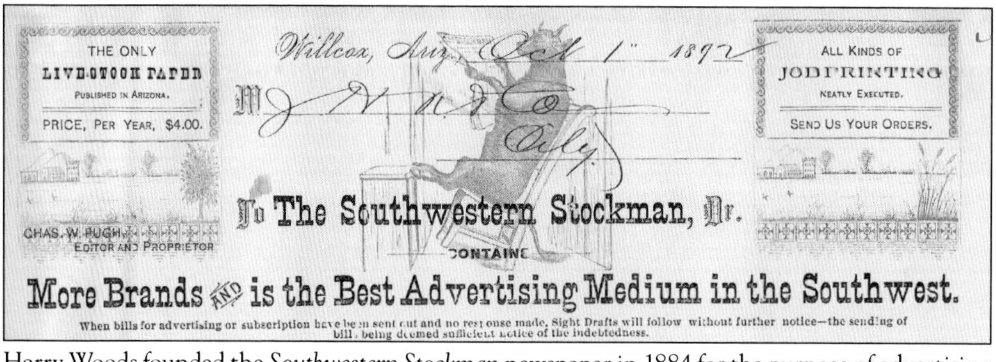

THE ONLY
LIVE-STOCK PAPER
PUBLISHED IN ARIZONA.
PRICE, PER YEAR, $4.00.
CHAS. W. PUGH,
EDITOR AND PROPRIETOR

Willcox, Ariz., Oct 1" 1892

ALL KINDS OF
JOB PRINTING
NEATLY EXECUTED.
SEND US YOUR ORDERS.

To The Southwestern Stockman, Dr.

CONTAINS

More Brands AND is the Best Advertising Medium in the Southwest.

When bills for advertising or subscription have been sent out and no response made, Sight Drafts will follow without further notice—the sending of bill, being deemed sufficient notice of the indebtedness.

Harry Woods founded the *Southwestern Stockman* newspaper in 1884 for the purpose of advertising the cattle brands, information on legislation, animal health issues, and items affecting the ranching business. But tidbits of local news were always included. In 1894, it coexisted with the *Sulphur Valley News* for a short while. The *Sulphur Valley News* became the *Arizona Range News* in 1897 and continues to this day.

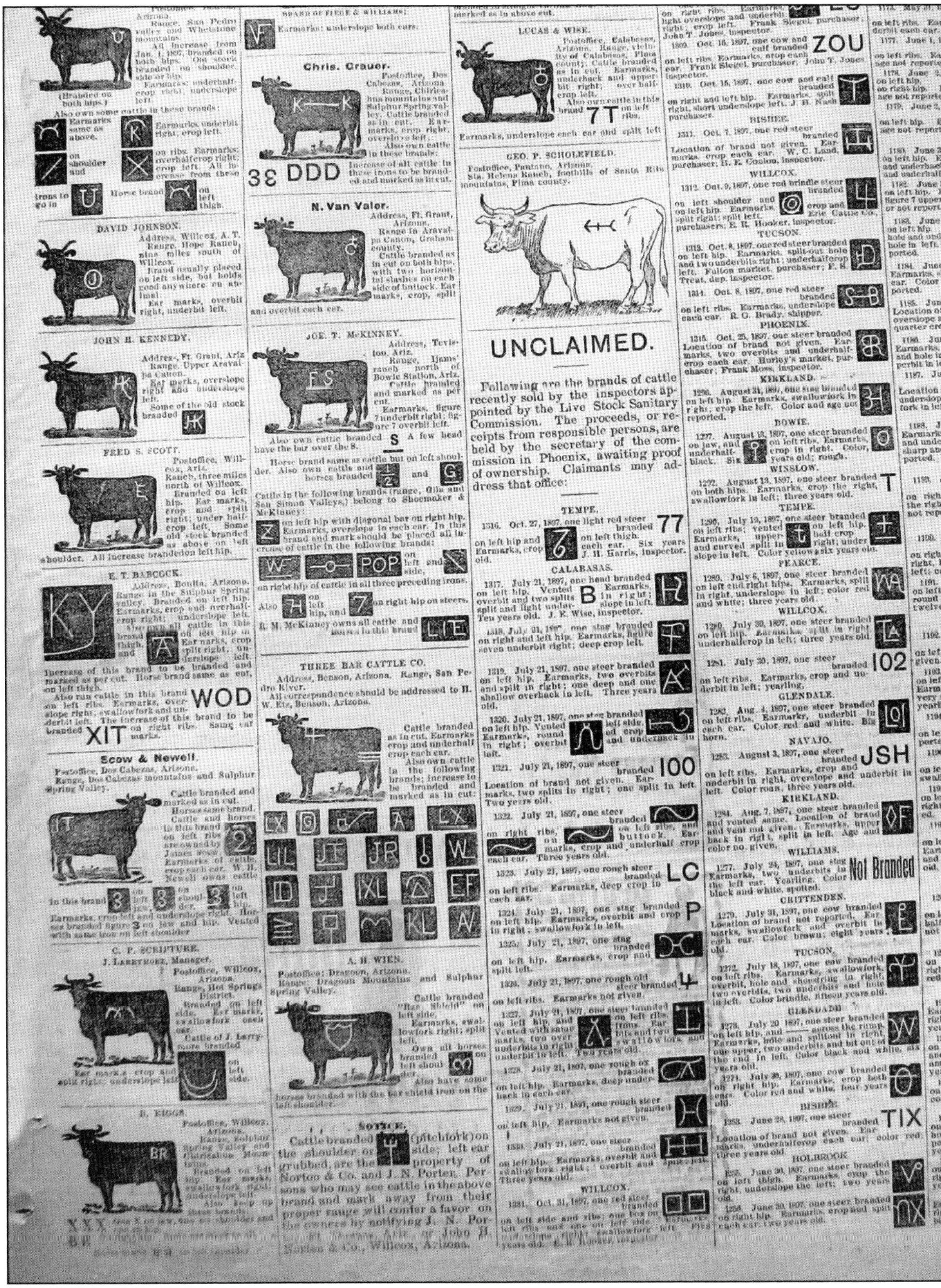
Chris. Grauer.

N. Van Valor.

DAVID JOHNSON.

JOHN H. KENNEDY.

FRED S. SCOTT.

E. T. BABCOCK.

Scow & Newell.

C. F. SCRIPTURE.

B. RIGGS.

JOE. T. McKINNEY.

THREE BAR CATTLE CO.

A. H. WIEN.

NOTICE.

LUCAS & WISK.

GEO. P. SCHOLEFIELD.

UNCLAIMED.

Following are the brands of cattle recently sold by the inspectors appointed by the Live Stock Sanitary Commission. The proceeds, or receipts from responsible persons, are held by the secretary of the commission in Phoenix, awaiting proof of ownership. Claimants may address that office:

At least one full page of brands continued to be shown each week in the *Southwestern Stockman* as new ones were added. Before barbed wire, cattle could roam for miles and this was the way to identify the animal's owner. At first, the brands were recorded with the county. Later an Arizona Livestock Sanitary Board would be set up for the recording of all brands, and brand books would be published. Ranchers tried to choose brands that could not easily be altered into another brand by those wishing to increase their herd the creative way.

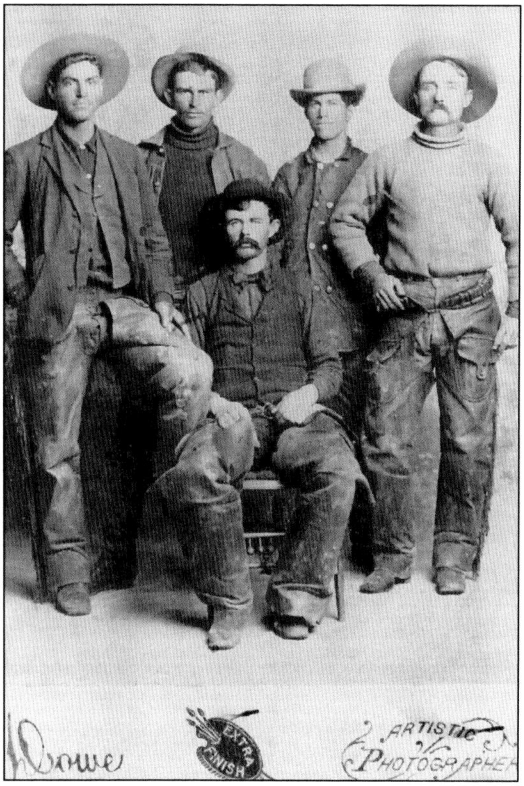

Pictured around 1897 are David Stuart Drew, seated, the son of William Henry Harrison Drew and Georgiana Stuart, and four unidentified cowboys outfitted in everyday working gear. Drew's family arrived in 1877 and ran Drew's Station between Benson and Contention in 1881. They later owned a ranch adjoining Col. Henry Hooker's ranch near Dr. Glendy King's Hot Springs. Dave Drew was foreman of the Monk Ranch and married Ora Virginia Roberts.

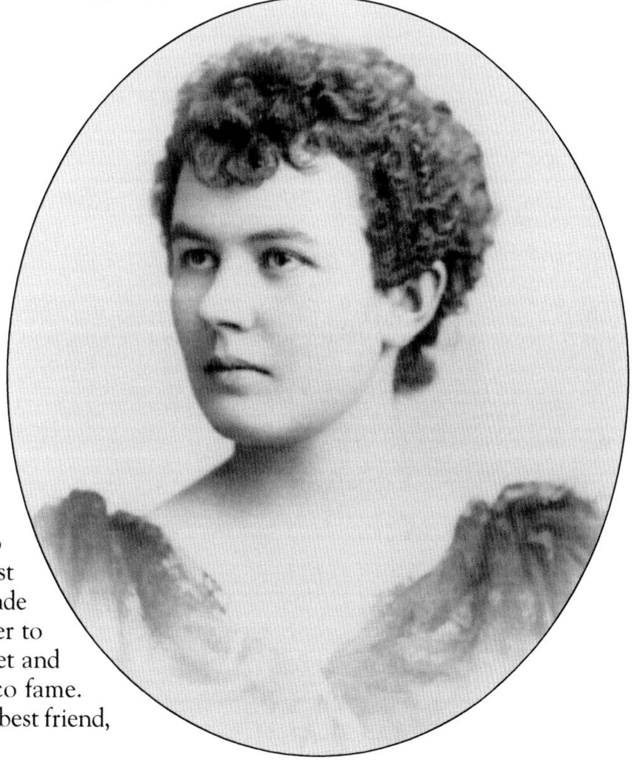

Cora Ann Drew entered her first horseback riding contest at 16 and held the championship in Arizona and New Mexico. In 1892, Buffalo Bill urged her to join his Wild West Show at Chicago. Her mother forbade her to participate but did allow her to go to the fair. While there, she met and married R. J. Reynolds of tobacco fame. Her daughter was named after her best friend, Forrestine Hooker.

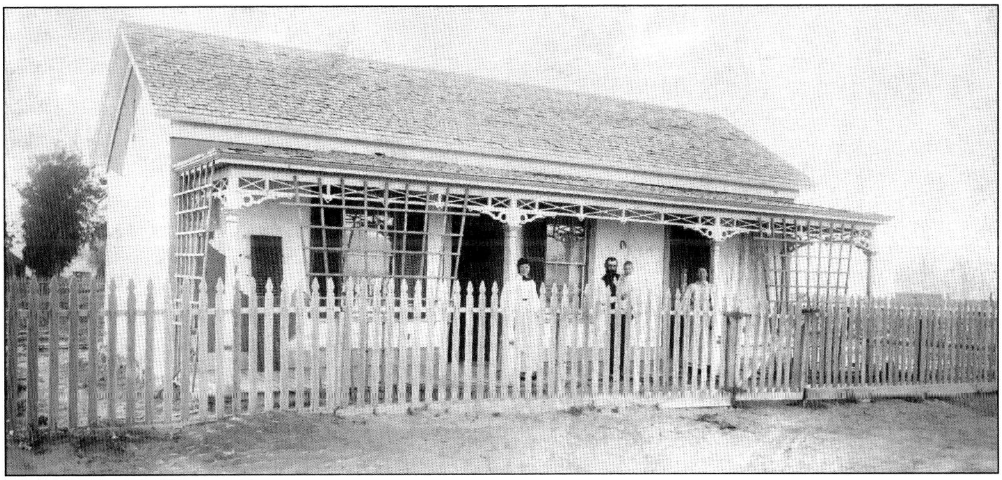

The Drew family home was located across the tracks on south Railroad Avenue between the John F. Crowley and J. B. Cook residences. Pictured from left to right are Ora Virginia Roberts Drew, John Redstone Gilman holding his son Albert, and his wife, Hattie (Ora's sister). Former postmaster and saloon owner Kasper Hauser, at age 93, was living in this house in 1945 when it burned to the ground.

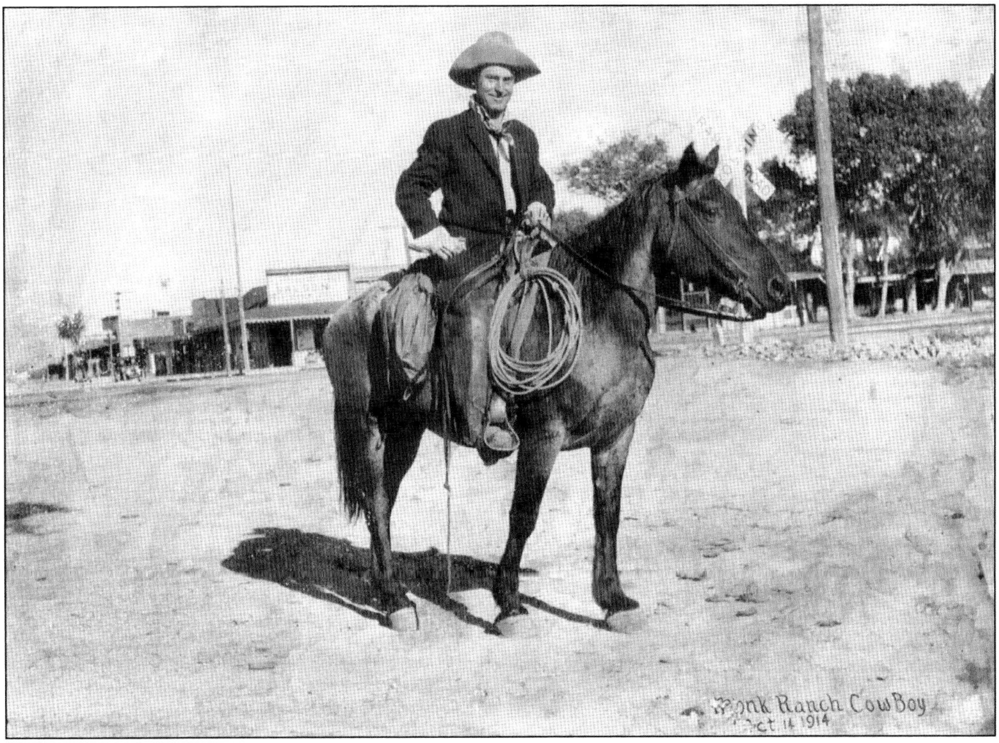

A Monk Ranch cowboy, looking cocky with his hat to the side, rode his horse into town on October 14, 1914. He was probably working the fall roundup, bringing cattle to ship on the train. At this time, the former Headquarters Saloon, on the corner of Maley Street and Railroad Avenue, had changed names to the Cattle Exchange Saloon with Bud Snow as proprietor.

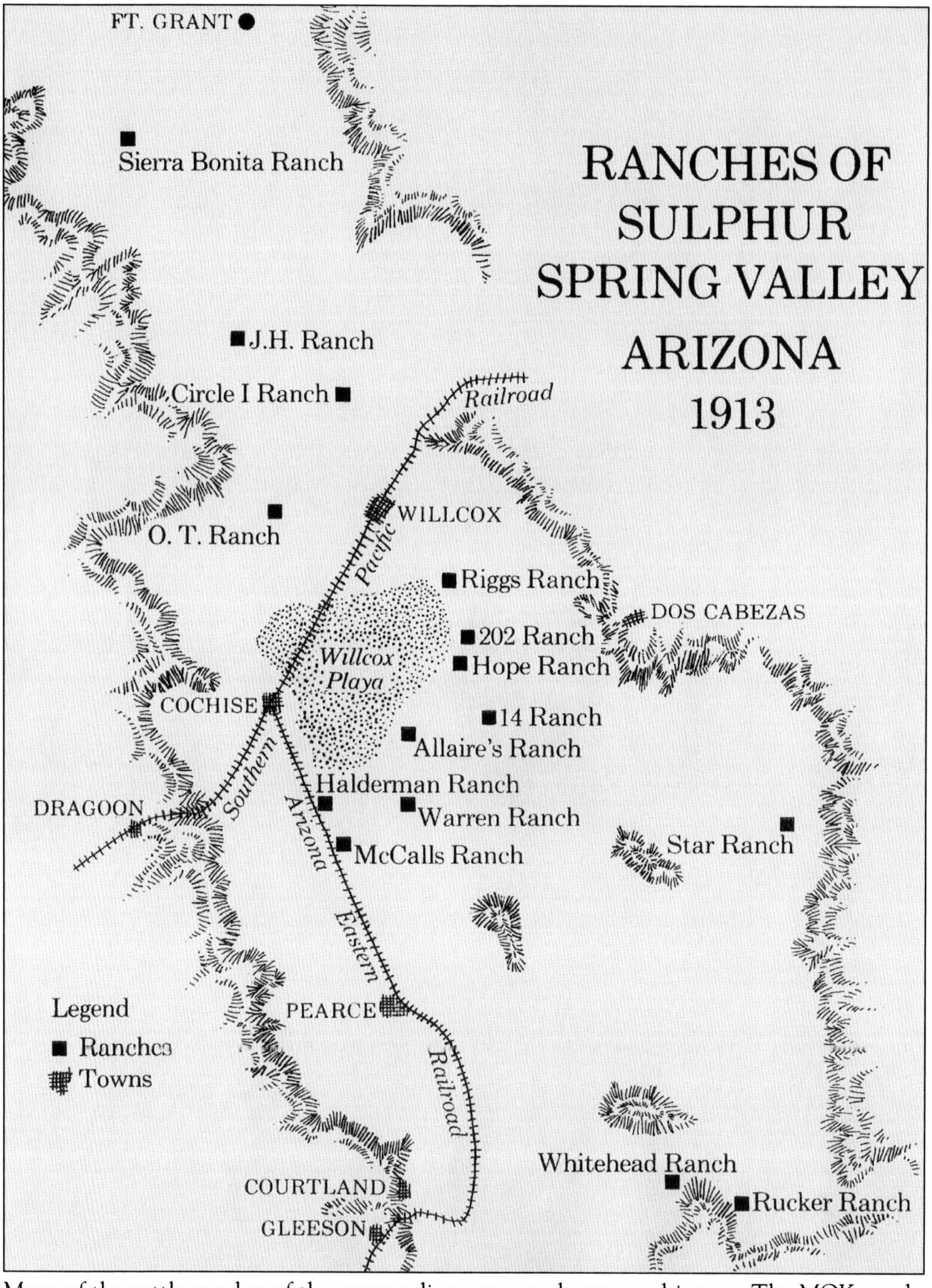

Many of the cattle ranches of the surrounding area are shown on this map. The MOK ranch, not shown, would have been on the north side of the Dos Cabezas Mountains. The majority of the Riggs ranch holdings were in the Chiricahua Mountains. The Klump family ranch, which became one of the largest ranches, was only beginning when this map was made in 1913.

Four

Doctors and Dentists

As early as 1884, J. Dorsey Sponogle, M.D., had a practice here as surgeon and physician. He operated the first drugstore, located next to the Norton and Stewart store, and was the U.S. examining surgeon for pensions. He was followed by Dr. Charles H. Porter in 1886, a specialist in throat, nose, and extraction of teeth. D. W. Hall was advertised as a dentist in 1889. By 1893, Joseph A. Bright had an electric bell telephone line from his drugstore to his residence. Part of it was the invention of Dr. Benjamin F. Holcombe, who had it connected to his and Dr. Porter's offices. Dr. Holcombe, a physician specializing in surgery and diseases of women, lived south of the depot. When his mother died, she was buried, as she requested, in the yard under her flowerbed. In 1893, J. A. Lord was a new dentist in town, and Dr. H. R. King had his dentist office at the Willcox House.

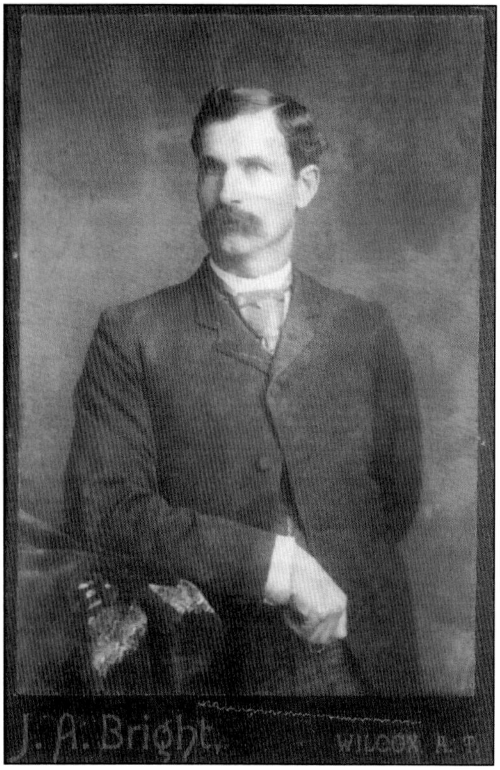

Joseph Aaron Bright, a pharmacist and photographer, operated the Willcox Drug Store and photography studio from July 1886 to October 1895. It was located two doors north of the Headquarters Saloon. He was married to Sarah Maxwell and had a daughter, Carrie Maxwell Bright.

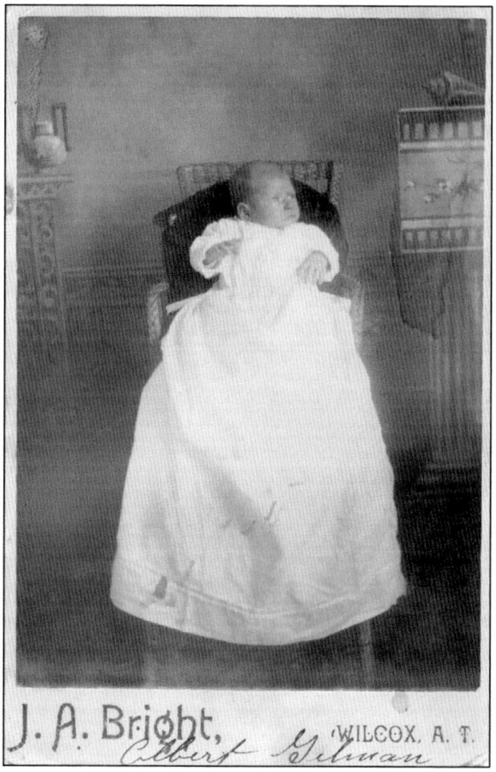

One of the many photographs by professional photographer J. A. Bright was of John and Hattie Gilman's son Albert. It was taken on October 11, 1890, at Bright's studio on Railroad Avenue. Albert's brother, Roy Anson Gilman, was born March 23, 1894, in Willcox. Ora Virginia Roberts Drew was their mother Hattie's sister.

Edgar A. Nichols, the Wells Fargo agent and railroad telegraph operator from 1882 to 1894, purchased the Willcox Drug Store from J. A. Bright in 1895 and sold it to Dr. M. J. Nicholson in 1897. Nichols was also the county school superintendent. In 1893, a long court battle ensued to determine whether Nichols or J. P. McAllister was the official appointee to the county board of supervisors. (Willcox Masonic Lodge.)

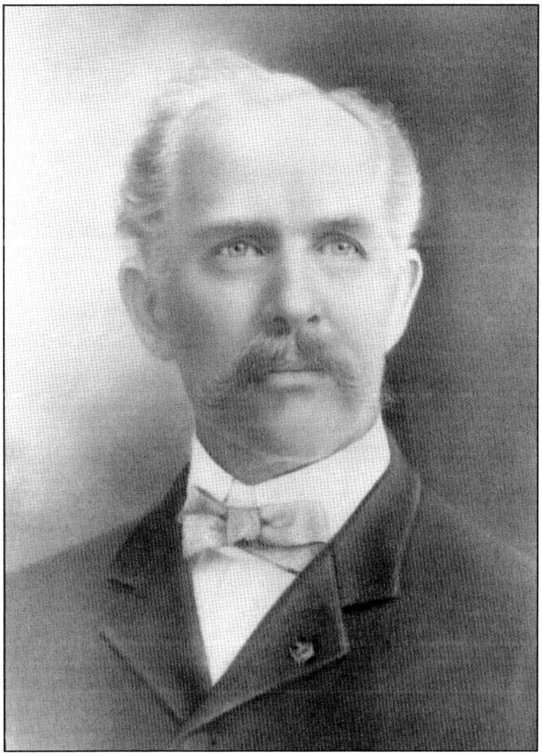

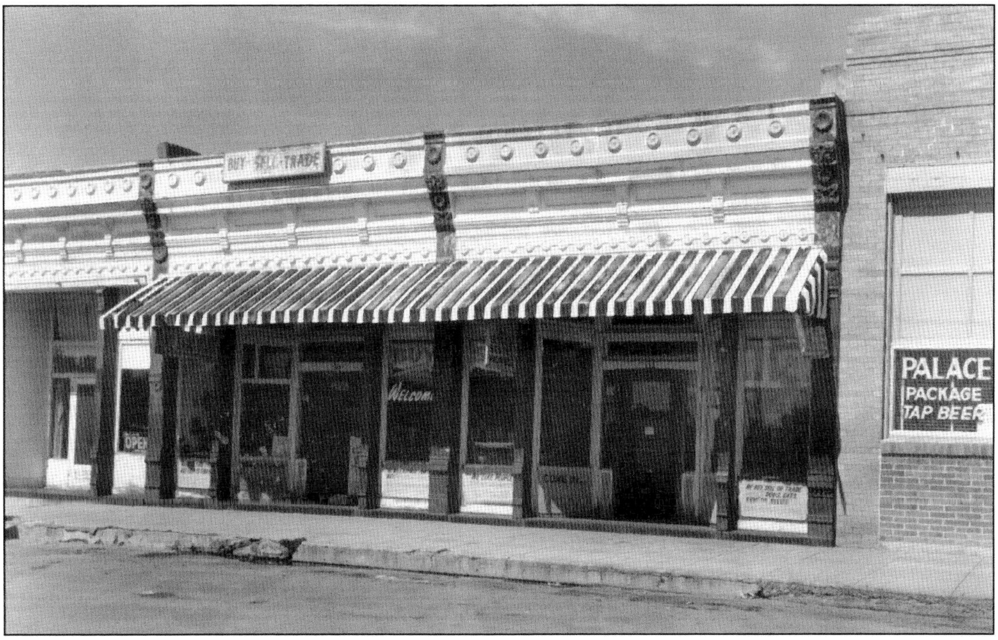

Now known as the Teeters Building, the barbershop, McCourt and Geddes store, and Willcox Drug Store were all located in this metal-fronted structure. John M. Nicholson was the pharmacist, and Dr. M. J. Nicholson was surgeon for the Southern Pacific Railroad Company. When John M. Nicholson died in 1901, the pharmacy sold to his brother Alexander Allen Nicholson, who later passed it on to his son Marshall.

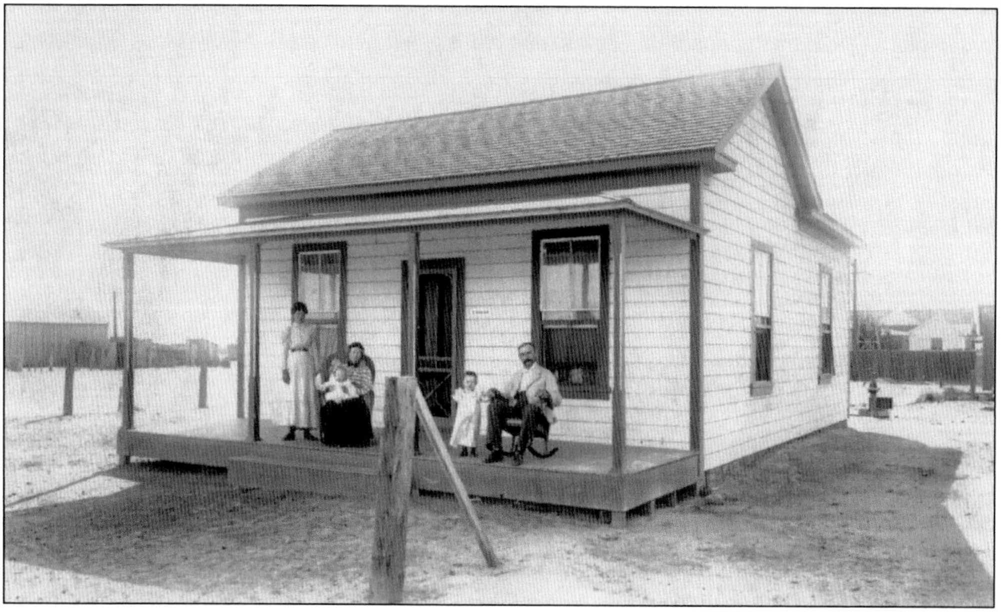

Dr. Malcom John Nicholson and family are relaxing on the porch of their home on Railroad Avenue. The Nicholsons had the first cement sidewalk in front of their business and the first glass wall cases. Dr. Nicholson examined the body of Warren Earp for the coroner's inquest. Even though the path of the bullet did not match the testimony of the witnesses, Johnny Boyett was exonerated.

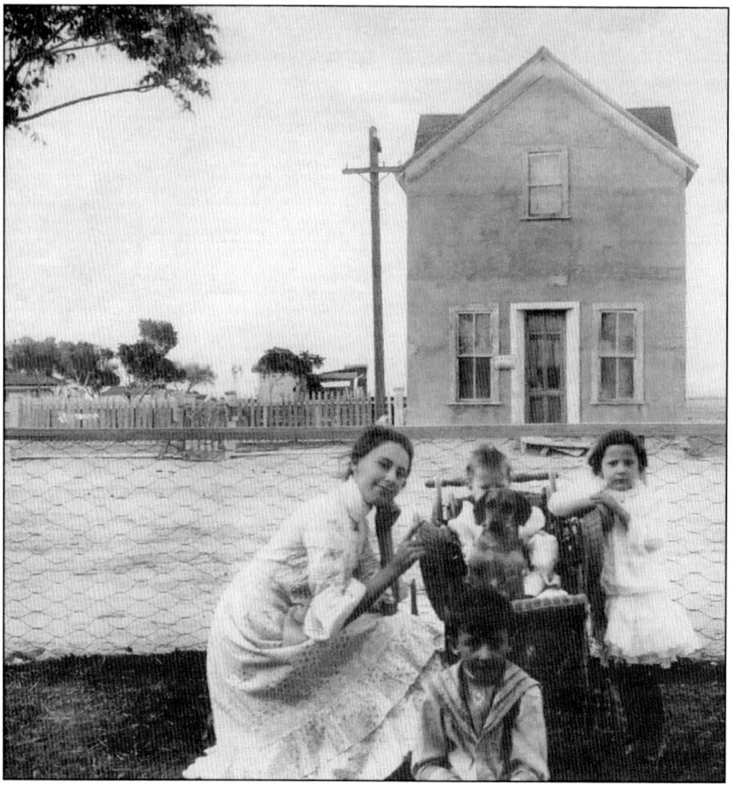

A sign by the door proclaims this to be Dr. Aiton's office; it was located on east Maley Street. Some old-timers called this the old cowboy hospital. Although it was not an official hospital, Dr. Robert Alexander Aiton may have kept some of his patients upstairs during treatment. He practiced here from 1899 to 1901 and opened the Red Cross Drug Store. The woman and children are believed to be one of his daughters and her children.

Dr. Robert Alexander Aiton's first wife, of four, was his cousin Mary Emma. Her parents, James M. and Mary McClintock, are buried in the old cemetery. All nine Aiton children were musical like their father, who played piano. He told his family that he secretly attended the gunshot wounds of Constable Burt Alvord's gang. While in Tucson, he was the first physician in Arizona to have an X-ray machine.

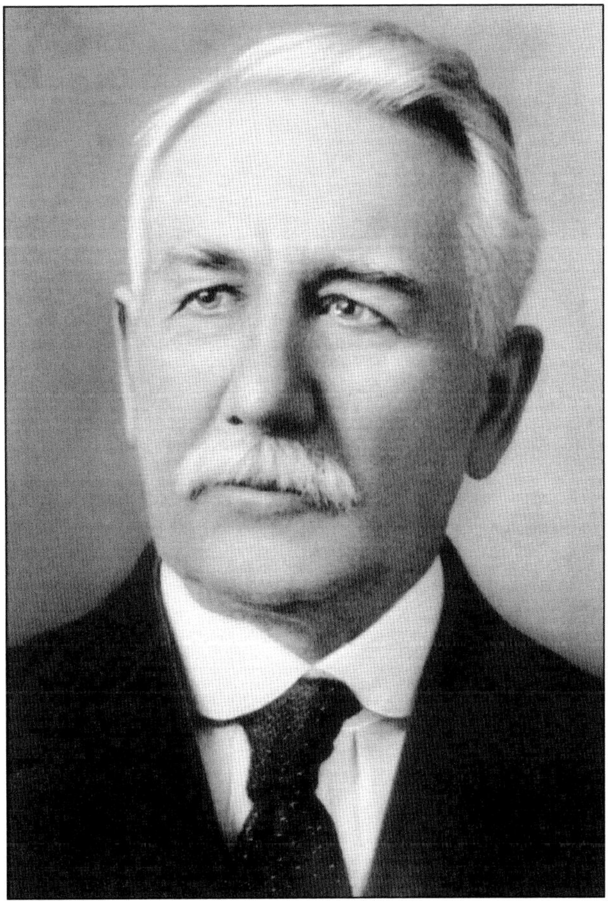

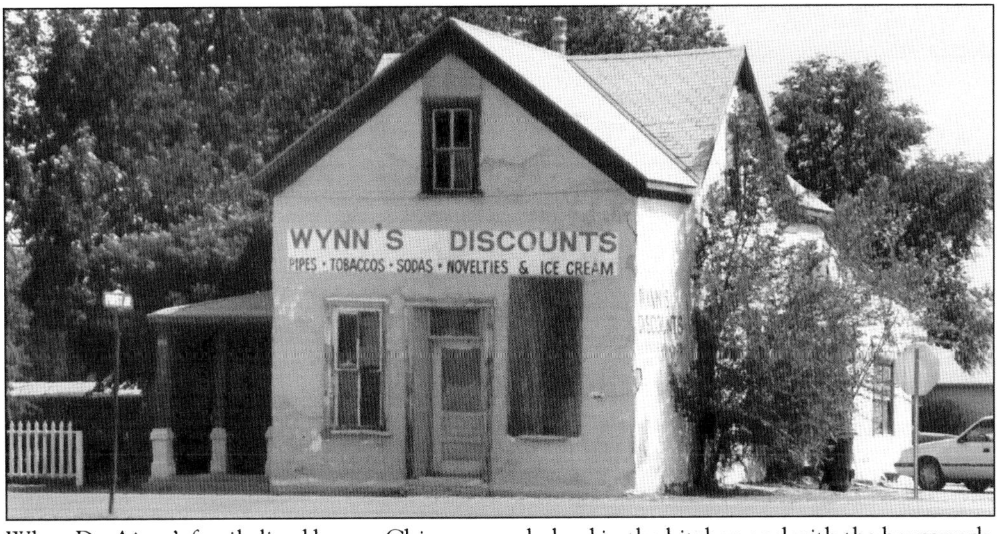

When Dr. Aiton's family lived here, a Chinese man helped in the kitchen and with the housework. Over the years, many different ranch families lived in this house during the school months. The sign for Wynn's Discount Store stayed on the building for years, even when it served as a home. The Shobe family owned the building when it was torn down in 1999.

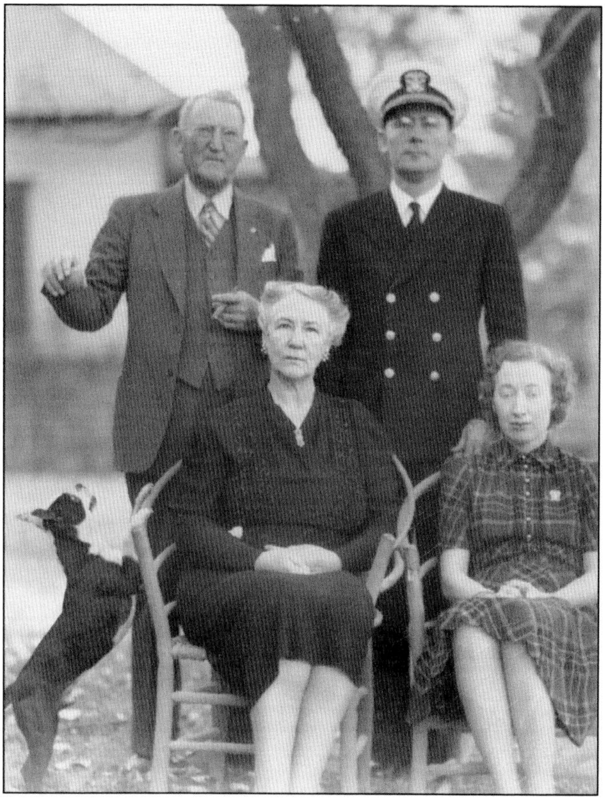

Just an "old country doctor," John Crofford Wilson (left) became district physician and surgeon for the Southern Pacific Railroad in 1904 and also for the Mascot Copper Company. His territory covered from Klondyke to Pearce, from Willcox to Bowie, and the Chiricahua Mountains. He delivered over 1,100 babies. With him are, from left to right, his wife, Carol; his son Jack (a local dentist); and Jack's wife, Edythe. (Butch and Kay Ellen Wilson.)

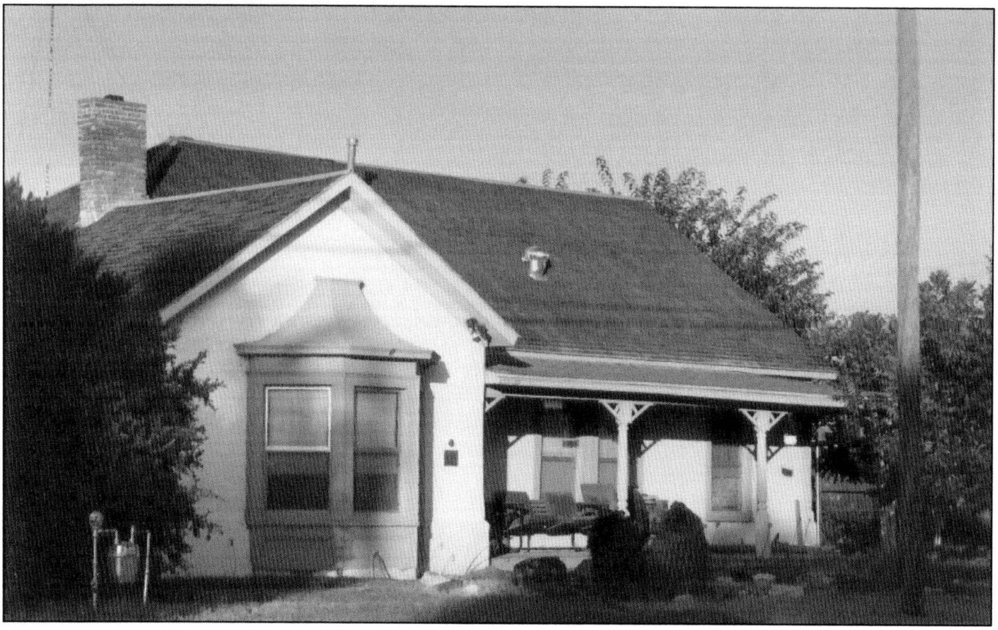

Dr. John Crofford Wilson lived in this home on Maley Street until his death in 1953. It was purchased in 1905 by Dr. Wilson and his first wife, Helen Gung'l. An old shed housed his buggy and Old Dobbin, the horse. Dr. Wilson was elected mayor three times, organized the American Legion post and Rotary Club, and started the first airport and first golf course. (Peta-Anne Tenney.)

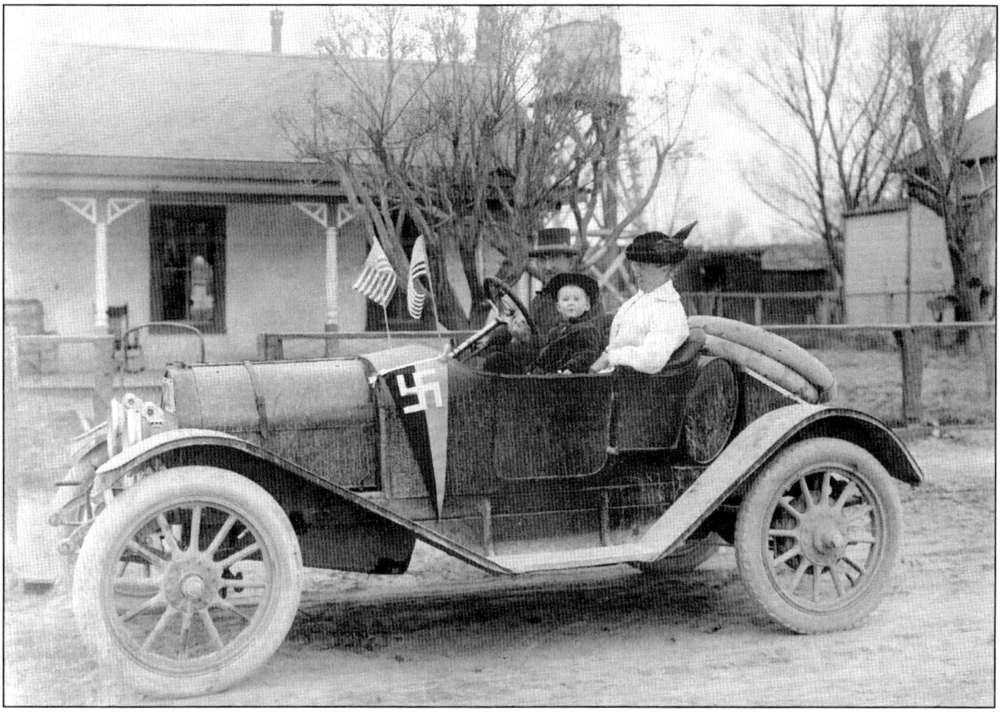

Dr. Wilson, Helen, and Jack are arriving home from the Mascot and Western Railroad parade in their new 1916 Model Overland Runabout. Wilson rode his horse to Safford to purchase his first automobile, the first car in town, and drove home after a few instructions from the dealer. The swastika logo, used by the Mascot Copper Company, had no association to Hitler. (Butch and Kay Ellen Wilson.)

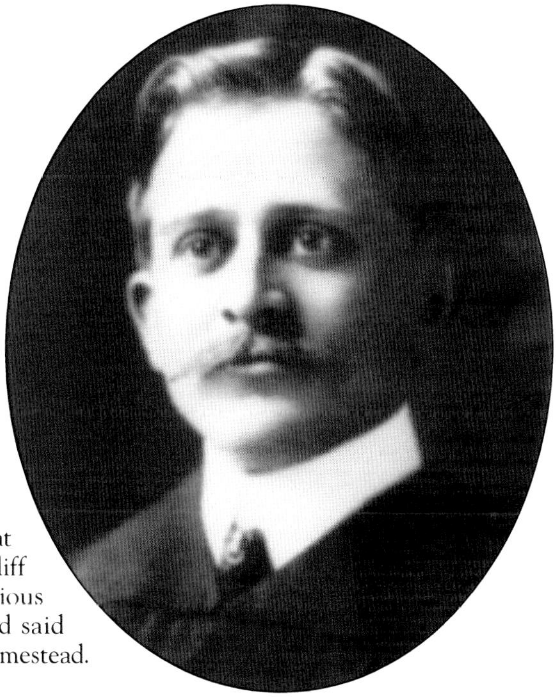

Dr. Frederick H. Ratcliff, licensed in Tennessee, mercifully treated neighbors for no fee, there being no dentists in Willcox. Funds were raised for an adjustable chair, tools, and an office in town. Notified that he was practicing illegally in Arizona, Ratcliff went to take the exam, came back furious without a license, closed his office, and said patients could come the 7 miles to his homestead. (Charlene Clark.)

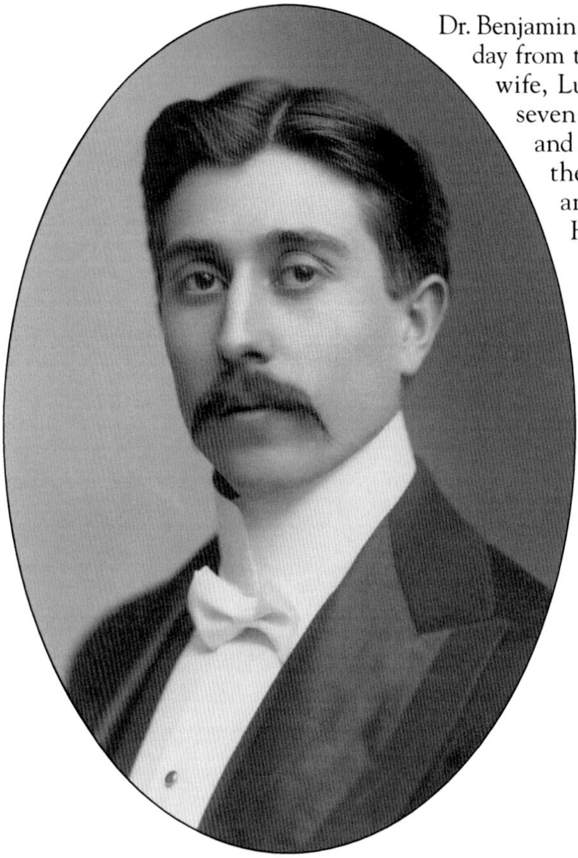

Dr. Benjamin Edward Briscoe is pictured on graduation day from the University of Tennessee. He and his wife, Lula, came here in 1909, and they had seven children. Lula's parents were James T. and Drusilla Cotner of Willcox. Briscoe was the Southern Pacific Railroad physician and practiced medicine here until 1949. He was elected to the Arizona House of Representatives in 1922 and served three terms. (Wanda Linam Perry.)

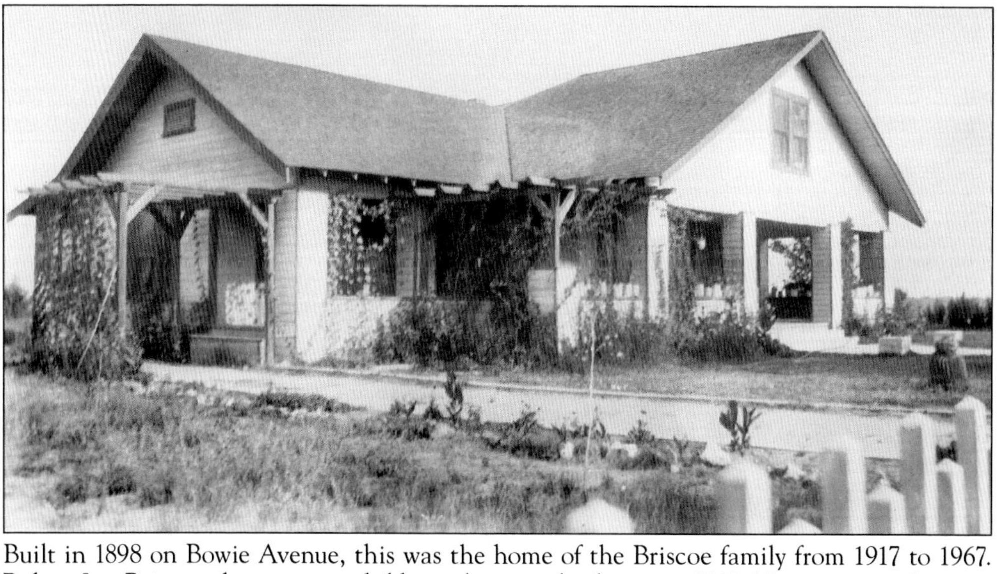

Built in 1898 on Bowie Avenue, this was the home of the Briscoe family from 1917 to 1967. Robert Lee Briscoe, the youngest child, was born in this house in 1918. He went on to become city manager of Coolidge, Arizona; Gunnison, Colorado; and Perris, California. A cutting from the famous Tombstone rosebush, which flourished, was the setting for many family wedding photographs. (Wanda Linam Perry.)

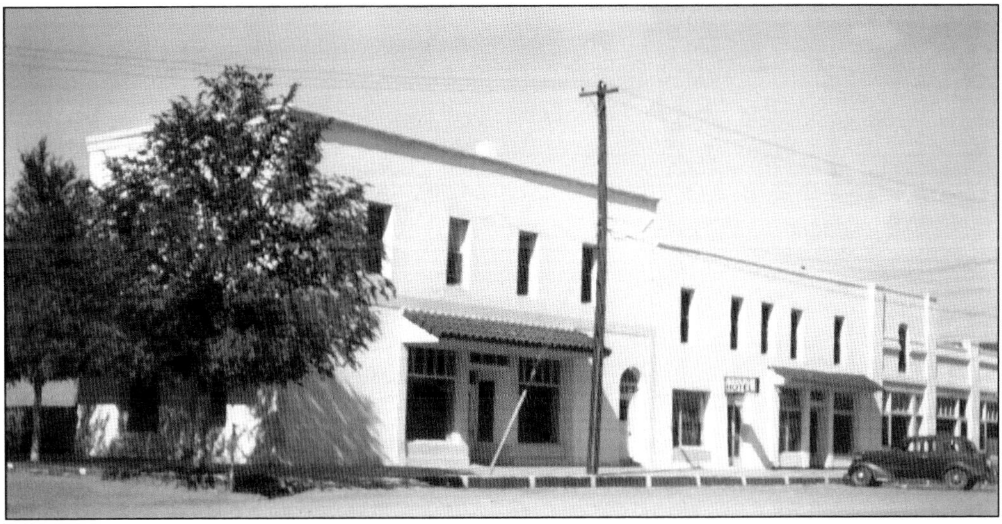

Dr. B. E. Briscoe's office was in this building on the corner of Maley Street and Railroad Avenue. His phone number for the office was 73; for his residence, it was 74. He owned the Navajo Hotel next door, managed by T. J. Davis. This building was demolished in 1970. Previous businesses that occupied the building were Kasper Hauser's Saloon, which opened there in 1897, and Harry Parks Curio Shop, which operated there from 1946 to 1951. (Wanda Linam Perry.)

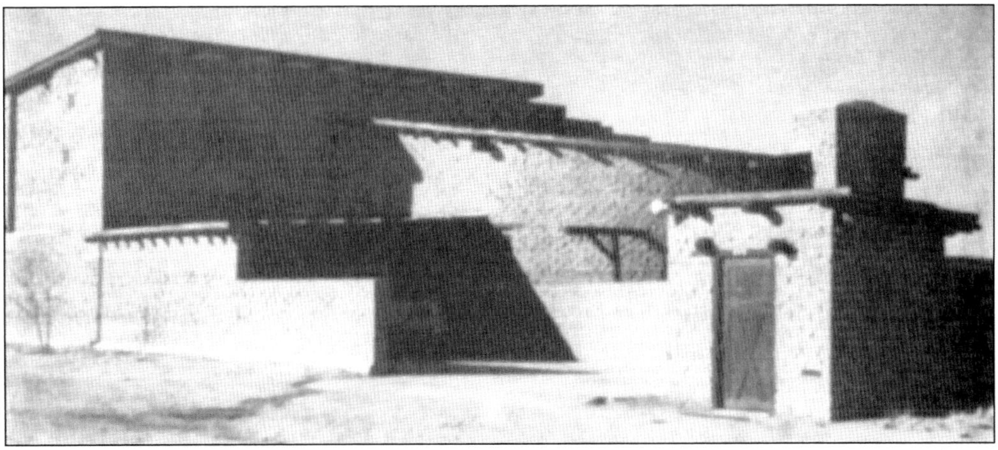

"The Fort" was built by Dr. Robert Hicks to resemble a battleship soon after taking over Dr. Wilson's practice in 1944. Hicks's license was suspended after he and his nurse went on a drinking spree with a heart attack victim still in the ambulance. At various times, the building was William Koehn's mortuary, the home of Rex Emrick (whose wife called it "the menopausaleum"), and Dr. Robert Patterson's house.

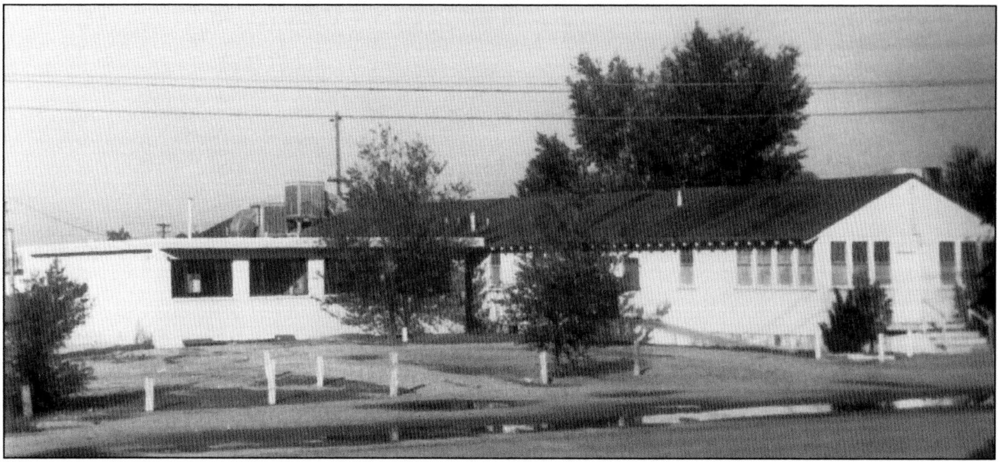

The Municipal Hospital on Maley Street, built in 1952 from barracks, served 12 patients. It replaced Dr. Robert Hicks's Valley Hospital Infirmary on Railroad Avenue, where a nurse would be signaled outside by a light over the patient's door. The infirmary became the Green Gables Apartments. In February 1967, the first patient was moved from the Municipal Hospital to Northern Cochise Community Hospital on Rex Allen Drive. The library was built here on Maley Street in 1969, with the Art League next door.

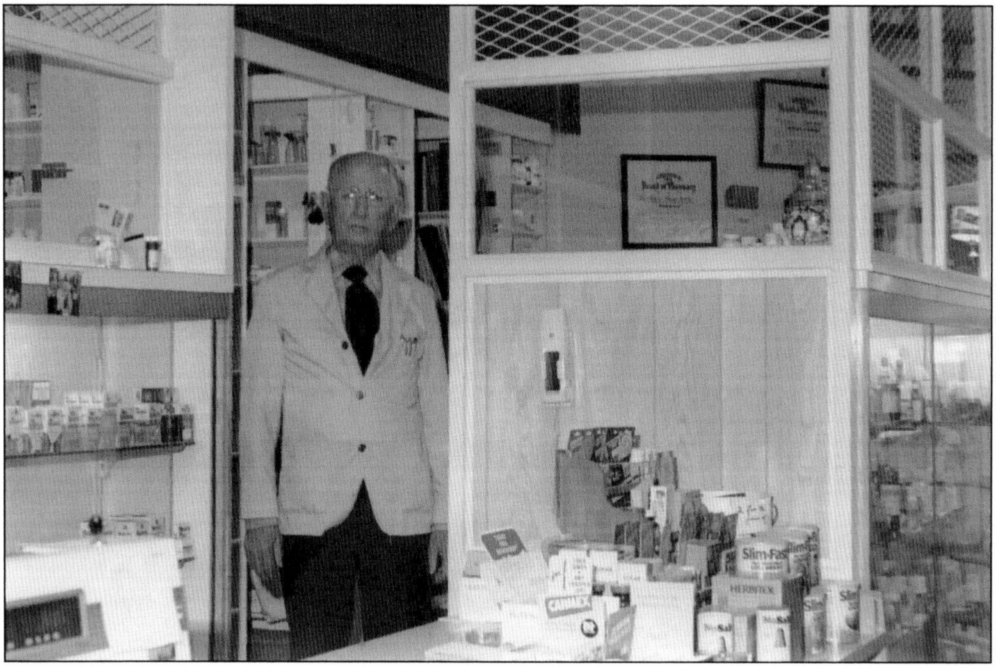

Inside Austin's Drug Store on Haskell Avenue is pharmacist George Austin. After World War II, he became partners with Marshall Nicholson in the Nicholson-Austin Drugstore. After Nicholson died, Austin became sole owner and moved to the new location in the Masonic Lodge. The governor appointed Austin to the State Board of Pharmacy for 10 years. El Paso Avenue was renamed Austin Boulevard after his death in 1989.

Five

Willcox Incorporates

January 1, 1915, marked the beginning of Prohibition in Arizona and the beginning of a new era for the town of Willcox. The *Arizona Range News* reported, "Willcox has needed incorporation more than any one thing. Trying to make headway with an unincorporated town is like trying to move a train of cars without an engine." On May 3, 1915, incorporation was passed by the county board of supervisors in Tombstone. Appointed to serve as councilmen until an election could be held were H. L. McCoy, L. V. McCourt, J. W. Angle, A. A. Nicholson, and Henry A. Morgan. At that meeting, $500 was appropriated for repairs on Fort Grant Road from Willcox to the Graham County Line, and bids were to be advertised for grading and labor to construct a road across the dry lake between Willcox and Cochise and to build the branch county jail at Willcox. The first city offices filled were as follows: Jesse Moore, city marshal and tax collector at a salary of $30 per month; Herbert Lowdermilk, city clerk and treasurer at $10 per month; Kasper Hauser, police judge at $10 per month; and John C. Gung'l, city attorney at $15 per month. Of the 16 ordinances passed that year, the first six set the time and place for meetings to be held, officers and salaries, and dog licenses. They also prohibited appearing in a state of nudity or in dress not belonging to his or her sex, any act of lewd or indecent behavior, being drunk or disorderly, vagrancy, and littering. It would be a misdemeanor to immoderately drive or ride horses or other animals, or to disturb any lawful assemblage of people, including discharging a gun or setting off fireworks. It was against the law to carry a concealed weapon. All vehicles must use a lighted lamp after sunset and before sunrise, carry a horn, and drive at no greater speed than 12 miles per hour. Ordinance number six enacted the collection of the annual street tax of $2 for every male over 21 and under 60 years of age.

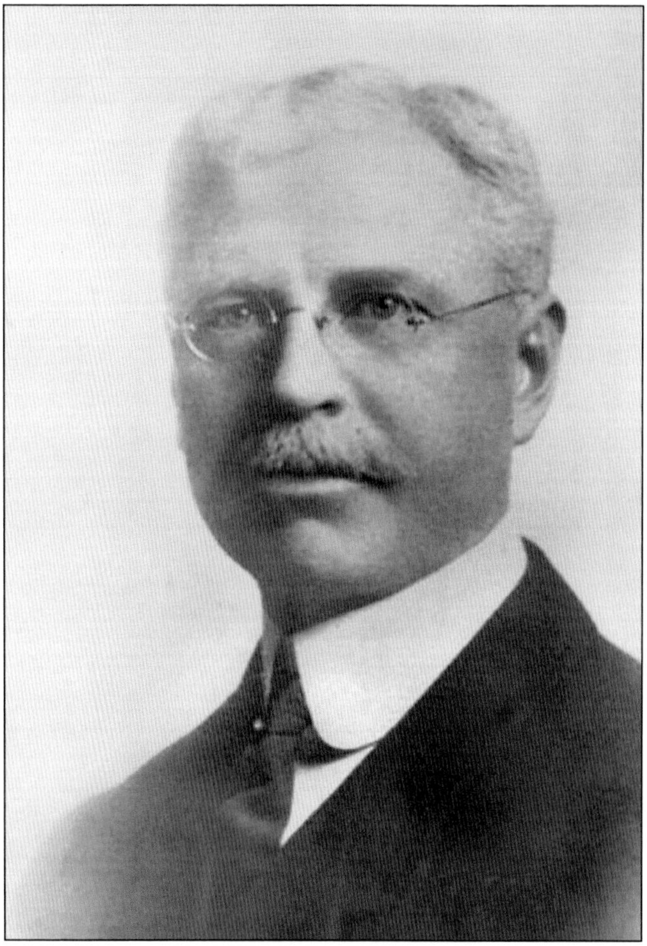

Henry A. Morgan was the first city mayor. He arrived on the overland stage and began as bookkeeper for John H. Norton at Fort Grant in 1881. They became partners in 1893 and changed the Willcox store to Norton–Morgan Commercial Company. Morgan was president of the Willcox Bank and Trust and very active in community affairs. He married Anna Dixon in 1886, and they had four children.

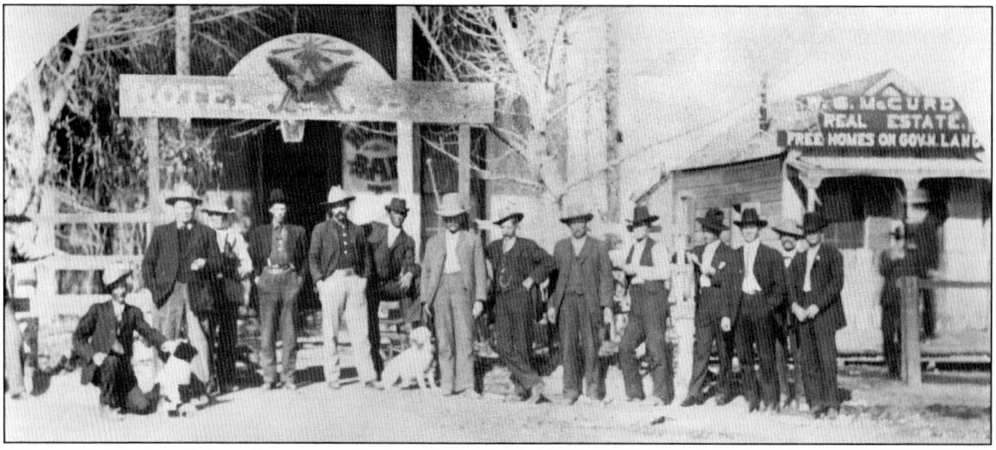

Walter S. McCurdy's real estate office was next to this hotel and bar with the Anheuser-Busch logo. In 1909, at the start of a building boom, he sold 60 lots in the Morgan and Angle additions. After his brother Rodolphes Clay McCurdy, a pool hall owner, died, Rodolphes's wife, Delia, operator of McCurdy's Boarding House, married Frank Tillotson, a photographer and owner of the local cleaners. (Linda Shaver.)

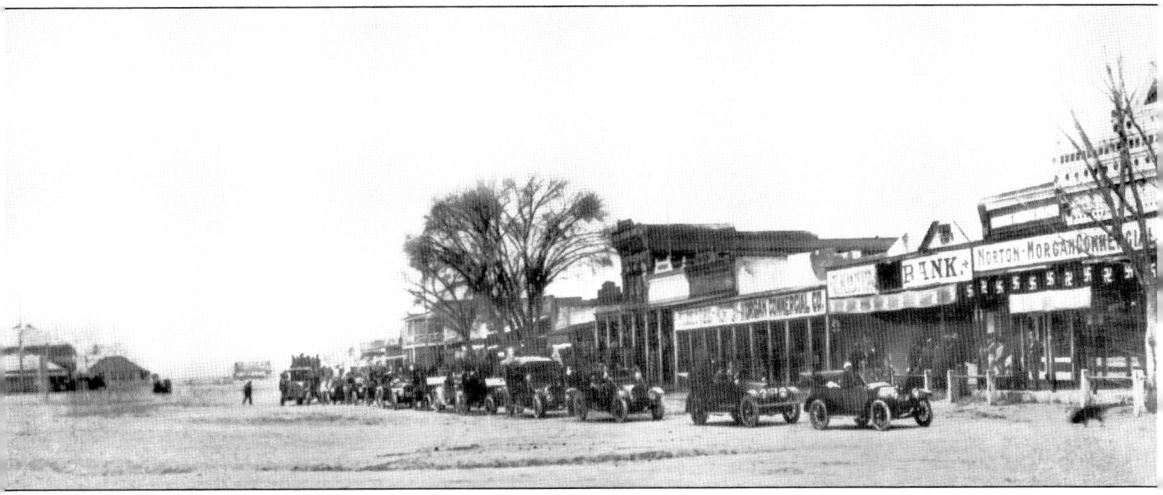

A huge celebration was held on January 27, 1915, as T. N. McCauley turned the first shovel of dirt for the new Mascot and Western Railroad from Willcox to Dos Cabezas. Flags and bunting (with the company's swastika logo) waved from the buildings, and the band played. Although the Mascot Mine created a great number of jobs, it turned out to be a huge stock-selling scheme.

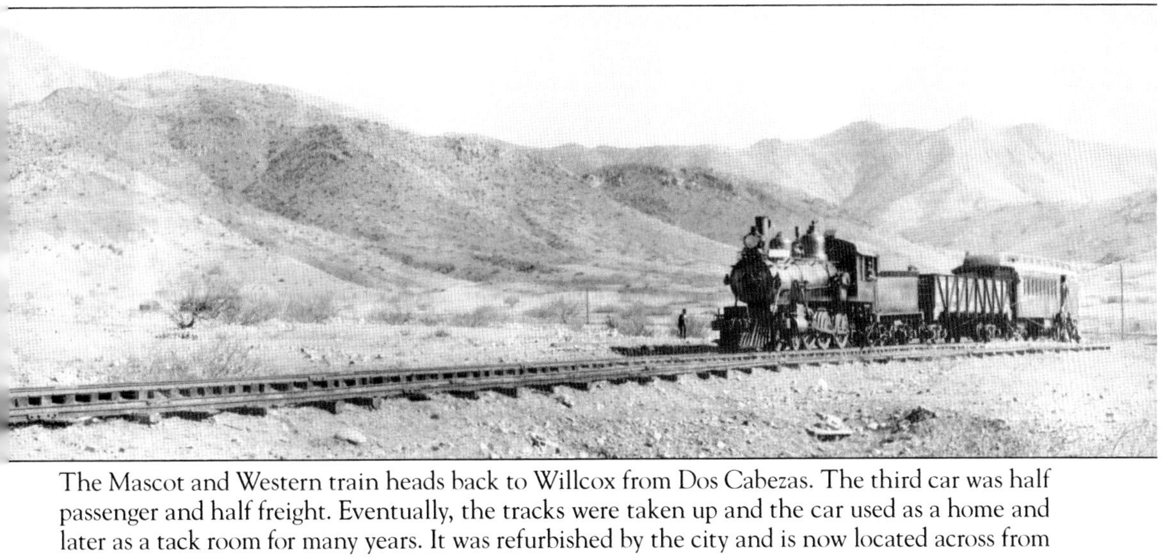

The Mascot and Western train heads back to Willcox from Dos Cabezas. The third car was half passenger and half freight. Eventually, the tracks were taken up and the car used as a home and later as a tack room for many years. It was refurbished by the city and is now located across from the railroad depot.

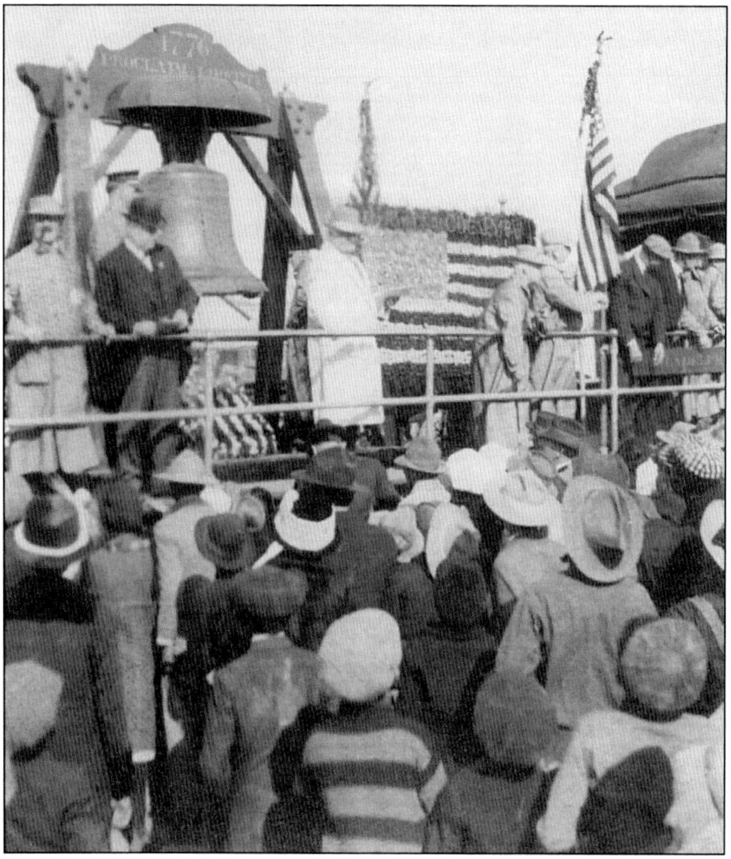

On November 16, 1915, people traveled from the farthest parts of the valley to see the special train carrying the Liberty Bell. Sid Page led the local band in patriotic songs. Souvenirs were thrown from the car, and Mayor Henry Morgan was presented with a silk flag, a badge, and a book containing the history of the bell. He boarded the train and rode as far as Bowie.

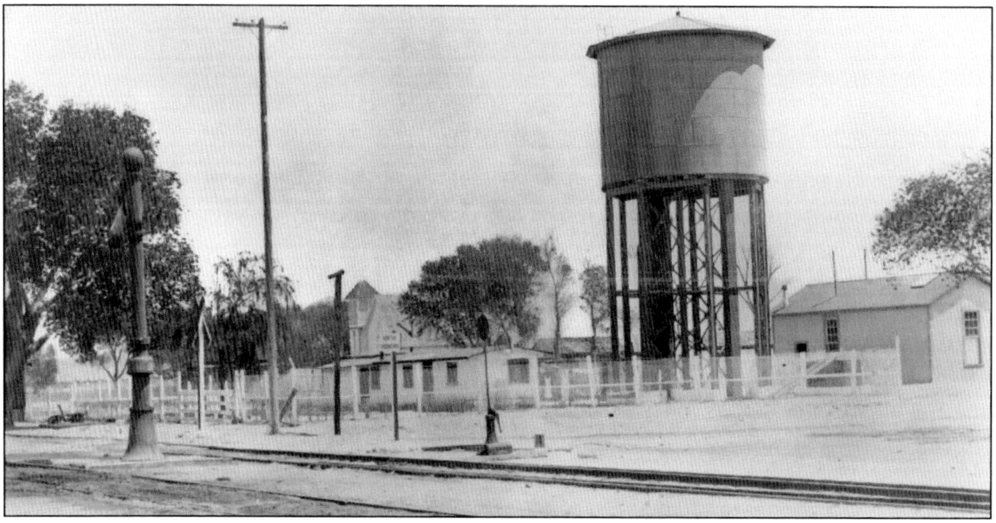

The Southern Pacific water tower, east of the tracks, stood from 1912 until 1956, becoming obsolete after the steam locomotives were no longer in use. In 1923, H. E. Lundquist sold oil he skimmed from on top of the water and from shallow wells on his lots southeast of the tower. The oil was leakage and overflow from the railroad's underground tanks and not a rich oil reserve.

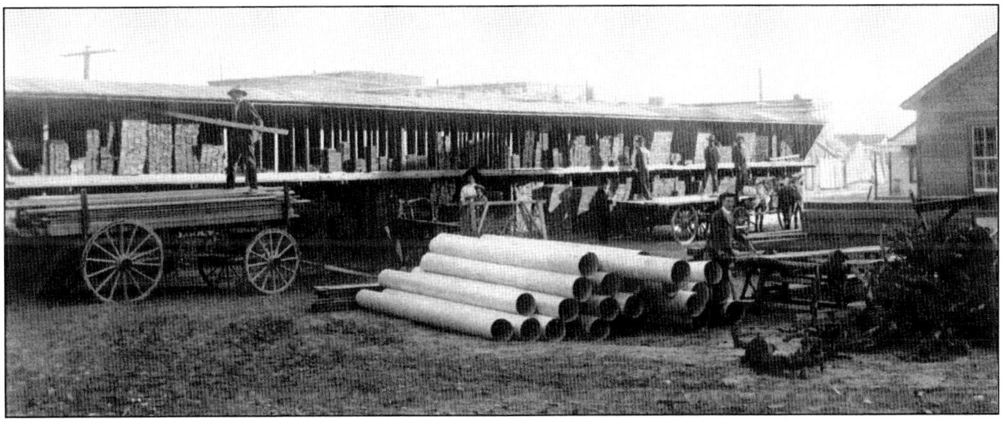

Angle and Bush Lumber Company's business was booming until their store at Mascot burned with a loss of $3,000 and no insurance. J. P. Cook, a bookkeeper, took over the lumber business, naming it the Arizona Lumber Company. The grain portion of the business was sold to Frank Rottman. Charles W. Bush learned the tinner's trade before going into the hardware business. He and his wife, Mahala Keeling, had two children.

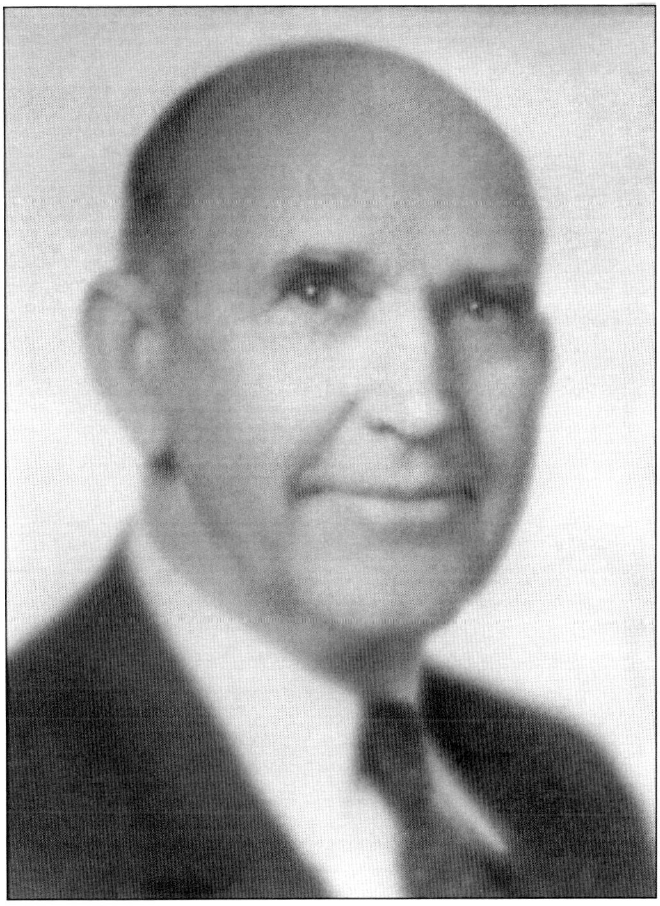

Joseph Wheeler Angle came to Willcox in 1908, after several years as a traveling salesman, and founded the lumber company with Charles W. Bush. Branch stores were opened in Bowie, San Simon, and Mascot, Arizona. One of the original city councilmen, Angle married Beulah Millican, with whom he had six children. They built a beautiful home on south Arizona Avenue, later the home of Harley and Irene Windsor.

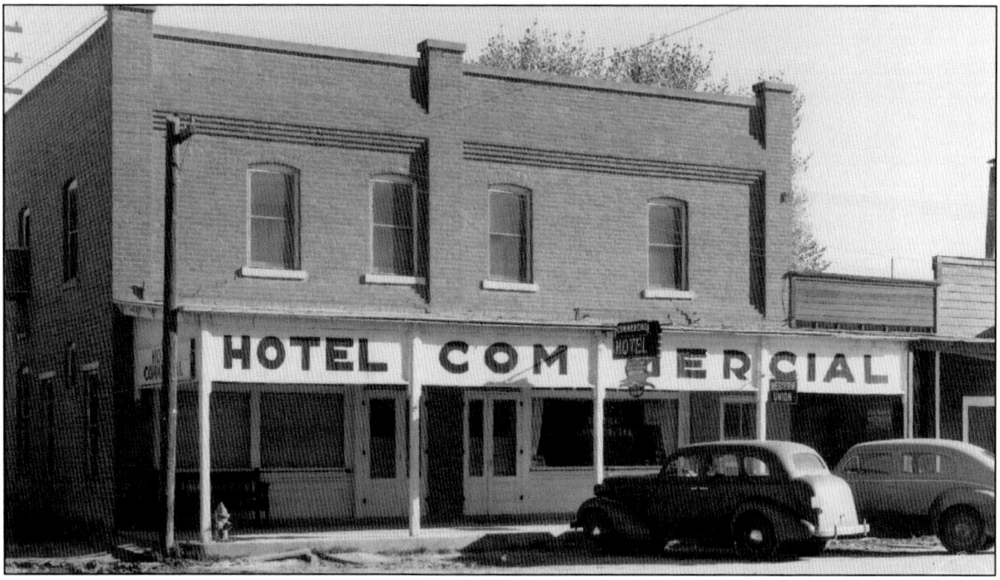

Originally known as the Moyer Building, the Commercial Hotel was built in 1916 on Maley Street to accommodate traveling salesmen and business people. In the television movie *Code of Vengeance* with Erin Gray, filmed here in the 1985, a truck was crashed through the door. The hotel was later restored and became Brown's Ice Cream Parlor, with law offices upstairs. (James and Sandra Thomas.)

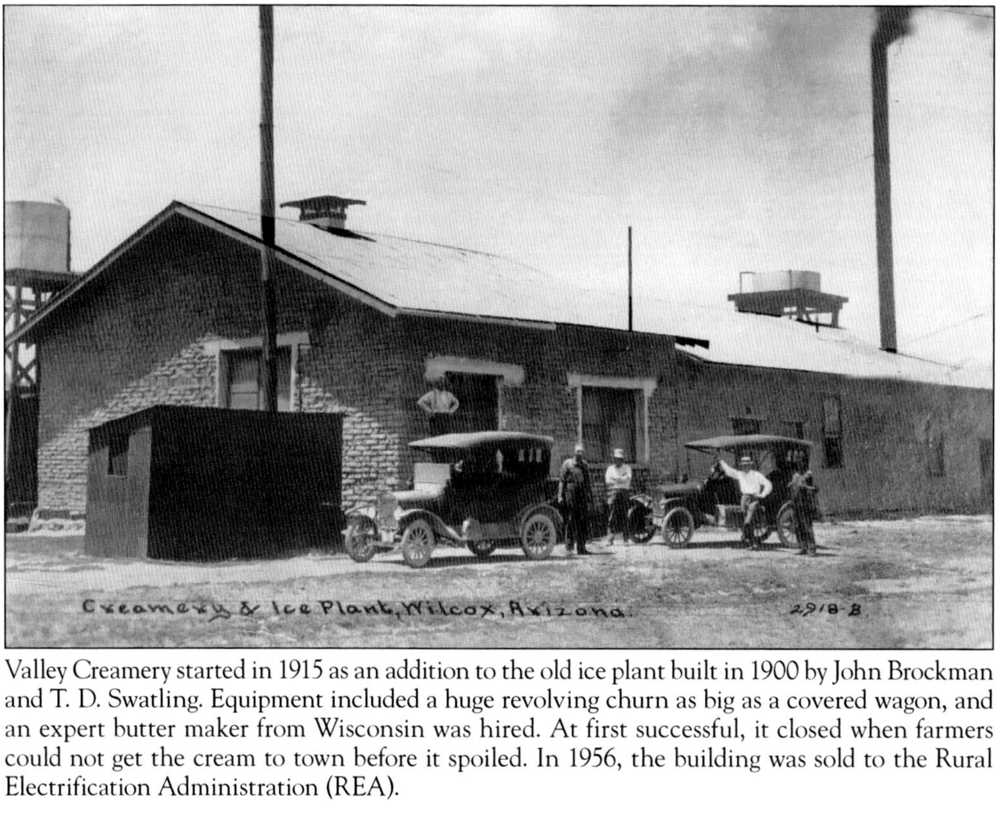

Valley Creamery started in 1915 as an addition to the old ice plant built in 1900 by John Brockman and T. D. Swatling. Equipment included a huge revolving churn as big as a covered wagon, and an expert butter maker from Wisconsin was hired. At first successful, it closed when farmers could not get the cream to town before it spoiled. In 1956, the building was sold to the Rural Electrification Administration (REA).

Thomas Avery Huffman and his wife, Julia, are shown with their son Bruce and daughter Katherine. Julia Redden came in 1910 to teach school and married Thomas in 1913. Bruce competed in boxing at the University of Arizona. A fund was named in his honor there after he established the Wildcat Club in Willcox to raise money for his alma mater. Katherine married Oscar Woods.

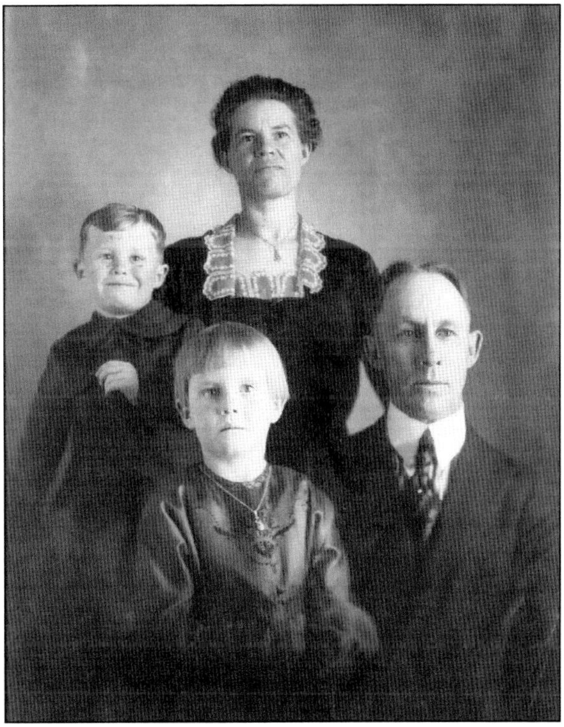

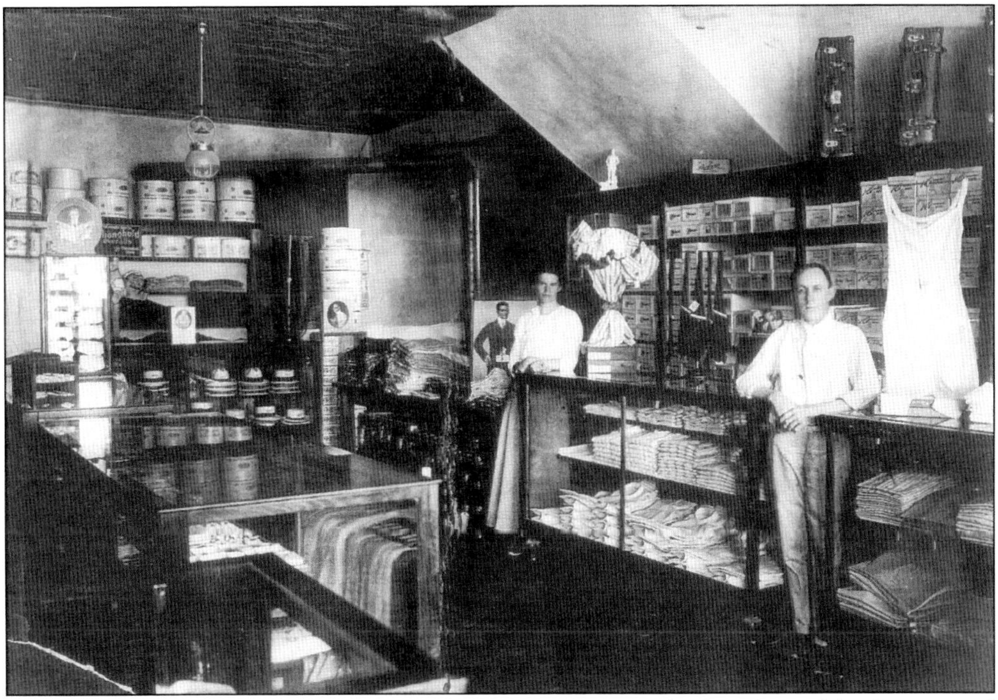

Thomas and Julia Huffman established the Toggery in 1916 on the first floor of the Commercial Hotel. Clothes were called togs in that day. The store moved across the street in 1925 into their brand new building. The Huffman family continued to operate the store until 2002. It is now the research library for the Chiricahua Regional Museum with displays in the original showcases.

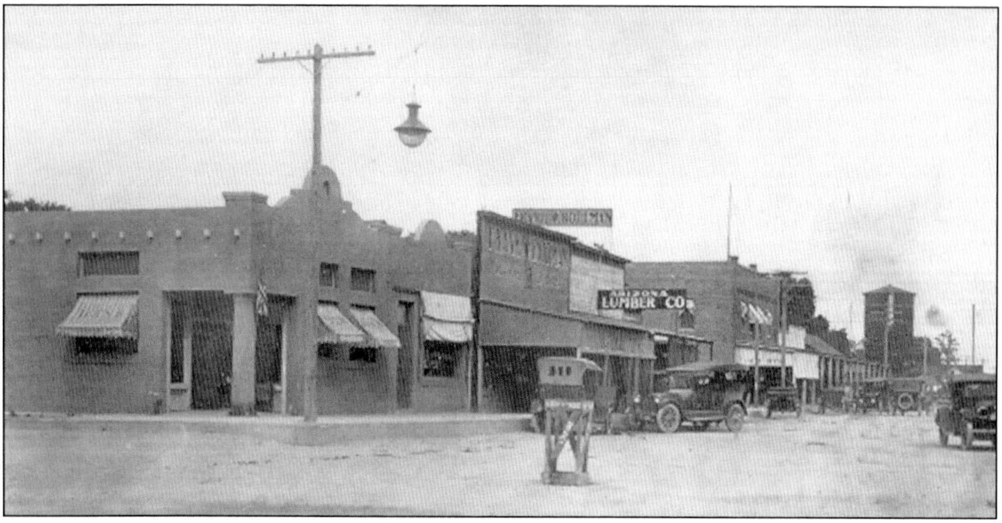

In 1915, the Central Bank of Phoenix built a branch on the corner of Haskell Avenue and Maley Street. Their motto was, "When you've got money we want it, when you want money, we've got it." Down the street are Frank Rottman's store, Arizona Lumber Company, Commercial Hotel, and the water tower. The Sulphur Springs Valley Bank on Railroad Avenue was liquidated that same year. (James and Sandra Thomas.)

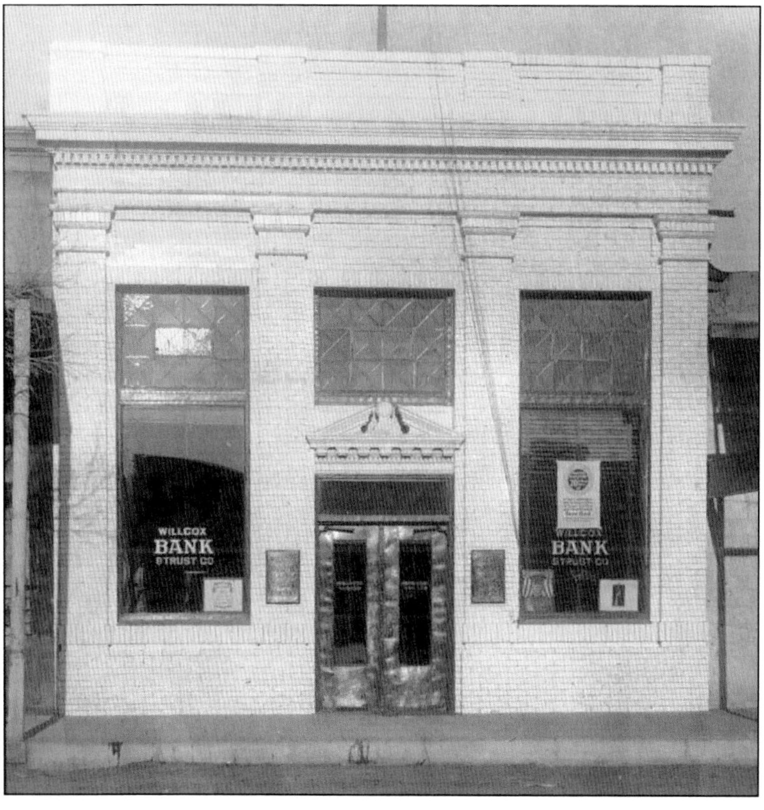

This white, Italian, glazed-brick building was the new home of the Willcox Bank and Trust in 1917. The bank was organized in 1909 with Henry Morgan, president, Horace Dunlap, cashier; and John H. Norton, Thomas Allaire, and A. Y. Smith, directors. The bank closed from difficulties during the Great Depression. It served as the Wildwood Gallery and Friends of the Library Book Bank from 1986 to 2007.

Six

Schools and Churches

The first school principal on record was Edwin Booth in 1893; he left town in a hurry after inappropriate behavior with one of the students. To date, there have been three grammar schools, three high schools, and only one middle school. Willcox High School was the first one in the state to offer an automobile driving instruction course. The longest serving principal of the elementary school was George J. Coleman, who was hired in 1932. At his retirement in 1959, Mayor W. B. Loving presented him with a gold watch. Remembered fondly for serving many years in the administration of the high school were Lloyd Eikenberry and Frank Jordan.

In the early days, it was noted that there were seven churches on Maley Street and seven saloons on Railroad Avenue. There are still at least seven churches on Maley Street but only the Palace Saloon survives on Railroad Avenue. Of the many different religions represented in Willcox, the Church of Jesus Christ of Latter-day Saints has become one of the largest. Their two wards cover from Willcox to Bonita, Bowie, and the Chiricahua Monument. Their first building was on Bowie Avenue where the Victory Baptist Church is today. On October 1, 1975, ground was broken for the new Latter-day Saints facility on Encanto Street.

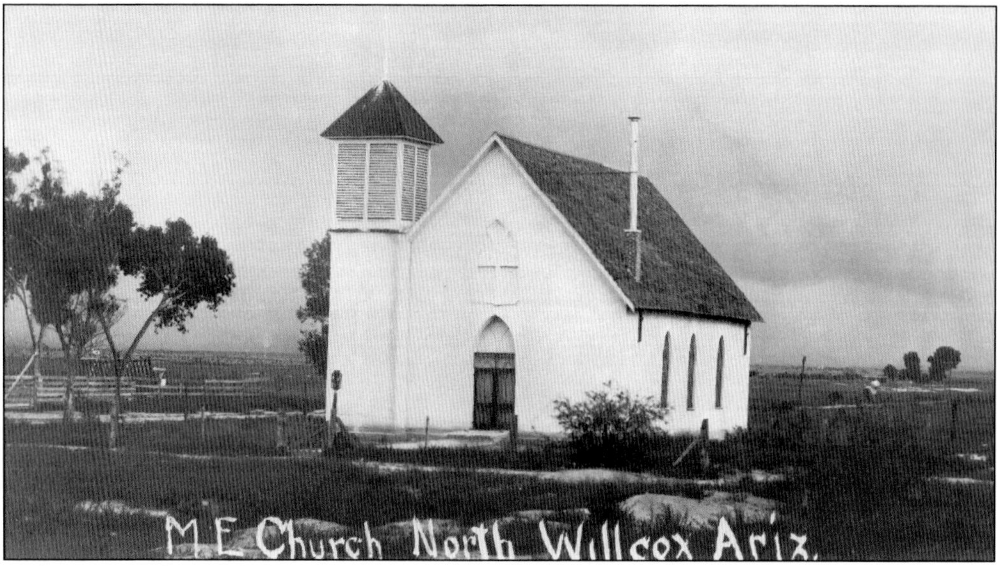

Built in 1886, the Methodist Episcopal (North) church was located over the railroad tracks on Stewart Street. Previously, Col. Henry Hooker had built a long adobe building for nondenominational use. John H. Norton donated the ornate pump organ, now in the Chiricahua Museum collection. The first permanent minister, Nathan L. Guthrie, came in 1887 from Flagstaff. He built a house in Willcox in 1890 but died in 1893.

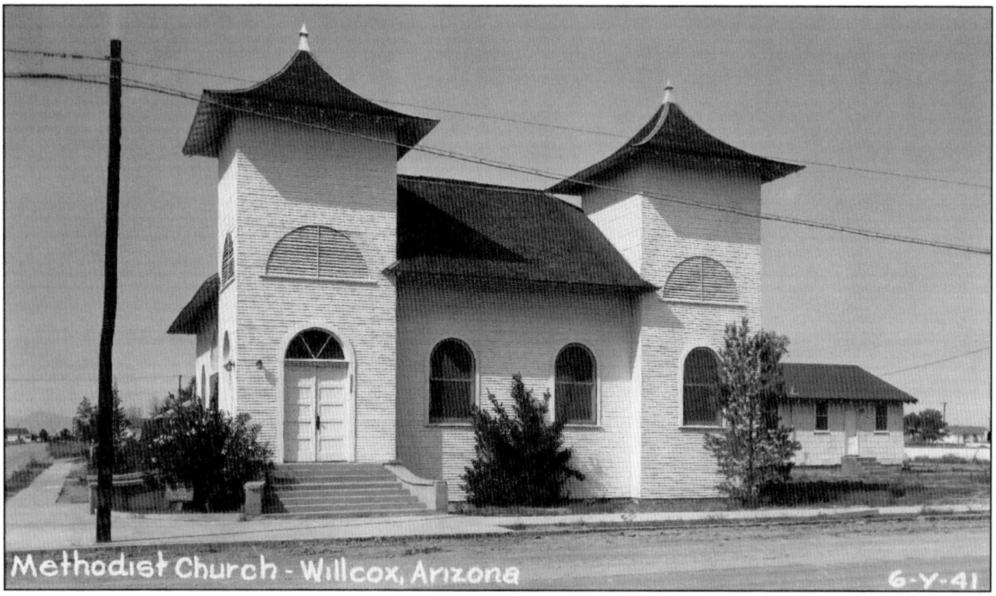

The Methodist Episcopal (South) church was built in 1911, replacing a tiny building constructed in 1909 on Maley Street. In 1912 and 1913, under the pastorship of T. A. Windsor (father of Harley Windsor), the North and South churches were combined and the old church on Stewart Street was no longer used. This building was dismantled in 1969 and replaced by the current building.

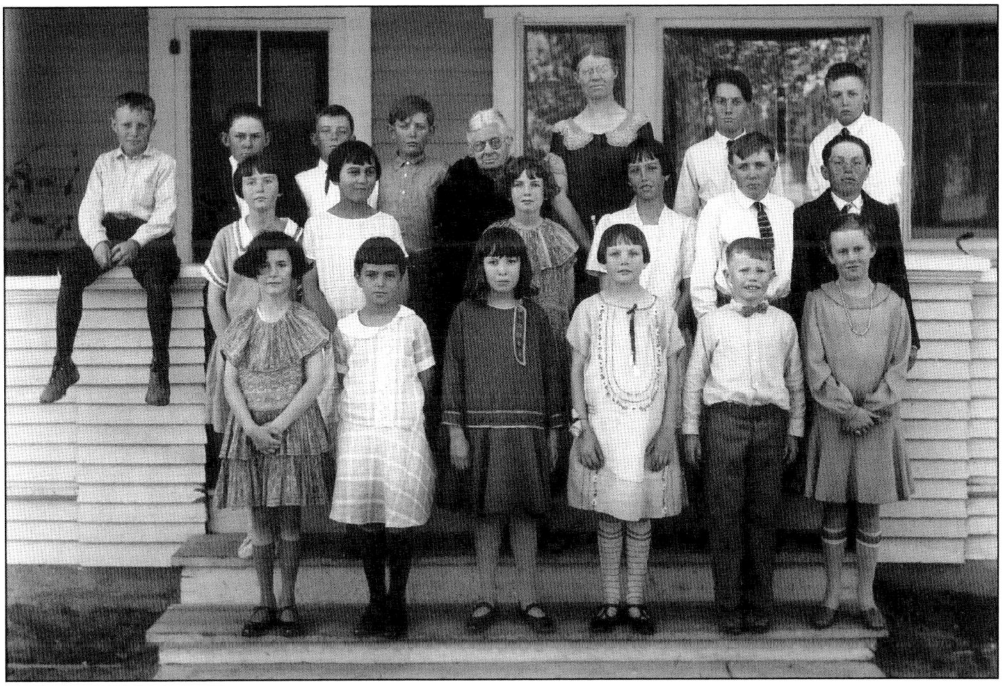

Standing in the middle of the top row is teacher Julia Huffman with her Methodist Sunday school class around 1925. Her mother, Kate A. Redden (with gray hair), stands fifth from the left in the top row, next to Julia. Julia's children, Bruce and Katherine Huffman, are in the bottom row at far right.

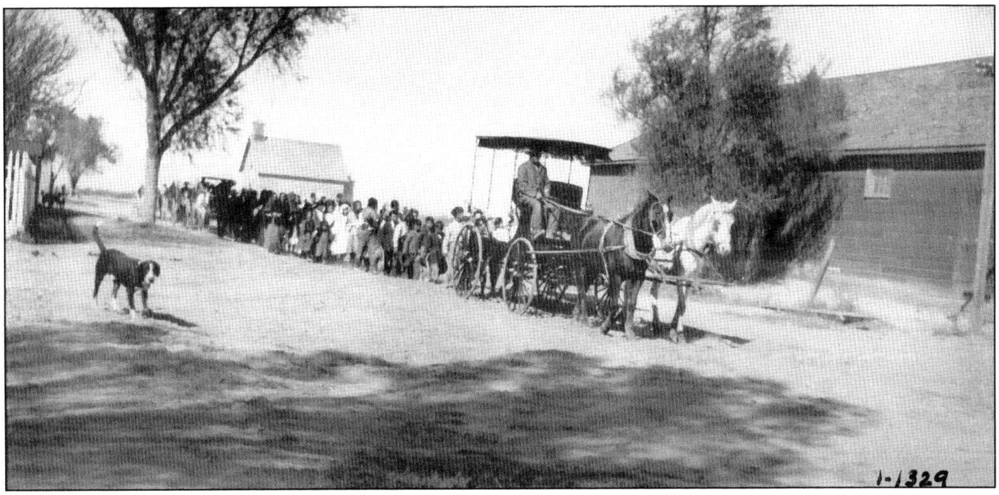

A horse-drawn carriage with a casket heads down Stewart Street to the old cemetery as mourners follow in this Mexican funeral procession. The first Catholic church is in the background. Started in 1887, the roof was completed in March 1889. Priests came weekly from Benson or Solomonville until Fr. Mariano Uson was called in 1934. The large building is Morgan Hall, originally Tully-Ochoa Hall then Norton Hall. (Arizona Historical Society.)

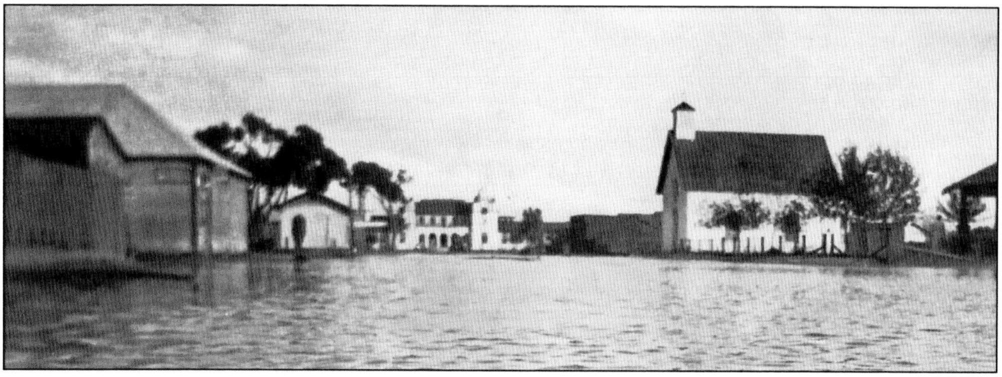

West Stewart Street is covered with floodwaters in 1923. Frank "Prairie Dog" Lewis's home and shoe shop were on the left. He was so named because the government hired him to eradicate all the prairie dogs in the area. The high school, with twin towers, is directly ahead. The Catholic church, on the right, burned on May 5, 1947, and was bulldozed down in 1959. (Wallace Lundquist family.)

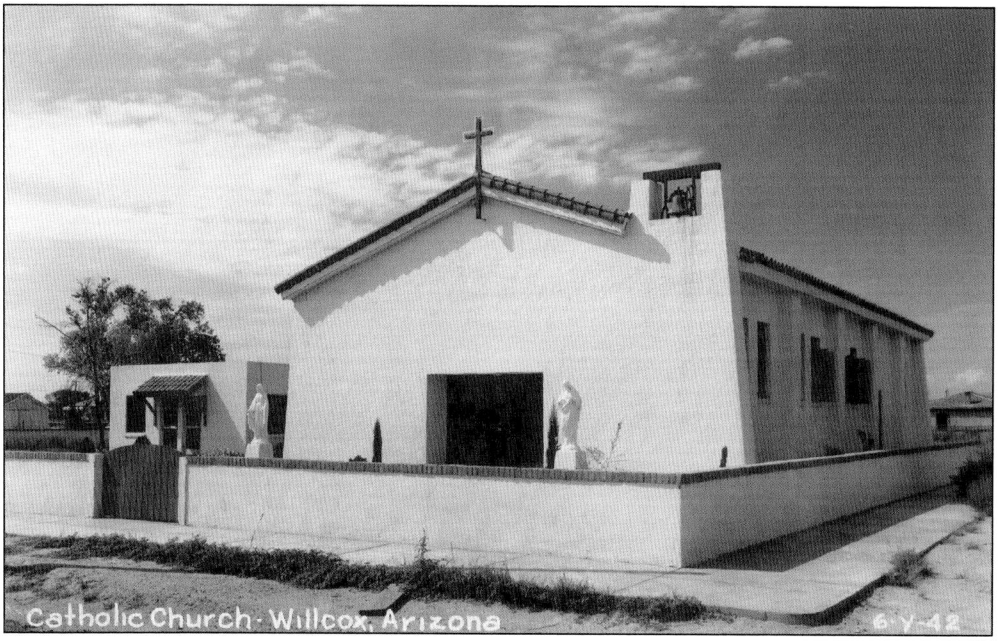

Construction began on Sacred Heart Catholic Church on Maley Street in October 1947. Designed by Tucson architect Terry Atkinson, all the pews, altars, and cabinets were made by hand and fashioned locally by Ed Garcia. Mrs. J. M. Brannen was the first parish organist. In 1964, a new building was completed for religious education. The building had a face-lift in 1996 with a new addition on the front.

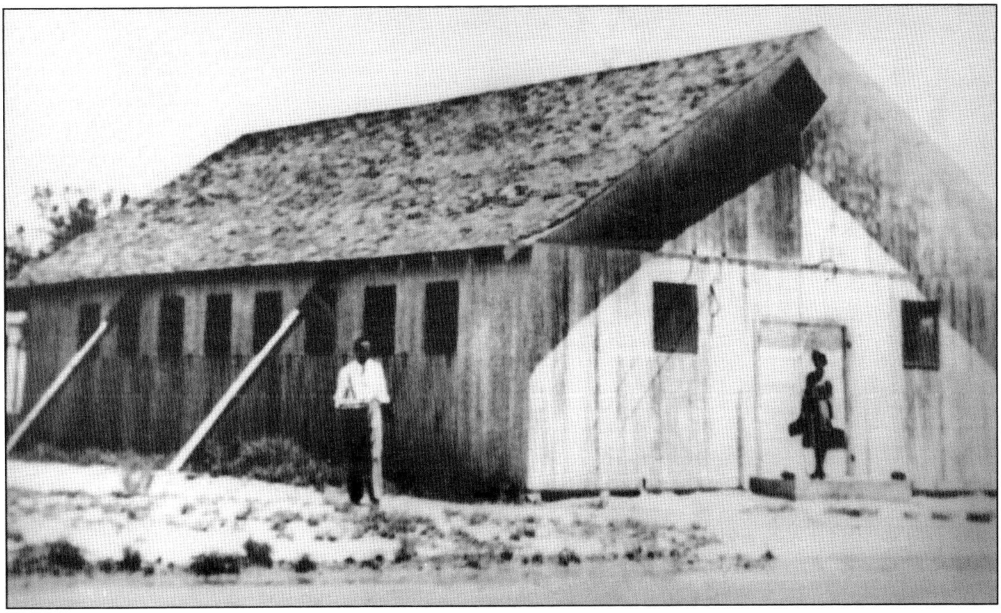

The Christian Tabernacle was established here in July 1911 on the corner of Maley Street and Austin Boulevard. Julia Huffman and Mrs. J. B. Cook (Rebecca) were two of the original members. The first building burned, and this structure was being constructed around 1940. (Richard Seidel.)

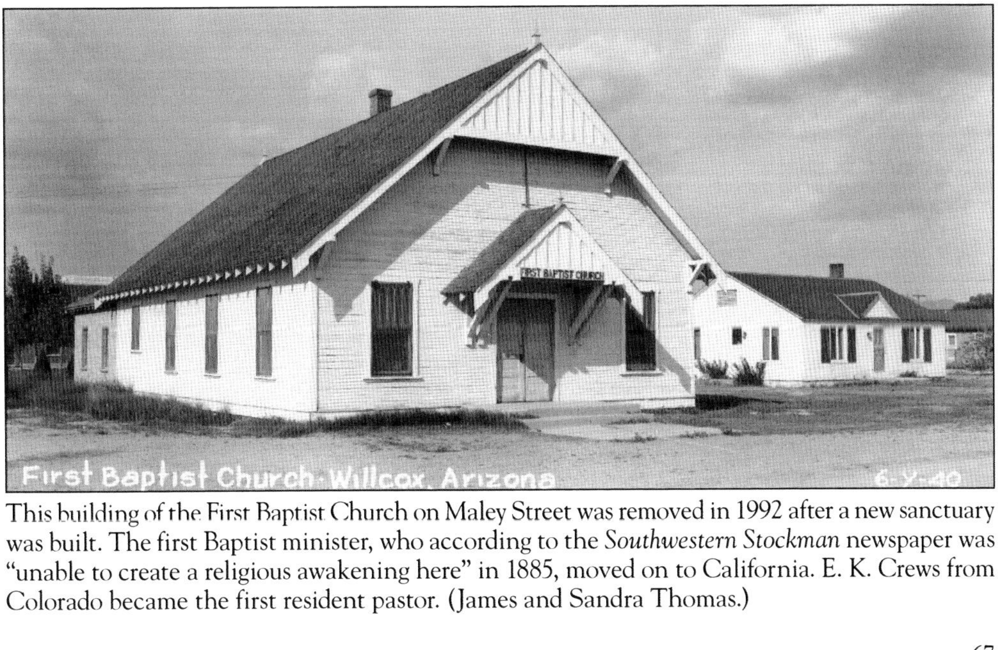

This building of the First Baptist Church on Maley Street was removed in 1992 after a new sanctuary was built. The first Baptist minister, who according to the *Southwestern Stockman* newspaper was "unable to create a religious awakening here" in 1885, moved on to California. E. K. Crews from Colorado became the first resident pastor. (James and Sandra Thomas.)

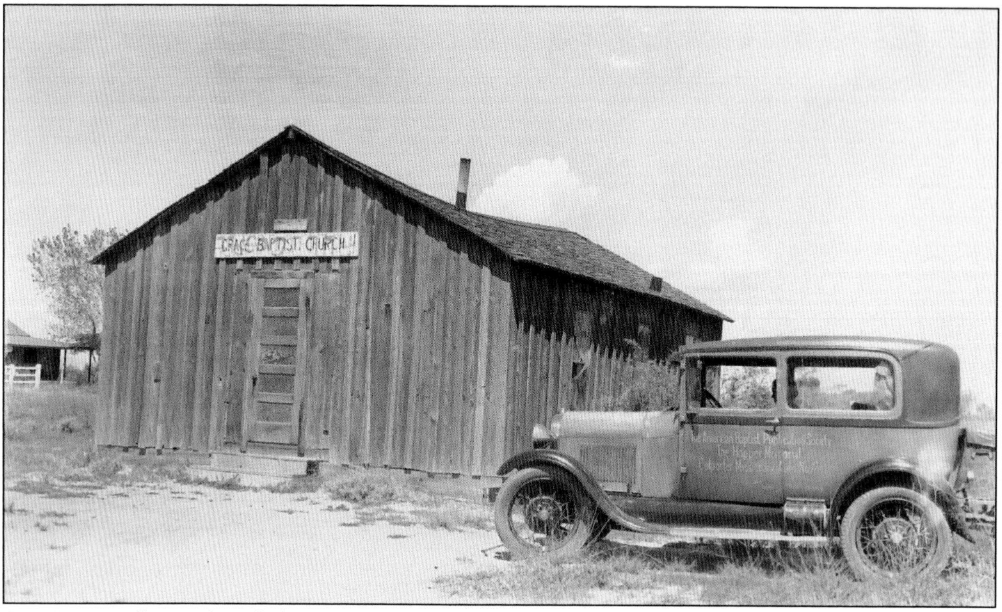

Rev. Dee Williams founded Grace Chapel in 1932. Located on Maley Street, it continues today in a nicely remodeled building. Dee and his wife, Ellen, homesteaded in Cochise in 1913. The family moved to Willcox in 1917 with their five children: Alvie, Raymond, Homer, Lillie, and Ruth. Reverend Williams was a blacksmith, carpenter, bricklayer, and plumber and ran a grocery and second-hand store. (Hansen family.)

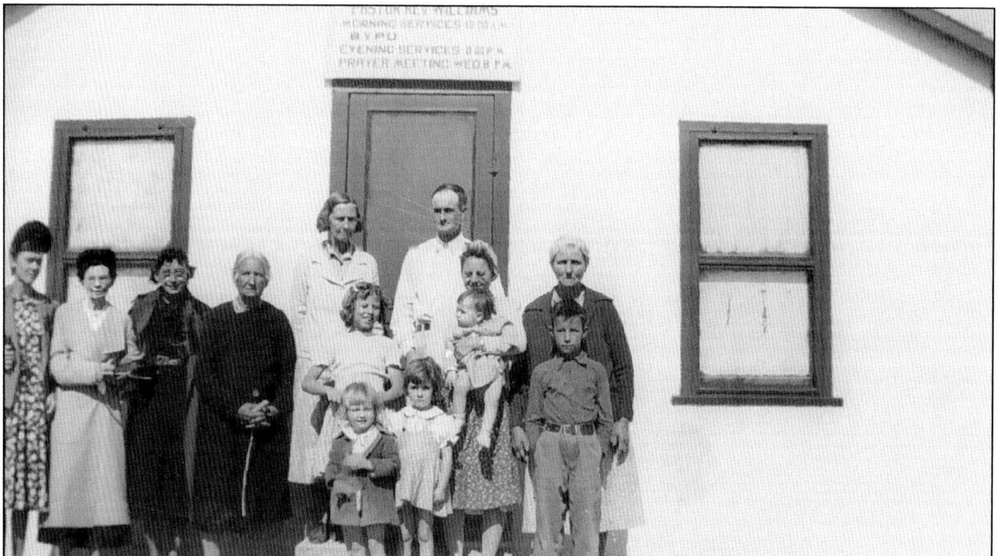

Members of the Grace Chapel congregation pose in front of the church in 1942. Identified are Julia Pope (second from left), Dee Williams (in front of door), and his daughter-in-law Georgie Belle holding Colleen. Georgie's children are Eileen, Vergene, Shirley, and J. O. (Hansen family.)

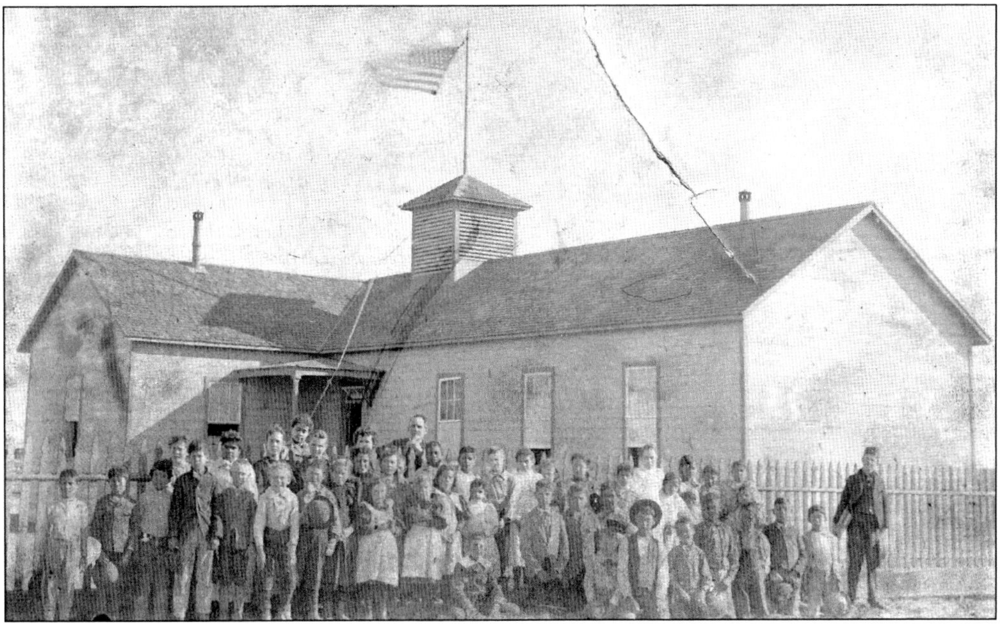

This two-room schoolhouse, built in 1893, was located at 322 East Maley Street. Teachers were Mercedes Shibell and ? Hendricks. Among the students in the 1897 photograph are Harry and May Parks, the Soto girls, Mabel and Gertie Kemp, and Julius Hauser. The newspaper announced that ladies were allowed to vote in the 1893 school election. This redwood school later burned to the ground. (Arizona Historical Society.)

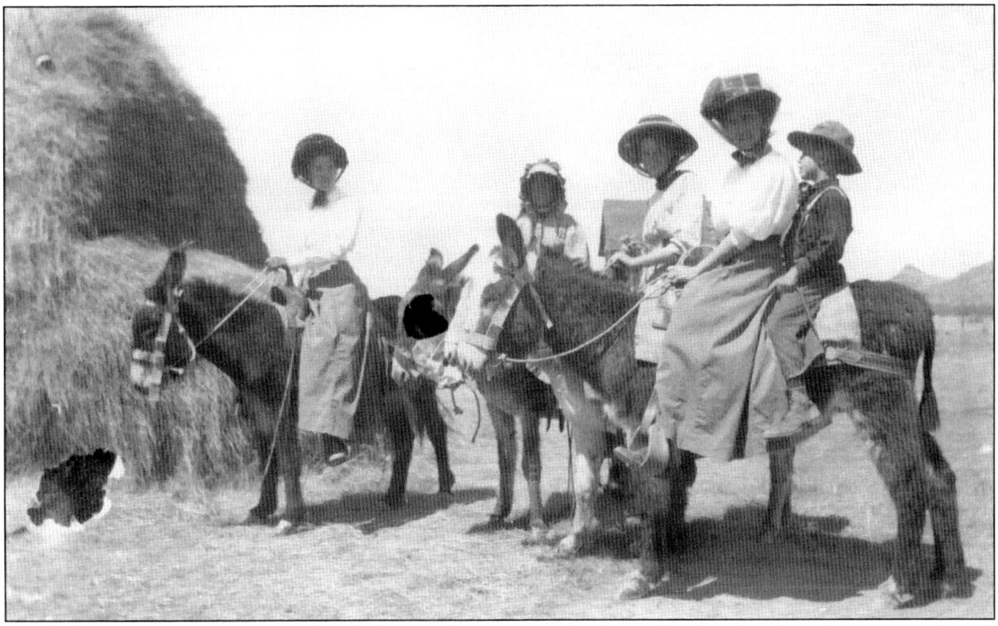

These Lawson family ladies include Margaret Lawson (right), a local schoolteacher around 1915. Sharing a ride on the burro with her is Irving Thompson. Daughters of Dr. Thomas Chalmers Lawson were Margaret, Elizabeth, Mary, and Alice. Elizabeth married Oscar McAda, the Arizona Ranger. Mary married Mabry Lawson (no relation), whose children, Richard, Chalmers, and Elizabeth Lawson Henderson, grew up on the Muleshoe Ranch. (Peta-Anne Tenney.)

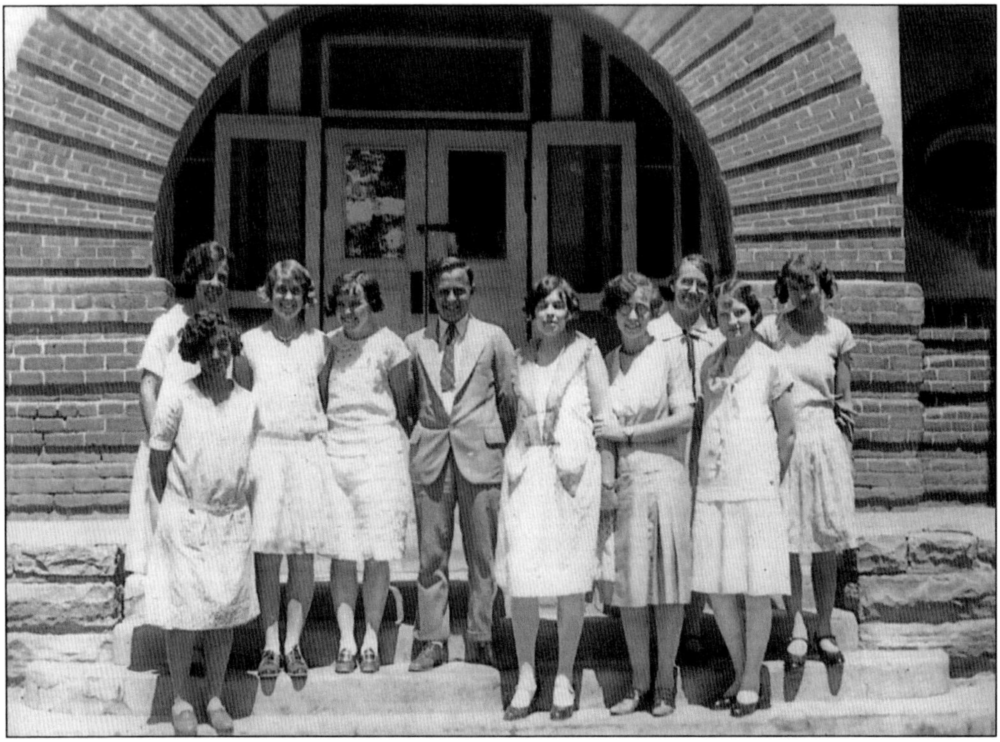

Principal Noble M. Hiser stands with the teaching staff of the Willcox Elementary School around 1928. Noble, wife Iona, and sons Donald and Leland lived in Willcox from 1926 to 1929. Donald became the Phoenix City archaeologist and director of Pueblo Grande Museum. (Donald H. Hiser.)

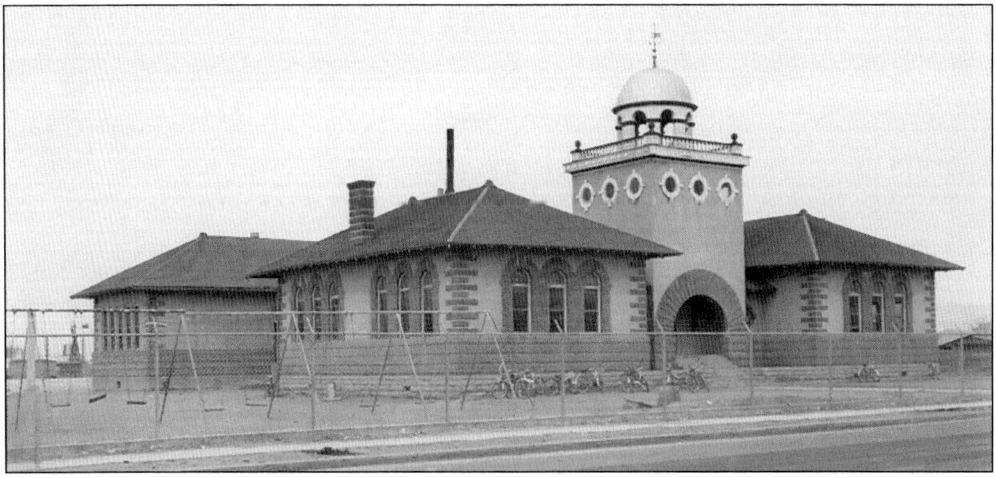

The second Willcox Elementary School, consisting of four rooms, was built in 1900 and abandoned in 1955. Sulphur Springs Valley Electric Cooperative purchased it as their office in 1957. The bell tower was removed and the bell placed at the new elementary school grounds in 1960. Frank Brown, custodian, rang the bell daily from 1914 to 1946. He lived across the street in the section known as Brownsville.

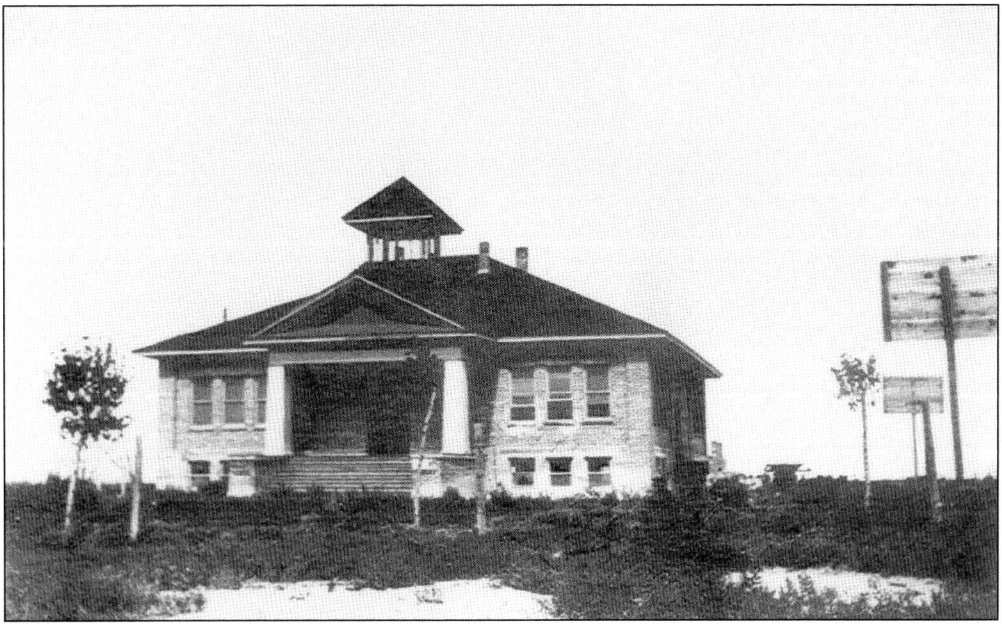

The first Willcox High School was built in 1911. The first graduation ever held in Willcox was at Norton's Hall on May 17, 1912, with one graduate, Florence Dickey. She was the valedictorian, salutatorian, class historian, and class prophet. Professor Campbell conducted the exercises, and William Riggs presented the diploma. The school was incorporated into the new high school building and became the auditorium when it was built in 1921.

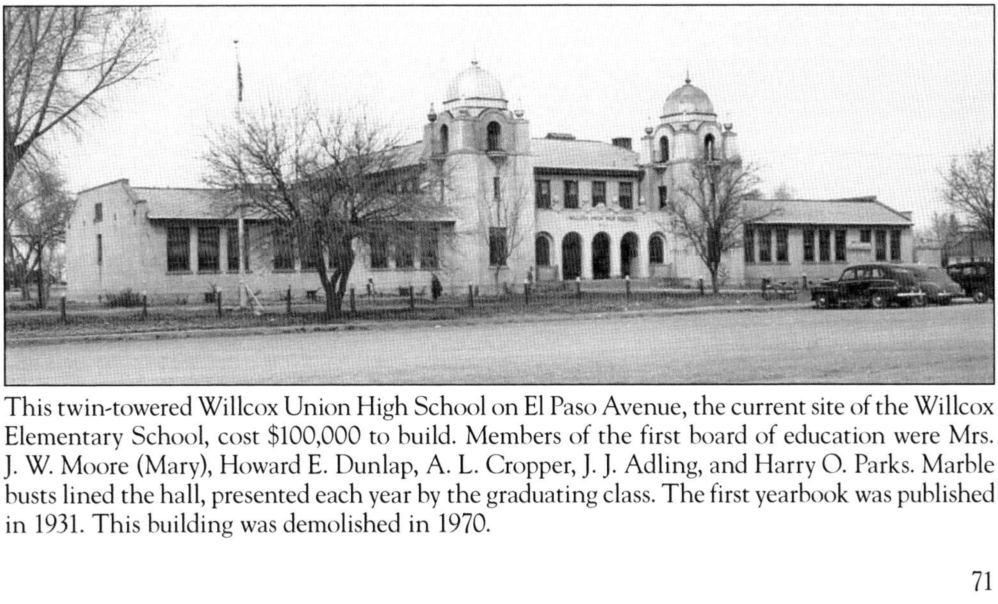

This twin-towered Willcox Union High School on El Paso Avenue, the current site of the Willcox Elementary School, cost $100,000 to build. Members of the first board of education were Mrs. J. W. Moore (Mary), Howard E. Dunlap, A. L. Cropper, J. J. Adling, and Harry O. Parks. Marble busts lined the hall, presented each year by the graduating class. The first yearbook was published in 1931. This building was demolished in 1970.

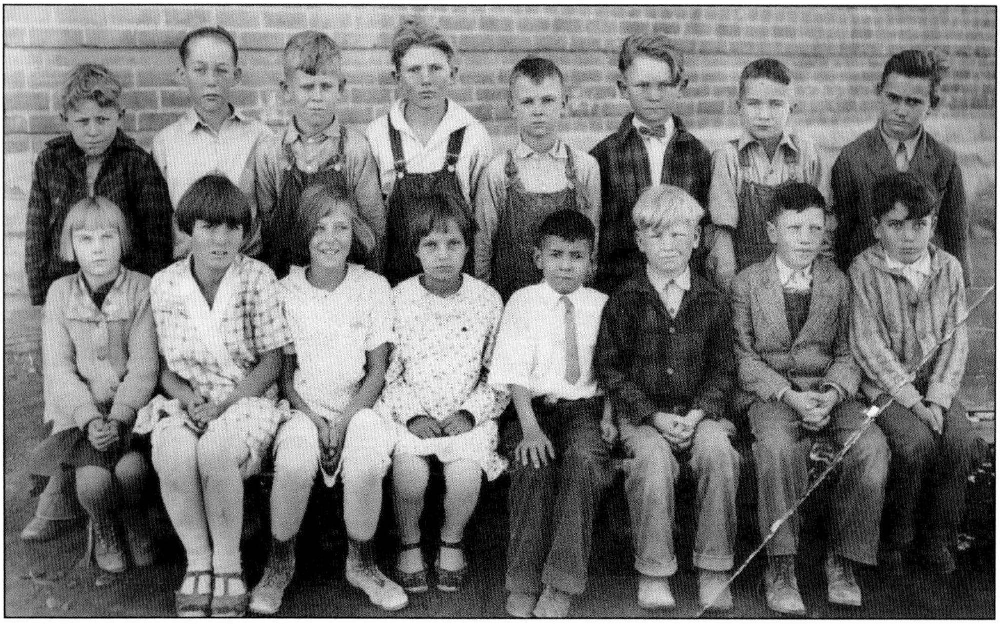

Ruth Briscoe taught this class around 1927. Students who would graduate in 1938 are, from left to right, (first row) Mildred Reed, Mary Wootan, Evelyn Shrode, Ethel Isaacs, George Takagi, Elvie (Rex) Allen, Granson Nash, and J. R. Gafford; (second row) Ray Collins, Bill Duncan, C. P. Winfrey, Kenneth Kuhn, Delton Hart, S. E. Rhea, Walter Ludwig, and Sidney Stevenson. (Wanda Linam Perry.)

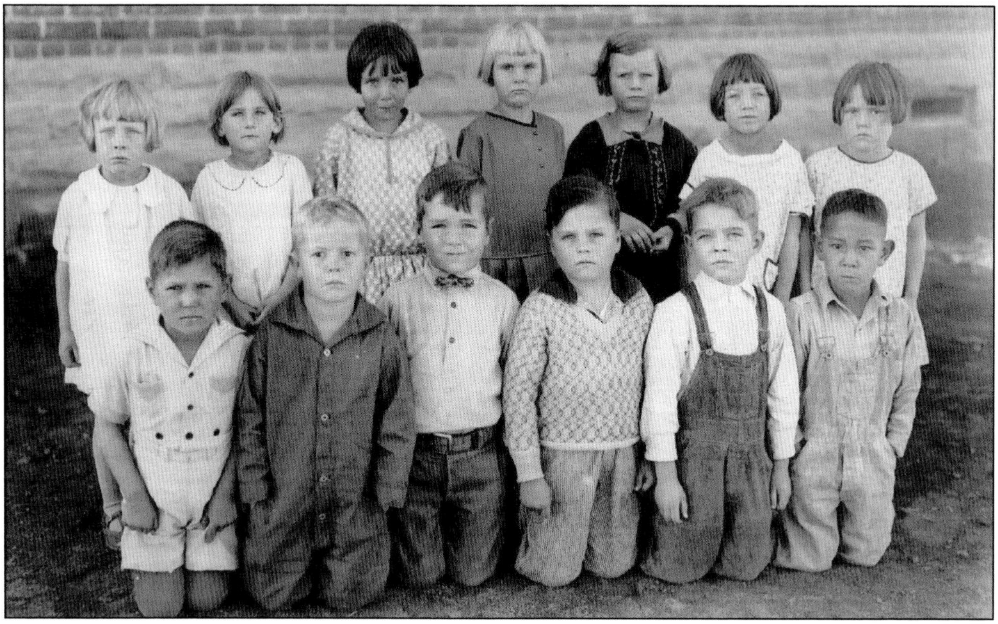

Allaire Browning had the mumps and was not in her school picture taken around 1929. These youngsters became part of the graduating class of 1941. From left to right are (first row) Donald McClure, Teddy Coxon, W. L. Cook, Joe Rice, David Schofield, and Henry Takagi; (second row) Gertude Davis, Isla Miller, Jean Maddox, unidentified, Bona Jean Moyer, Mabel Ward, and Marie Nicholson. (Peta-Anne Tenney.)

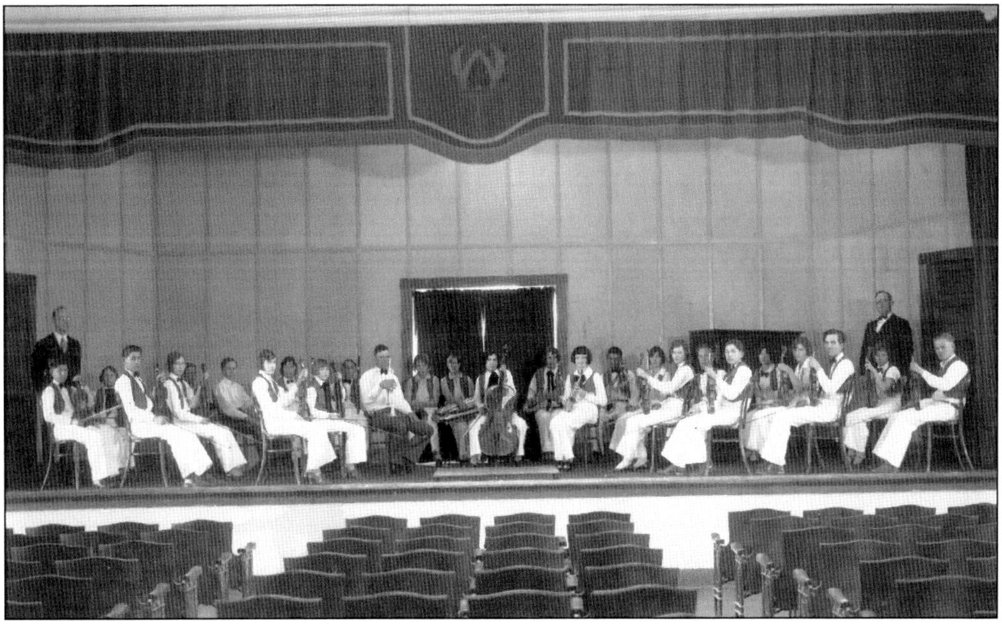

Members of the Willcox High School orchestra are pictured as they prepare to perform in the high school auditorium in 1935. Their uniforms were white waists and trousers with white and red jackets. The school budget allotted $25 for band and a like amount for the glee club.

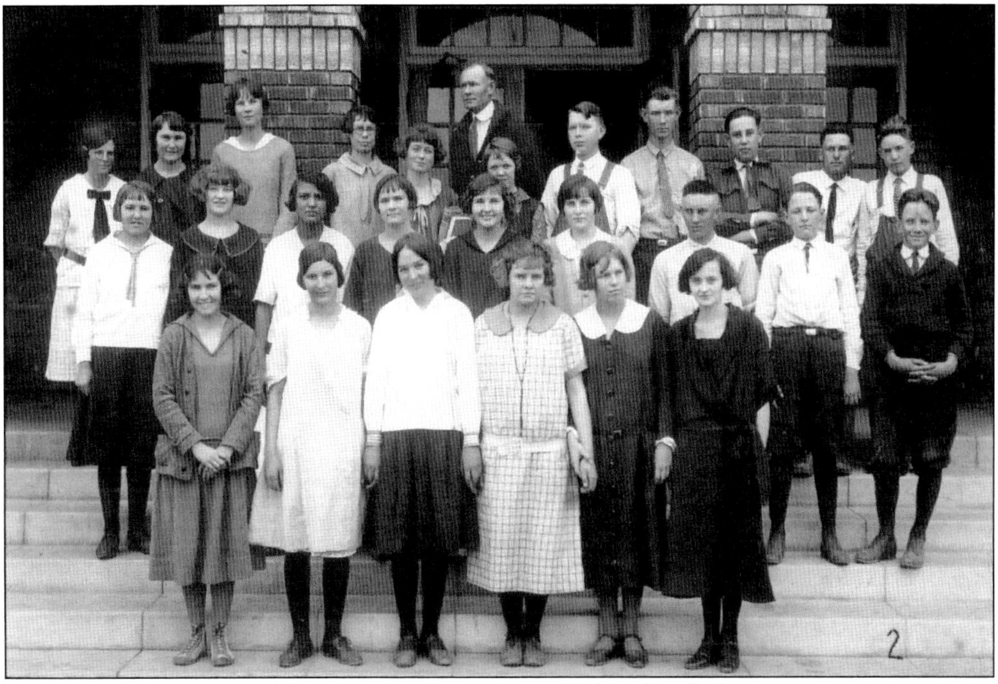

High school graduates and teachers gather in front of the school about 1919. J. W. Laird, the principal, is in back, and Wanda Browning, sister of Ernest Browning, is fifth from left in the third row. Wanda married Clarence Falk, taught school in Bowie, was president of the Tucson Woman's Club, and wrote a book titled *Mrs. J. A. B.* about her grandmother, Jeanetta Angelina Browning. (Janice Falk.)

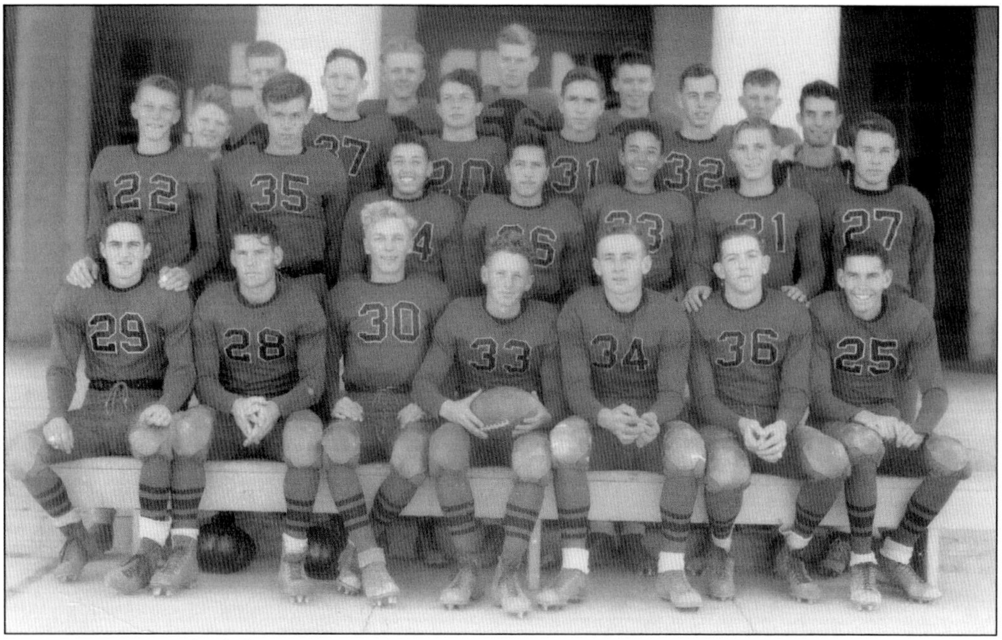

Ken Pearson coached the 1940 Cowboys football team. Those identified are Bill McAleb, No. 29; Gene Lewis, No. 30; Ed Kuhn, No. 33; Lee Gardner, No. 34; Sonny Swanner, No. 36; Don Thompson, No. 22; Ray Gardner, No. 35; Joe Anaya, No. 24; Tiny Hurtado, No. 23; LaVern Isaacks, No. 21; Joe Moore, No. 27; Hardy Kirby, No. 20; Bill Cook, No. 31; Dick Thompson, No. 32; Lynn Kirby, No. 39 (no number visible); Bob Crookshank; Bill Ewing; and Bob Bliss.

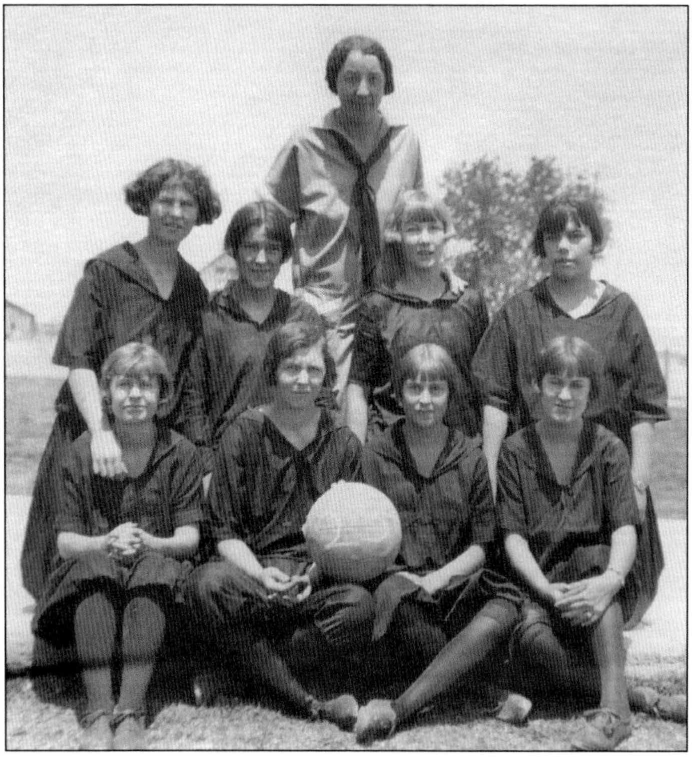

Hazel Bendure Johnson coached the girl's basketball team in 1924. She was married to W. L. "Bill" Johnson and was mother to Marvin "Swede" Johnson and Anne Johnson McPherson. The Hazel Fund and a park were named after her. Players are, from left to right, (first row) Juanita McCurdy, Naomi Goodwin, Ruth Briscoe, and Margueretti Faulconer; (second row) Margaret Duffey, Louise Jones, coach Johnson, Edna Boyd, and Dorothy Keeth. (Wanda Linam Perry.)

Majorettes in 1949 are, from left to right, (kneeling) ? Hammond, ? Wootan, Ruth Ann Eikenberry, and Betty Jo Wear; (standing) Jo Ann Sommer, ? Downey, Mary Anne McHenry, ? Sorgen, and Mary Lou Harris.

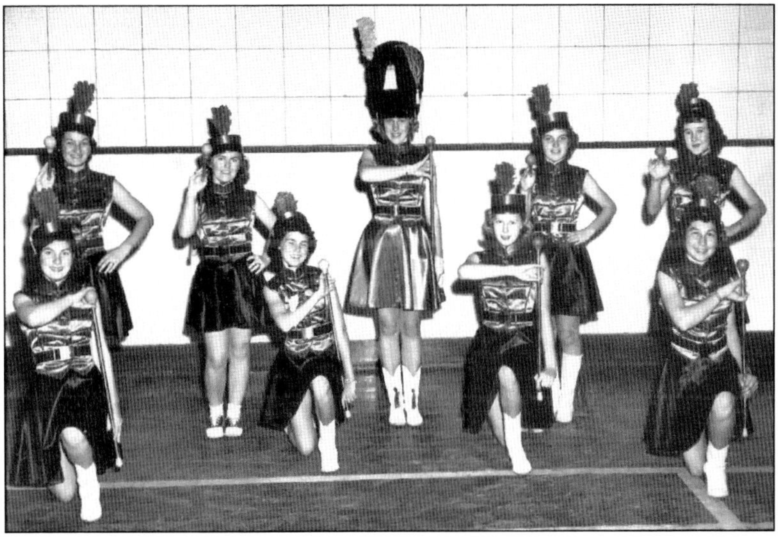

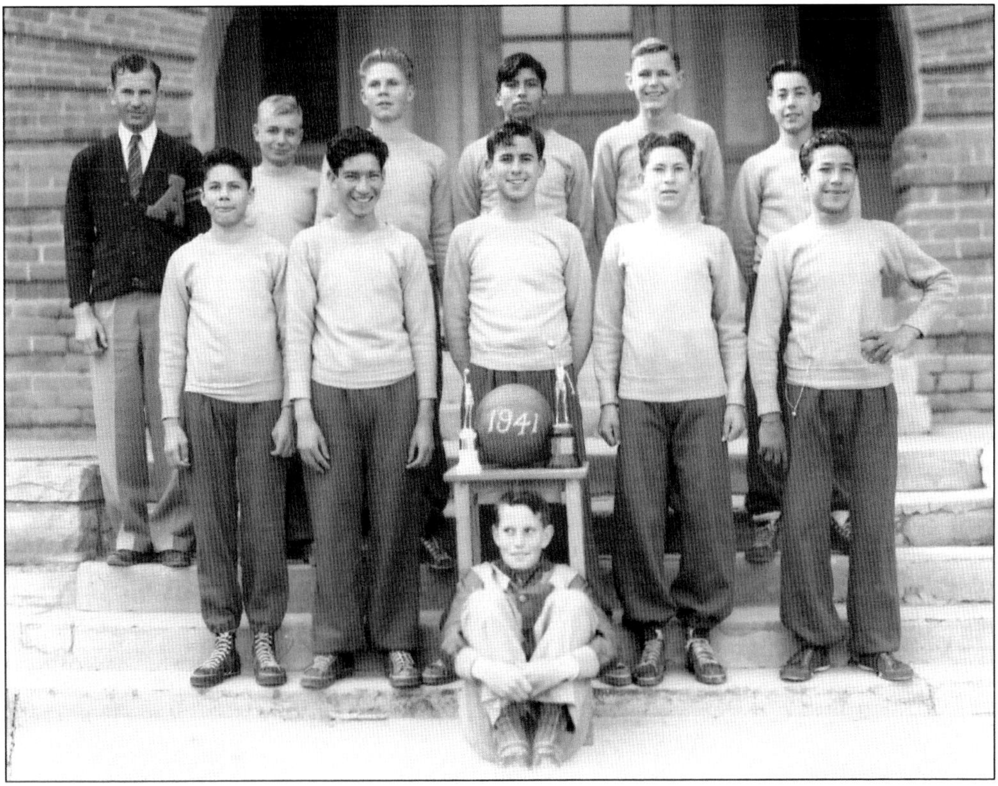

The 1941 basketball team is pictured in front of the elementary school with coach Duane Clapp. Besides coaching, he also taught wood shop and was a member of the Civil Air Patrol. The Clapps were early settlers in the Willcox area.

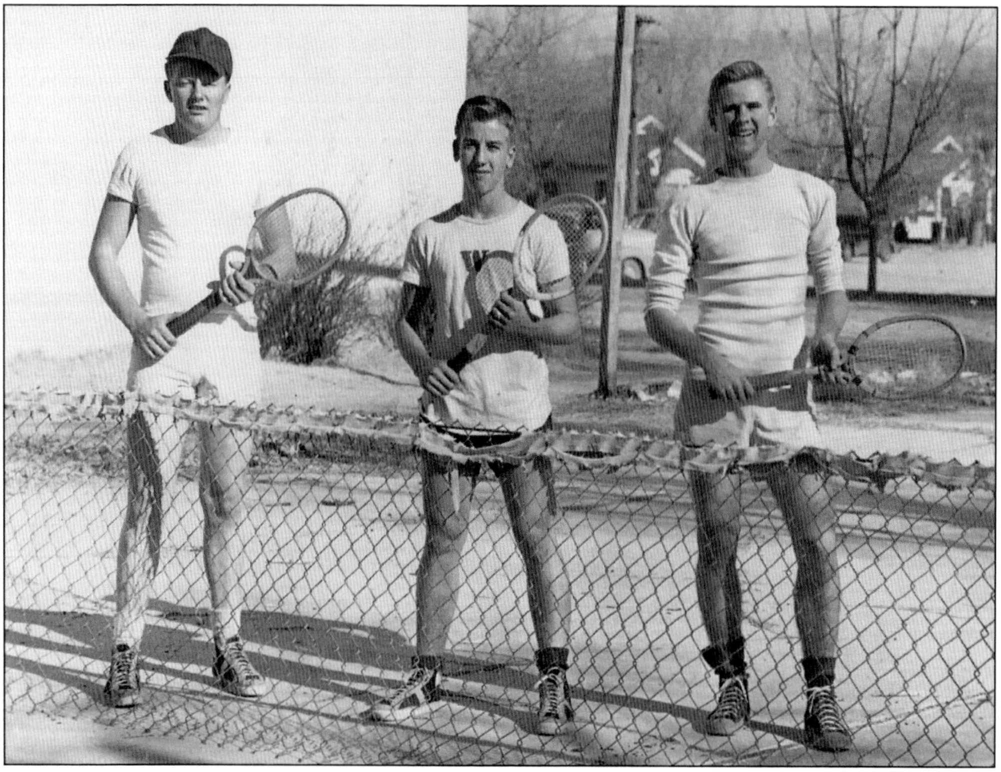

The three tennis players shown here are, from left to right, Robert McHenry, Delle Ferris, and Tom Fleetham. They had been practicing hard for the 1949 interschool and district meets.

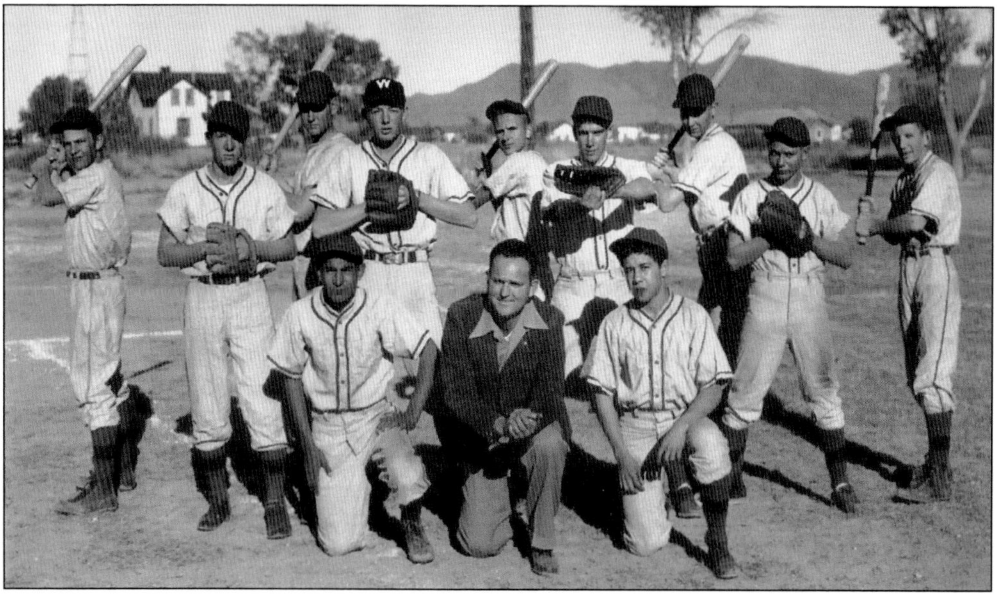

Coach Frank Jordan is kneeling in the midst of the championship baseball team of 1949. Players are, from left to right, (kneeling) Nasario Bedolla, coach Frank Jordan, and Albert Ward; (standing) John Kimzey, Harold George, Melvin Shilling, Don Bethel, Keith Seiler, Ben Meyers, Kenneth Wilson, Richard Cox, and Berl Byrd.

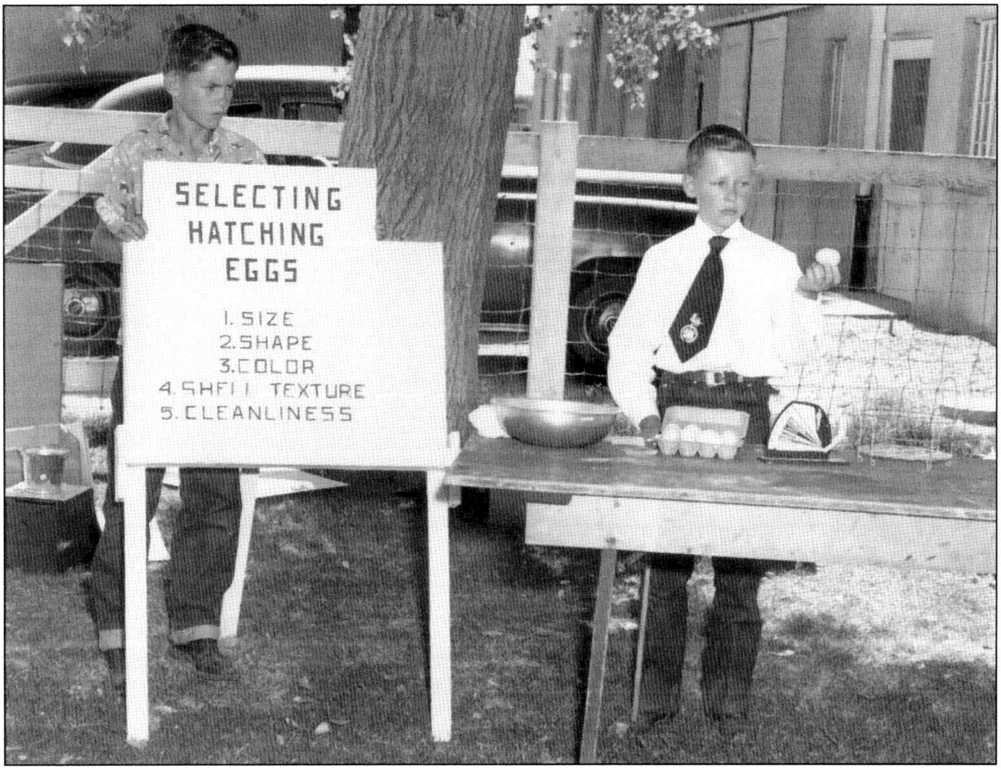

Carmy Page Jr. (right) was a member of the Up and Comers 4-H Club under the auspices of the University of Arizona Cooperative Extension Service. His father, Carmy G. Page Sr., was the county agricultural agent. Young Carmy demonstrates choosing the best eggs for hatching in 1952. These clubs, along with school-sponsored Future Farmers of America (FFA) and Future Homemakers of America (FHA), teach skills for rural youth.

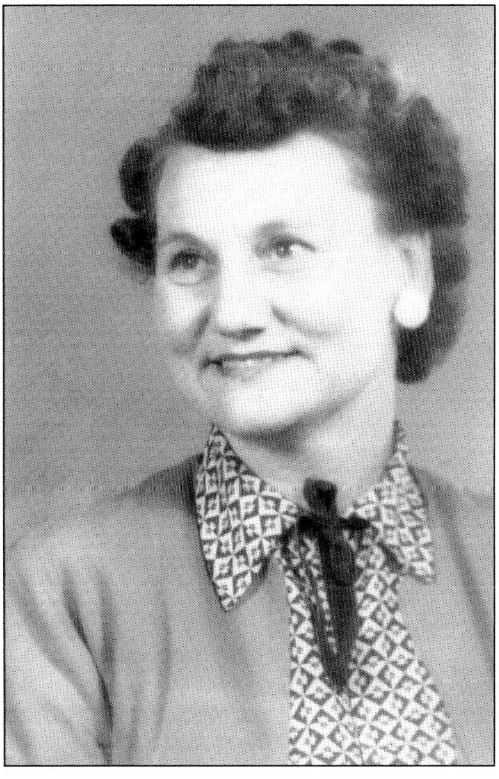

Ruth Nichols Troutman, photographed in 1954, was a graduate of Willcox High School and a favorite teacher for many years. Soon after graduation, she worked as a personal secretary to John W. Proutt, engineer at the Central Copper Company's Mascot Mine at Dos Cabezas. She married fellow teacher Herman Troutman. (Betty Kowalczyk.)

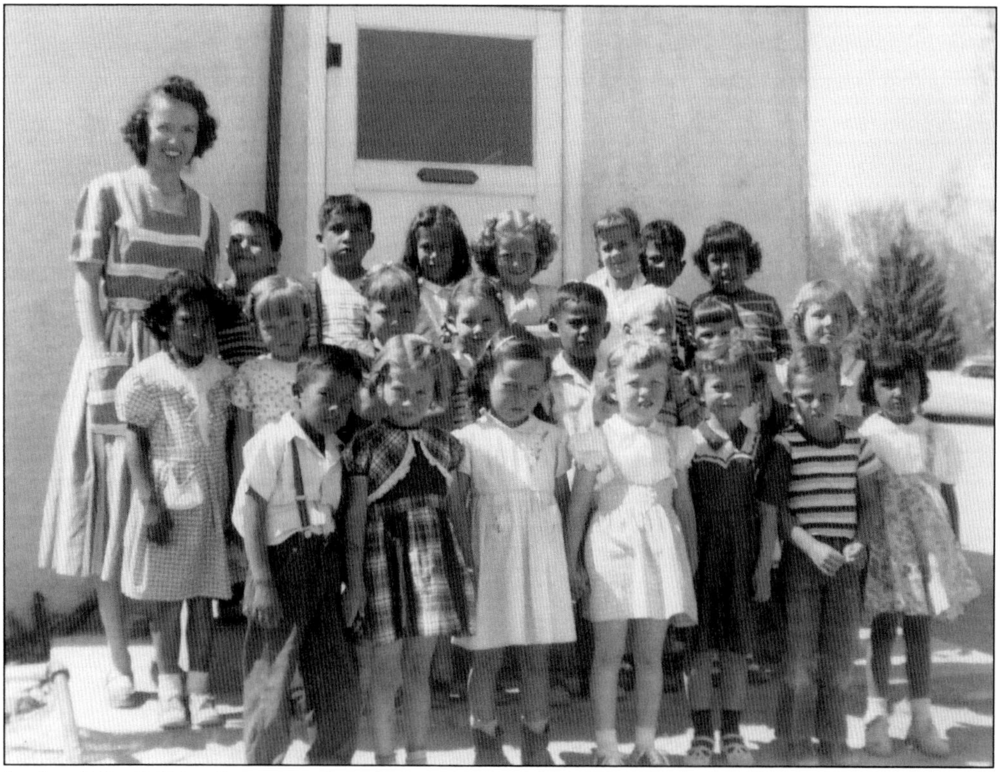

In this 1951–1952 kindergarten class photograph are, from left to right, (first row) Danny Rodriquez, Ida Ann Motes, Sharon Byrd, Ann Huffman, Charlotte Duncan, Wayne Brown, and Margaret Hernandez; (second row) Vicenta Bedolla, Nell Harris, Gae Nell Freeman, Sharon Gaskill, Tommy Lopez, Alfred DeWall, Leslie Noble, and Carol Higgins; (third row) teacher Verna Chambers, Dennis Owen, Xavier Rios, Sarah Sundheimer, Sally Gordon, Kathleen Flynt, Lee Saenz, and Eugenia Moreno. (Kathleen Poquette.)

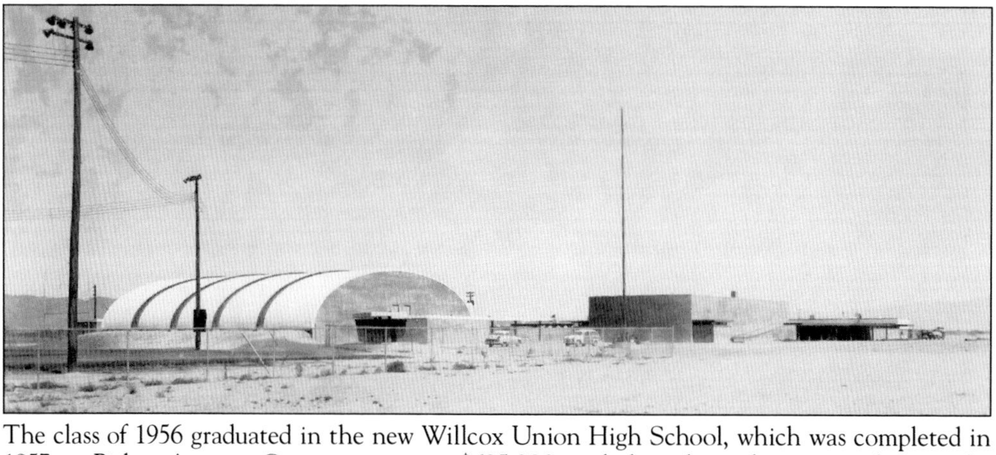

The class of 1956 graduated in the new Willcox Union High School, which was completed in 1957 on Bisbee Avenue. Construction cost $625,000, including the auditorium and gym. The architects were Scholer, Sakellar, and Fuller of Tucson. J. R. Porter Construction built the facility plus a new Willcox Elementary School between Delos and Stewart Streets on El Paso Avenue. (James and Sandra Thomas.)

Seven

SERVICE CLUBS AND ORGANIZATIONS

Willcox has benefited significantly from the services performed by clubs and organizations over the years. Most businessmen and their wives belonged to at least one organization. Besides being a social outlet, great strides were made in improving the town through cultural activities, recreation, beautification, helping construct buildings, numbering the streets, and improving conditions for the poor. People took pride in holding offices in these organizations and were faithful and dependable members. The first organizations for the men were the Masons, Ancient Order of United Workmen (AOUW), Woodmen of the World, Knights of Pythias, and the Rotarians. The women belonged to the Order of the Eastern Star or organized community events through their church organizations. Later the Woman's Club was formed and then the Garden Club and Stewart Homemakers. The Junior Women's Club, Lions Club, Kiwanis Club, Vets Club, Civil Air Patrol, and MANPO (Mexican-American Nonprofit Organization) were also active here at one time. Some of those most active today are the Elks Club, Rotary Club, Hospital Auxiliary, Friends of Elsie S. Hogan Community Library, Sulphur Springs Valley Historical Society, Willcox Cowbelles, Lambda Chi Omega, and Art League of Willcox.

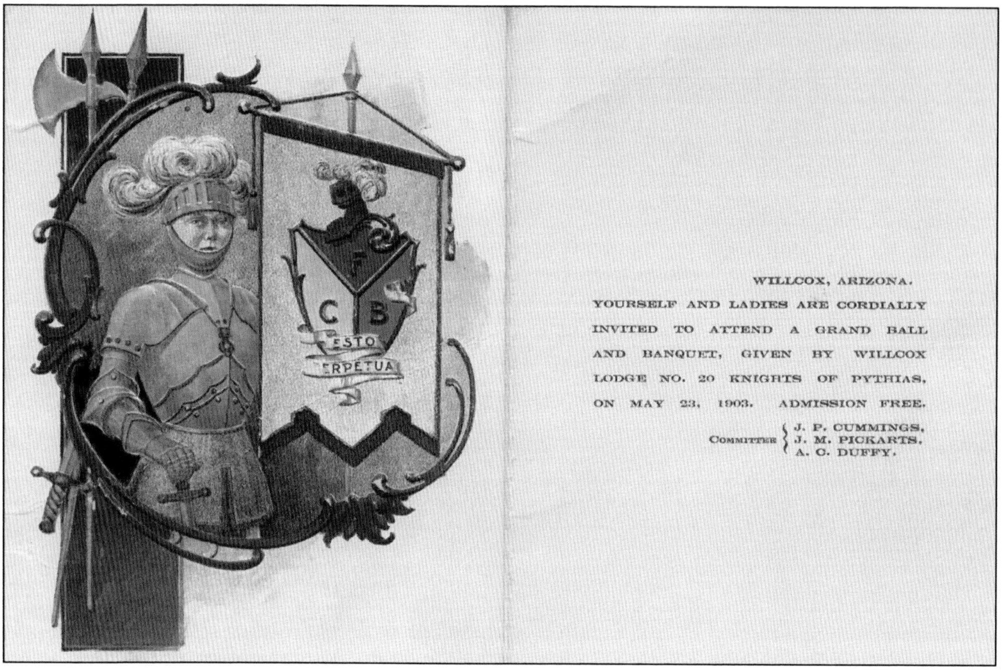

WILLCOX, ARIZONA.

YOURSELF AND LADIES ARE CORDIALLY INVITED TO ATTEND A GRAND BALL AND BANQUET, GIVEN BY WILLCOX LODGE NO. 20 KNIGHTS OF PYTHIAS, ON MAY 23, 1903. ADMISSION FREE.

COMMITTEE { J. P. CUMMINGS, J. M. PICKARTS, A. C. DUFFY.

The Knights of Pythias was the first fraternal organization to receive a charter under an act of Congress in 1864. Loyalty, honor, and friendship are the central ideals of the order. John Perry Cummings, organizer of this ball, was the local barber, vice-president of the Riggs Bank, and president of the Rotary Club. His wife, Edith, was Worthy Grand Matron of the local and state Eastern Star.

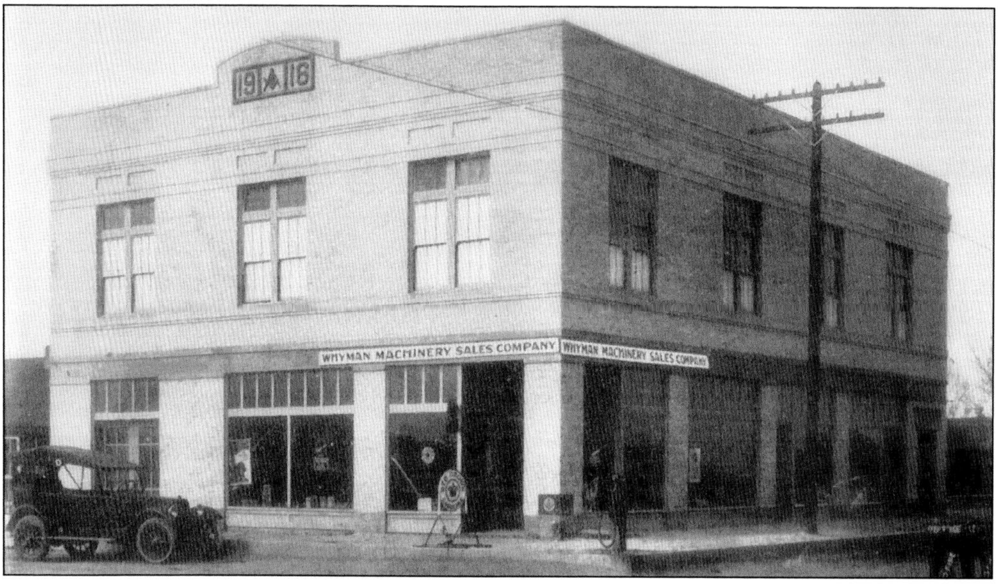

Pictured about 1921, the second home of the Masonic lodge was built on the corner of Haskell Avenue and Maley Street at a cost of $8,750. The first Worshipful Master, in 1891, was Rev. Nathan L. Guthrie. Mark Allen Cook was the first Master Mason in this temple. The first-floor businesses have included the county agricultural agent, Austin's Drug Store, a hobby shop, and now a clothing store.

Kasper Hauser was secretary for the Masonic lodge when the new building was constructed in 1916. He also became Worshipful Master. A Willcox citizen for 57 of his 93 years, he was a city clerk, police judge, postmaster, saloon owner, and operator of the Willcox Hotel. He once said he had done everything in order to make a living except stealing cattle or horses. (Willcox Masonic Lodge.)

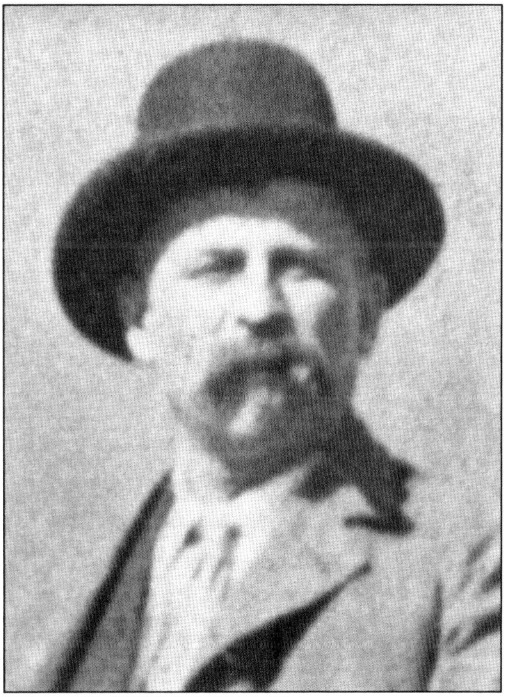

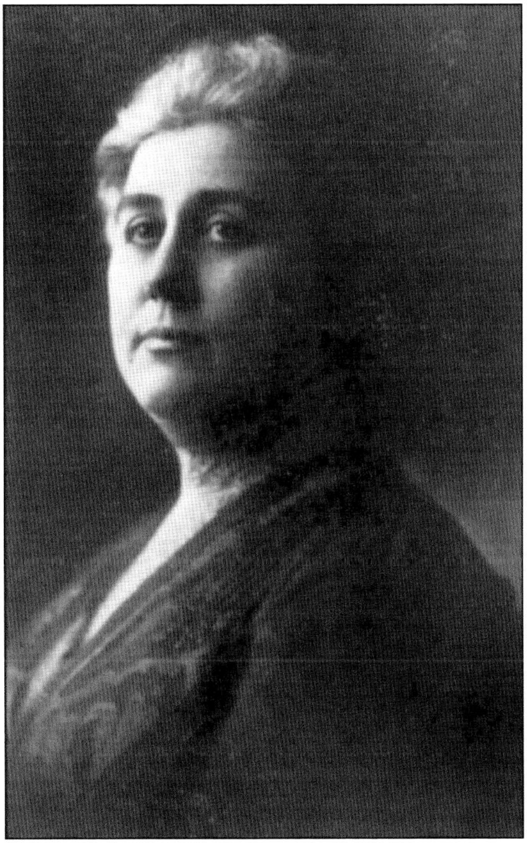

Anna Morgan, wife of Mayor Henry Morgan, was well educated and cultured and very active in society circles. She was Grand Matron for Arizona Order of the Eastern Star and president of the Woman's Club. In 1925, a cookbook published by the Ladies Aid Society of the Methodist church was dedicated to her for her constant example of loyalty, devotion, and service as president.

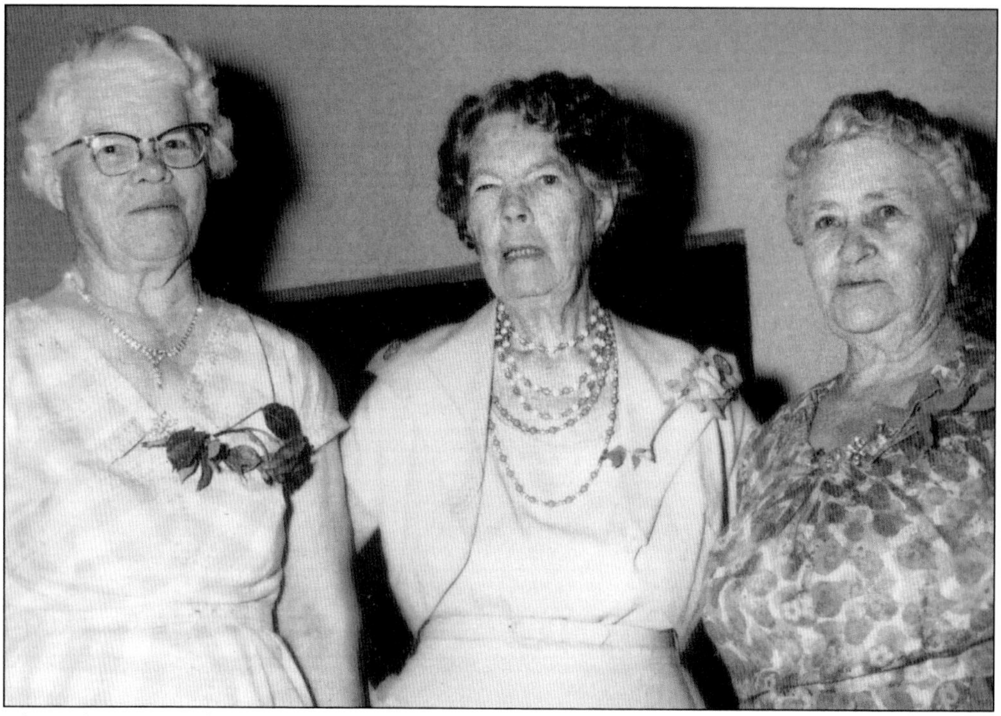

Three charter members of the Woman's Club, which organized in 1911, were, from left to right, Julia Huffman, Elizabeth Johnson, and Edith Cummings. The first officers were Lulu Anderson, Anna Morgan, and Mary Moore. The Woman's Club goals stressed cultural opportunities, community service, education, and youth.

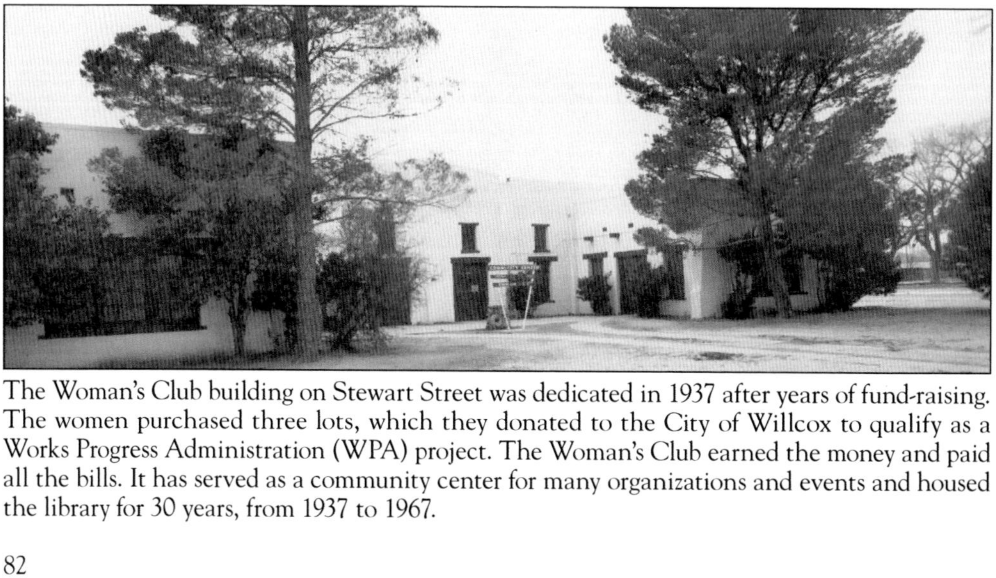

The Woman's Club building on Stewart Street was dedicated in 1937 after years of fund-raising. The women purchased three lots, which they donated to the City of Willcox to qualify as a Works Progress Administration (WPA) project. The Woman's Club earned the money and paid all the bills. It has served as a community center for many organizations and events and housed the library for 30 years, from 1937 to 1967.

Rosemary Robbs (right) and Mrs. Lee Childress (Shirley) of the Junior Women's Club renovated the children's book section in 1959. The Woman's Club started the library in 1923 in the high school, and Hazel Bendure Johnson was the first volunteer librarian. From 1930 to 1936, the library was in Masonic Hall. It was moved to the Woman's Club building until 1967, when all 8,000 books were transferred to the city.

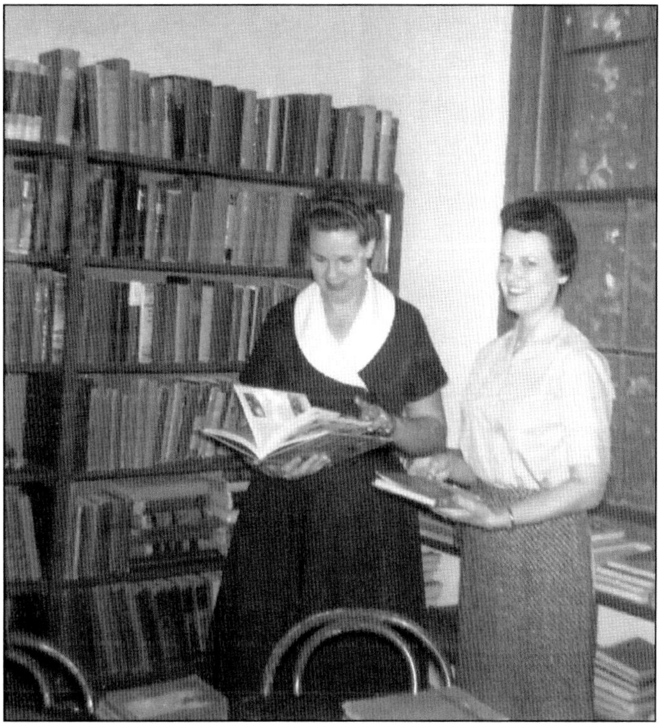

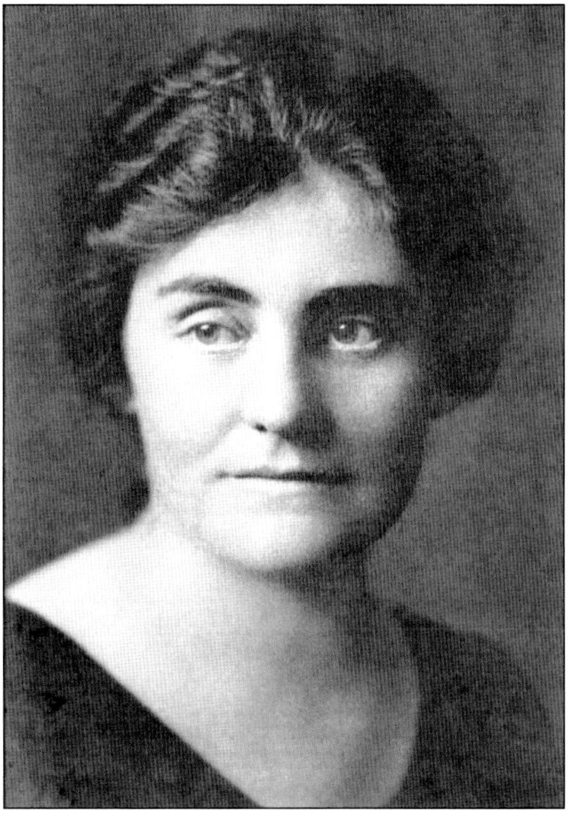

Elsie Sackett Hogan, the first paid librarian, held the position from 1961 to 1975, when she turned 85. Much loved, she always had cookies, candy, and coffee on hand for the patrons. The new library, built in 1969, was named the Elsie S. Hogan Community Library in her honor. The Friends of the Library held their organizational tea on her 92nd birthday, July 1, 1981.

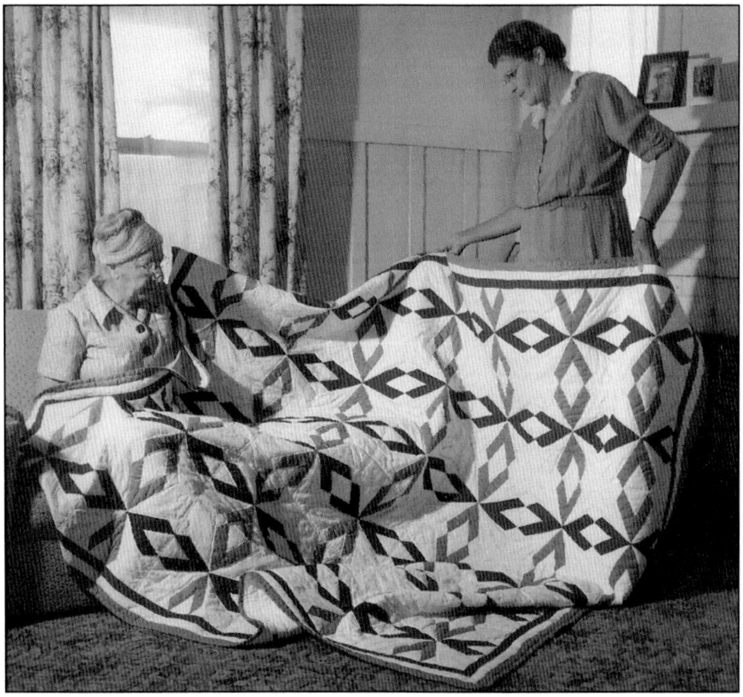

As county home economist, Bertha Virmond's guidance was a great help to families from 1929 to 1946 as they persevered during the Great Depression and World War II. She organized homemakers' clubs to teach such skills as quilting, sewing, food preparation, and childcare, conservation of farm and household goods, and planting of victory gardens. The local Stewart Homemakers was founded in 1931 and continues today.

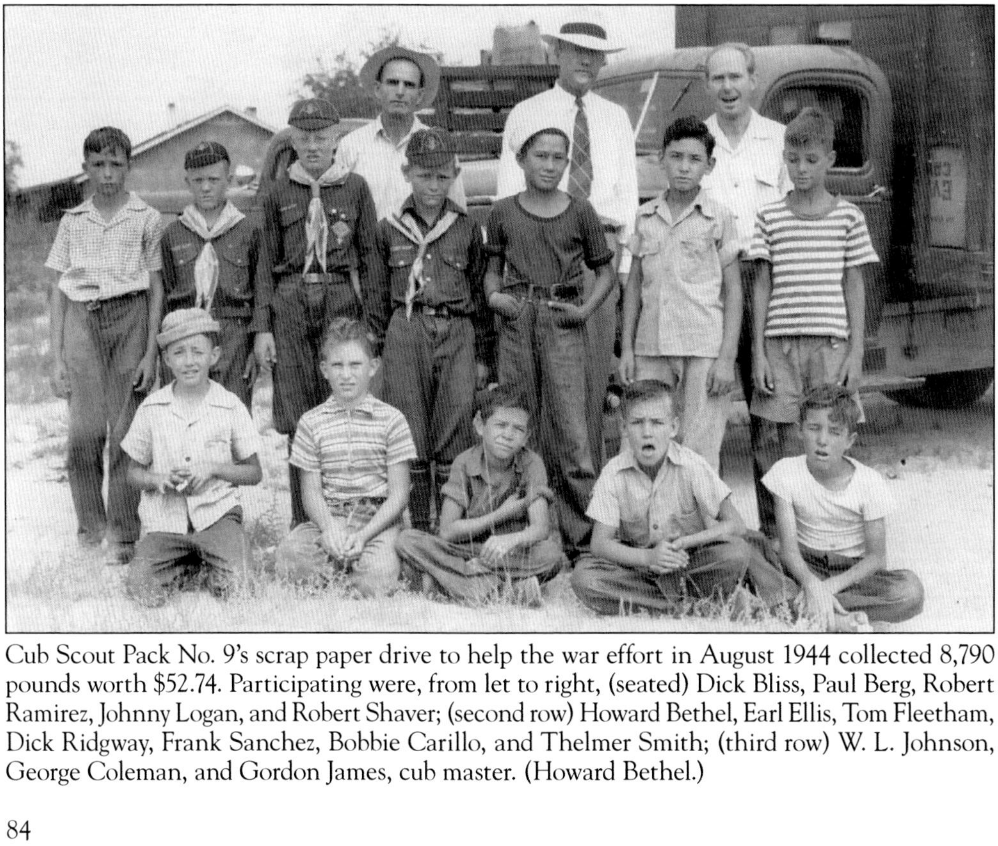

Cub Scout Pack No. 9's scrap paper drive to help the war effort in August 1944 collected 8,790 pounds worth $52.74. Participating were, from let to right, (seated) Dick Bliss, Paul Berg, Robert Ramirez, Johnny Logan, and Robert Shaver; (second row) Howard Bethel, Earl Ellis, Tom Fleetham, Dick Ridgway, Frank Sanchez, Bobbie Carillo, and Thelmer Smith; (third row) W. L. Johnson, George Coleman, and Gordon James, cub master. (Howard Bethel.)

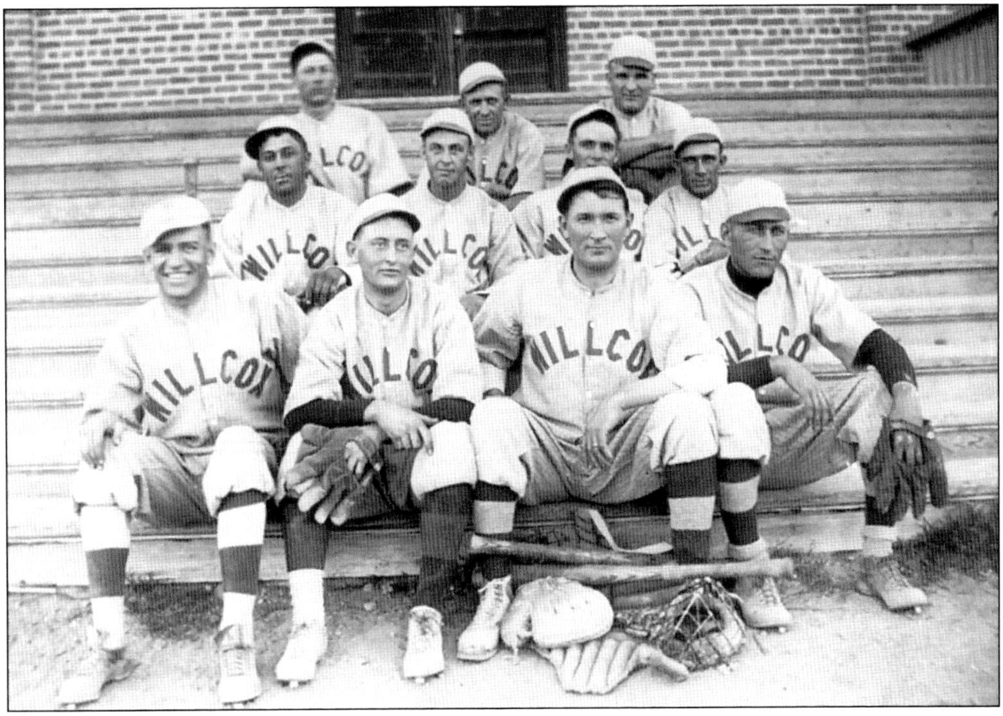

This 1920s Willcox baseball team consisted of, from left to right, (first row) Clay Johnson, Ernest Browning (Piggly Wiggly store), D. D. Simms (theater and Sweet Shop), and B. G. Honeycutt (Standard Oil dealer); (second row) Rafael Gonzales, Charlie McGuigan, Dick Misenheimer, and Joe Willie Ellis; (third row) Harley Windsor (Valley Hardware), Ed Kuhn, and Dutch Taylor. (Bisbee Mining and Historical Museum.)

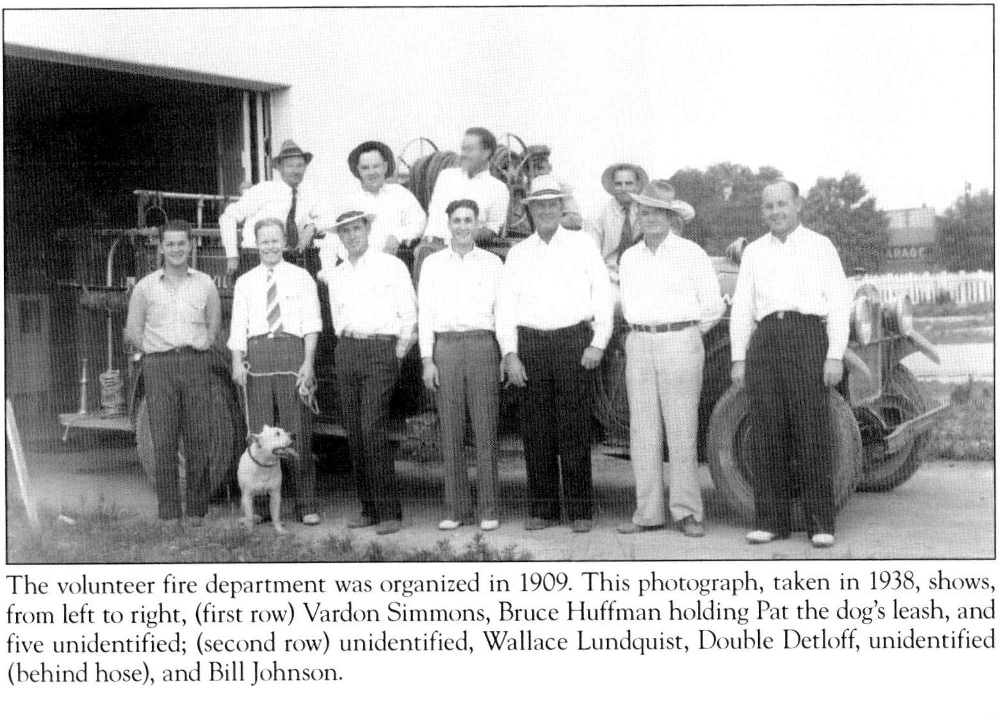

The volunteer fire department was organized in 1909. This photograph, taken in 1938, shows, from left to right, (first row) Vardon Simmons, Bruce Huffman holding Pat the dog's leash, and five unidentified; (second row) unidentified, Wallace Lundquist, Double Detloff, unidentified (behind hose), and Bill Johnson.

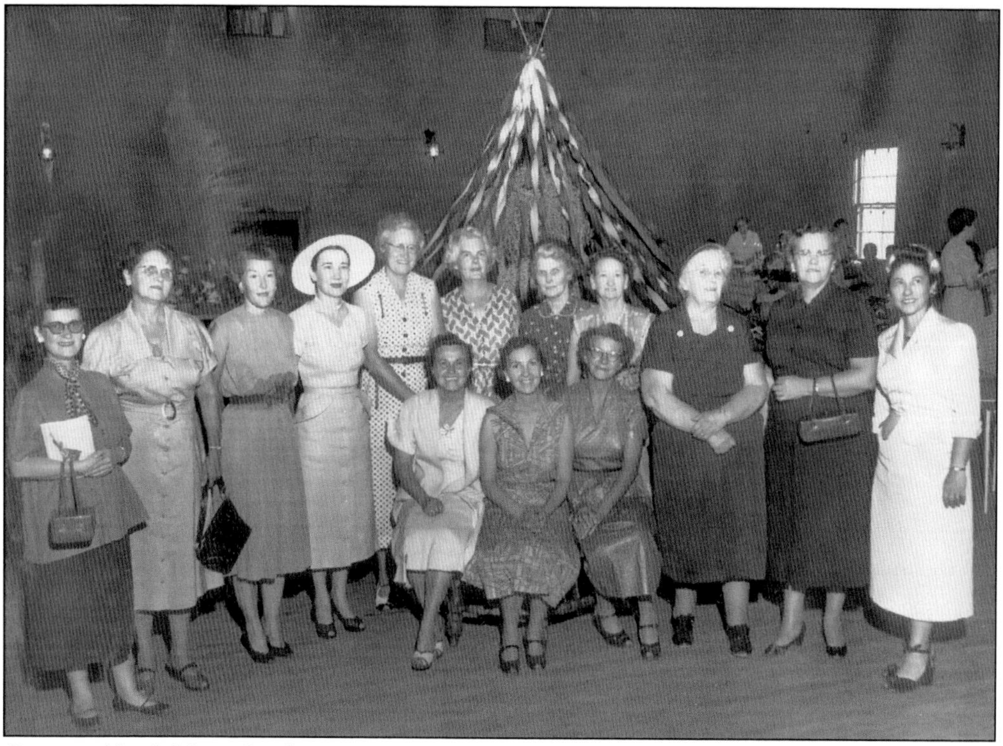

Organized by Adeleen Gordon in 1940 as Better Homes and Gardens, the name was changed in 1943 to the Willcox Garden Club. Members identified in this 1957 photograph include Beatrice Grove, Gretna Coleman, ? Donnelley, Sabina Larson (in white hat), ? Nicholson, Elsie Crookshank, Virginia Hatley, ? Wagoner, Mary Plough, Lorraine Detterback, and Lula Briscoe.

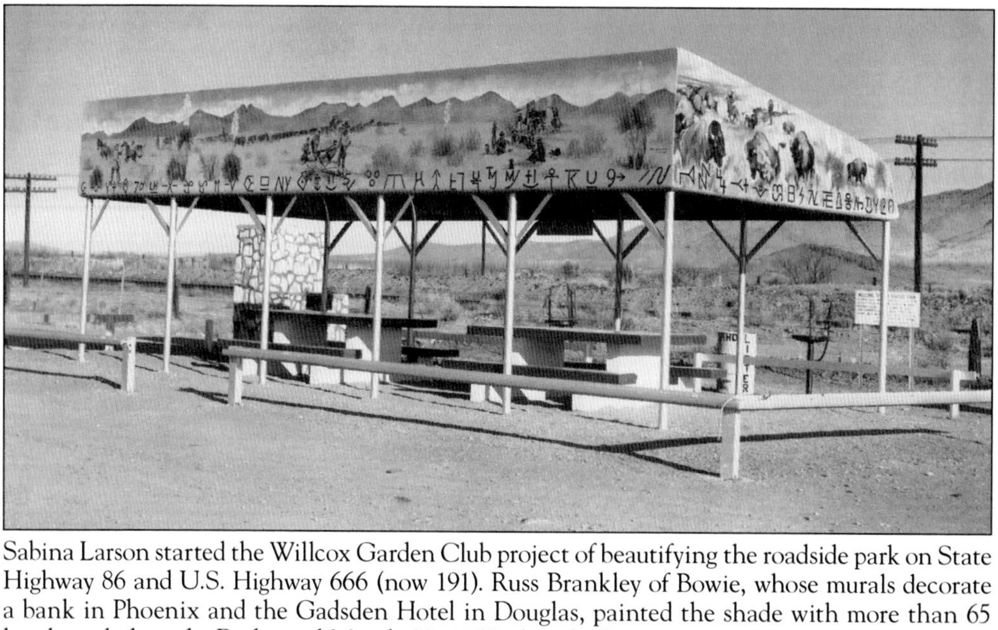

Sabina Larson started the Willcox Garden Club project of beautifying the roadside park on State Highway 86 and U.S. Highway 666 (now 191). Russ Brankley of Bowie, whose murals decorate a bank in Phoenix and the Gadsden Hotel in Douglas, painted the shade with more than 65 local cattle brands. Dedicated March 29, 1957, this shade was moved to Railroad Park after I-10 was built.

Lula Briscoe (right) was honored with a life membership from the Arizona Children's Home Association. For over 25 years, her house was a collection center for children's clothing and articles to be used at the home. She also fed lunch to the high school teachers daily at her home. The county Homemakers Clubs donated a quilt each year for the Children's Home. (Wanda Linam Perry.)

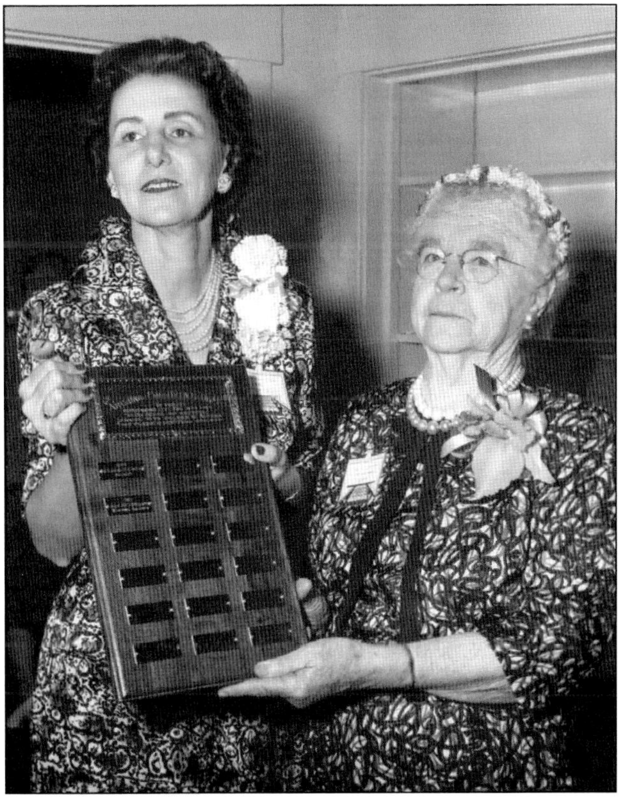

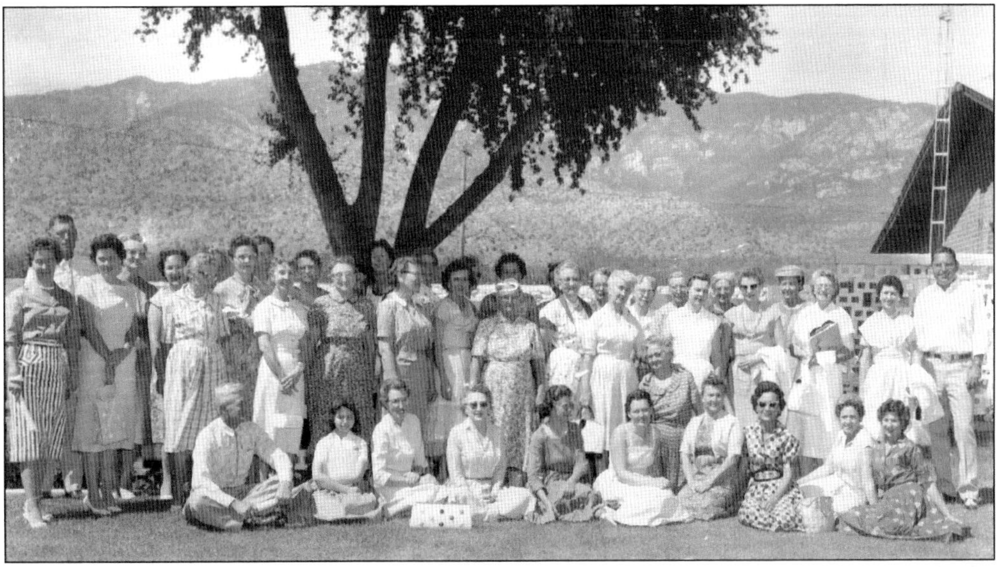

The Willcox Cowbelles, organized in 1946 with 61 charter members, promote cooperation for the best interest of the cattle industry and the community. Among those meeting in May 1960 at Fort Grant are Lorene Bull, Margaret Prestridge, Tyne Jernigan, Marjorie Monzingo, Katie Deering, Margaret McClintock, Millie Ellis, Polly Browning, Irene Windsor, Jean Riggs, Chuckie Hudson, Steve Vuchevich (host), Melba Houser, Irene Mills, Liz Gunter, Ruby Spurgeon, Jessie McAleb, Margie Cook, Peggy Wear, Norma Lee Riggs, and Julia Riggs. (Peta-Anne Tenney.)

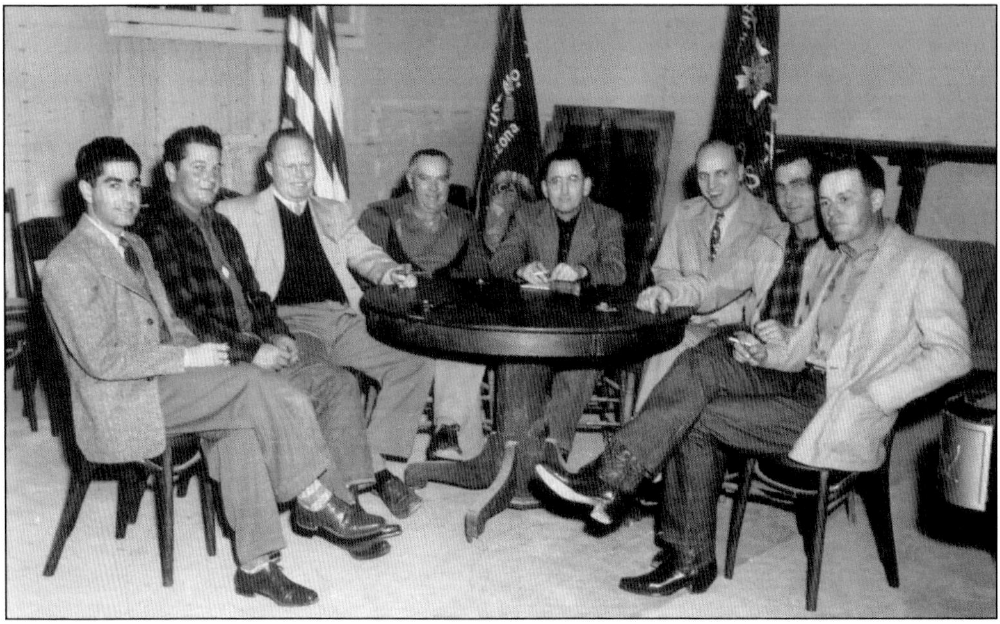

The Board of Directors of Willcox Veteran's Club includes, from left to right, Bob Briscoe, Llandon Simmons, Bruce Huffman, Wallace Lundquist, George Austin, Vernon Lybeck, Fred Ditmars, and Carlton Gordon. The club was organized in 1948 consisting of members of the American Legion and Veterans of Foreign Wars. The Elks Club purchased their club building on east Stewart Street in 1971.

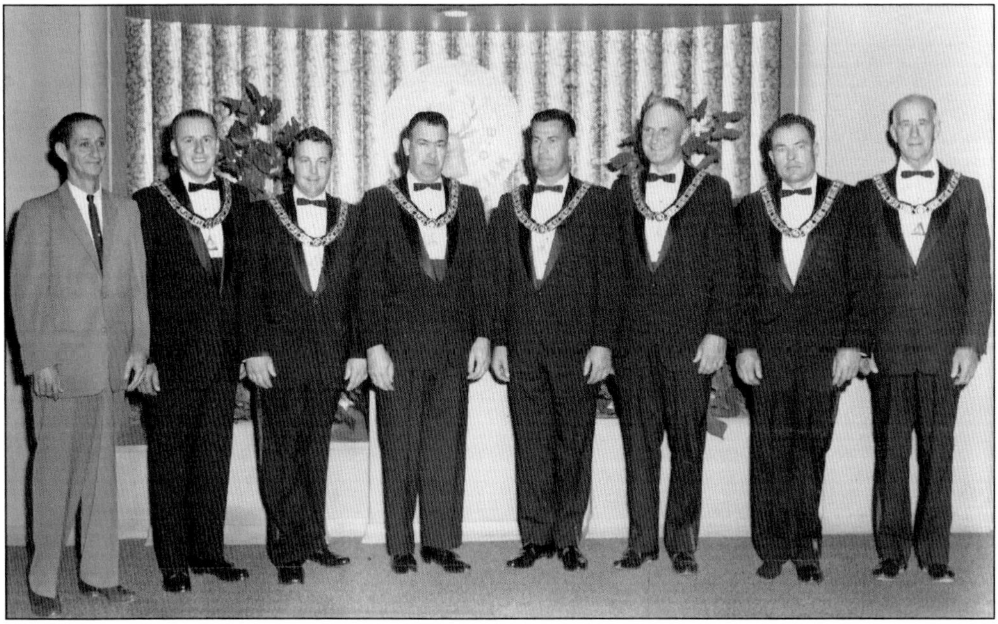

Elks Lodge No. 2131 was chartered June 17, 1959, at the Community Center. Charles Torpey was the first Exalted Ruler. They moved into their new lodge in December 1960. When it became too small, they purchased the Vets Club building. Pictured here about 1965 are, from left to right, Albert Armagnac (left), George Teeling, unidentified, Milo Miscovich, Larry McCarty, Jeff Thomason, Buck Clayton, and Albert Schwertner.

Eight

The 1920s and 1930s

The first half of the 1920s saw a boom in building and an increase in population. In 1920, over 200 cars could be seen parked on the streets, and the fire department had a man-powered cart with a foamite tank. Bill Severin served as the refuse collector with a horse-drawn wagon until Nick Ludwig took over using a Model T truck. Jesse Moore, the city marshal, patrolled his rounds with a horse as his means of transportation. Jack Tyndall kept the unpaved streets in good shape with the county grader. Frank Harris was the new real estate agent. Mrs. Stone ran a rooming house in the Navajo Hotel building. Joseph and Minnie Ellis operated the Commercial Hotel on Maley Street.

The 1930s saw more progress for the town. The Medlock and Hines Dairies brought milk to doorsteps. Mr. A. E. Keeth owned the bakery. The Detloffs ran the theater and sweet shop. Guy Holt was the owner of the Willcox Commercial. Haircuts were available from Ernest Perkins, the barber on Railroad Avenue. Gas stations, garages, cafés, and motor courts were becoming plentiful as more people were traveling. Laurence and Bessie Fulmer were the editors of the *Arizona Range News*. If there was land to be surveyed, one called Albert Schwertner. People could get a drink at W. E. Johnson's Palace Club. Myrtle's Beauty Shoppe offered "natural croquignole" (permanent waving). Street paving projects and a sewer system began in 1938, and the Sulphur Springs Valley Electric Cooperative was founded the same year, making electricity available through the Rural Electrification Act.

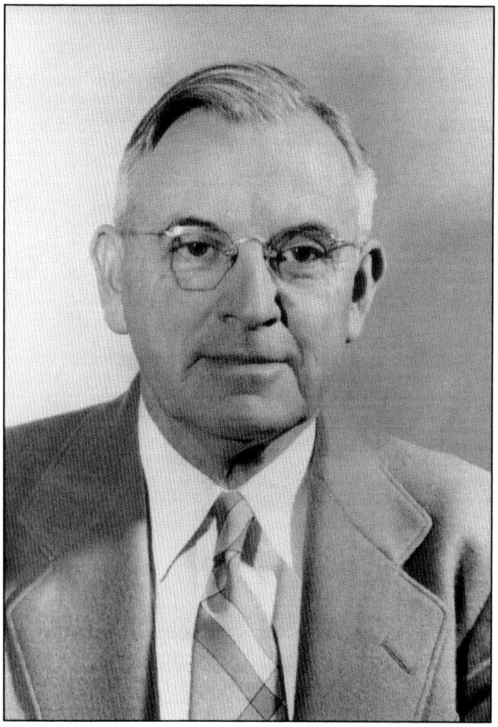

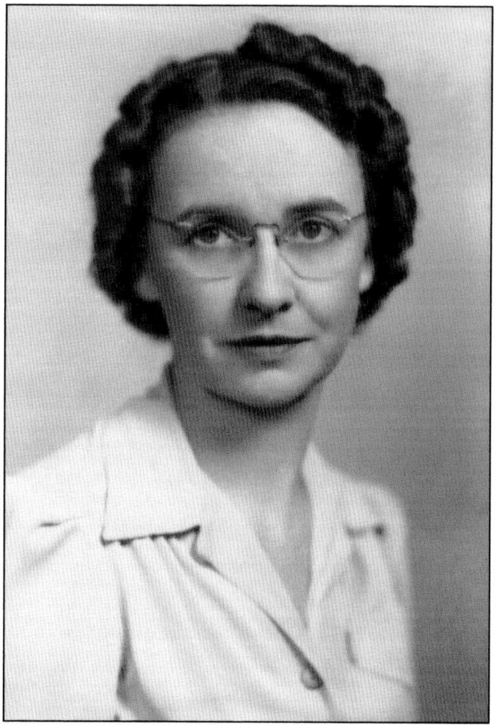

Dana T. Milner, once voted most outstanding citizen of Willcox, purchased a controlling interest in Riggs Bank in 1931 when it became the Bank of Willcox. He remained president and manager for 10 years after it was sold to Valley National Bank in 1936. Mildred Clapp worked for the bank for years and greeted everyone by name. Her son Carl Clapp became a famous artist.

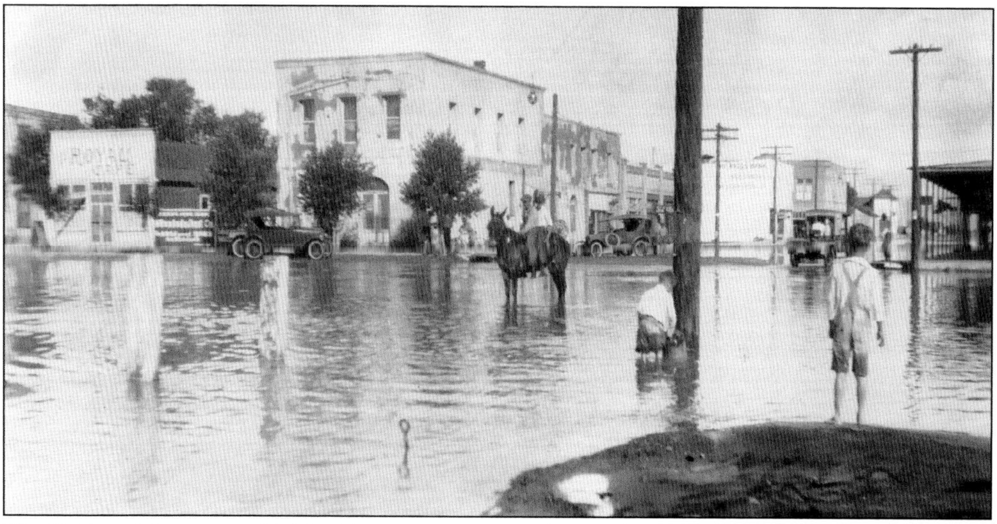

The Railroad Avenue and Maley Street intersection during the 1923 flood shows the Riggs Bank building to the right of the large pole. Brothers William M., John C., and B. K. Riggs organized the bank in 1920. J. B. Gersbach operated the Palace Hotel here, leasing it to R. J. German in 1915. The first owner of record for this lot was R. H. McDermott in 1883; he sold it to ? Clark and Henry Sidle, blacksmiths.

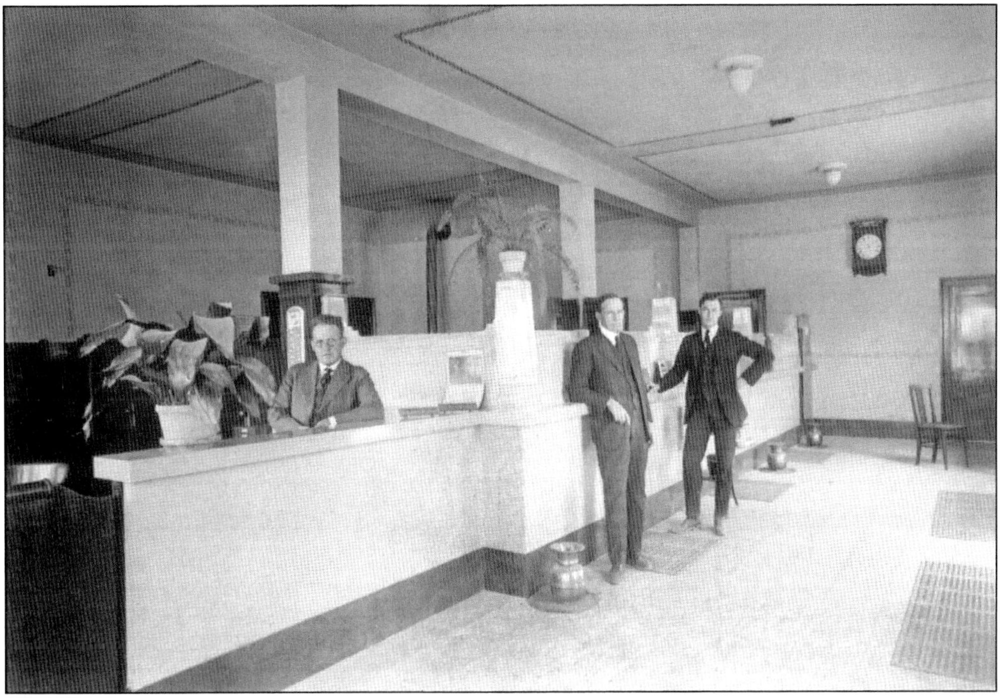

The interior of the Riggs Bank, on the corner of Haskell Avenue and Maley Street, is pictured during the 1920s. E. B. McAleb is behind the counter with William C. Riggs (center) and Dana T. Milner (right). Note the spittoons at each teller's window. The bank took up only one-third of the lower floor. The theater and sweet shop were in the same building.

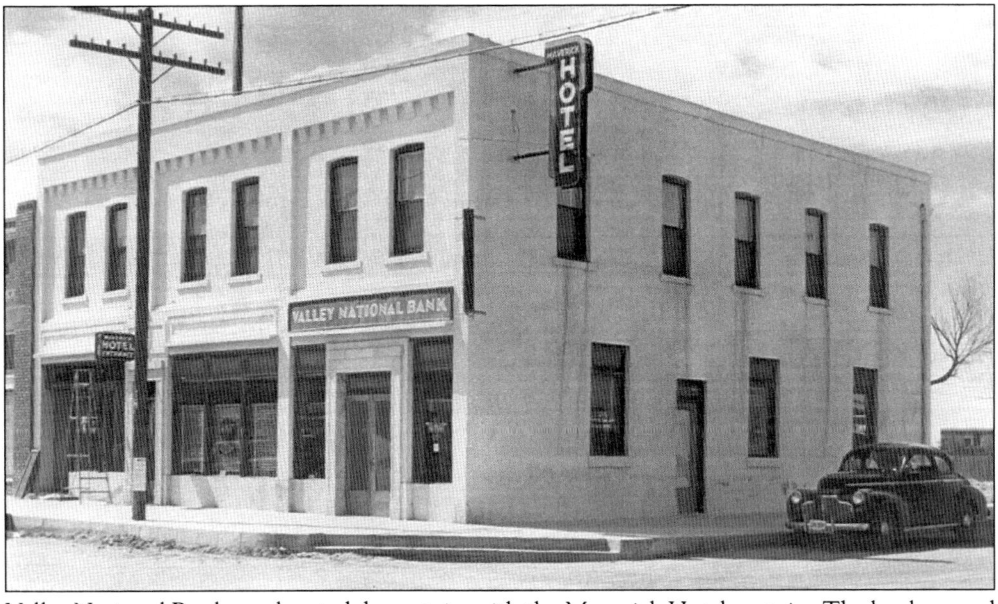

Valley National Bank was located downstairs with the Maverick Hotel upstairs. The bank moved to Grant Street in 1966 with Terry Lunt as manager and Harold Skinner as assistant manager. It later became Bank One and then Chase Bank. Rex Cotherman, with his real estate office, was one of the last businesses to use the building.

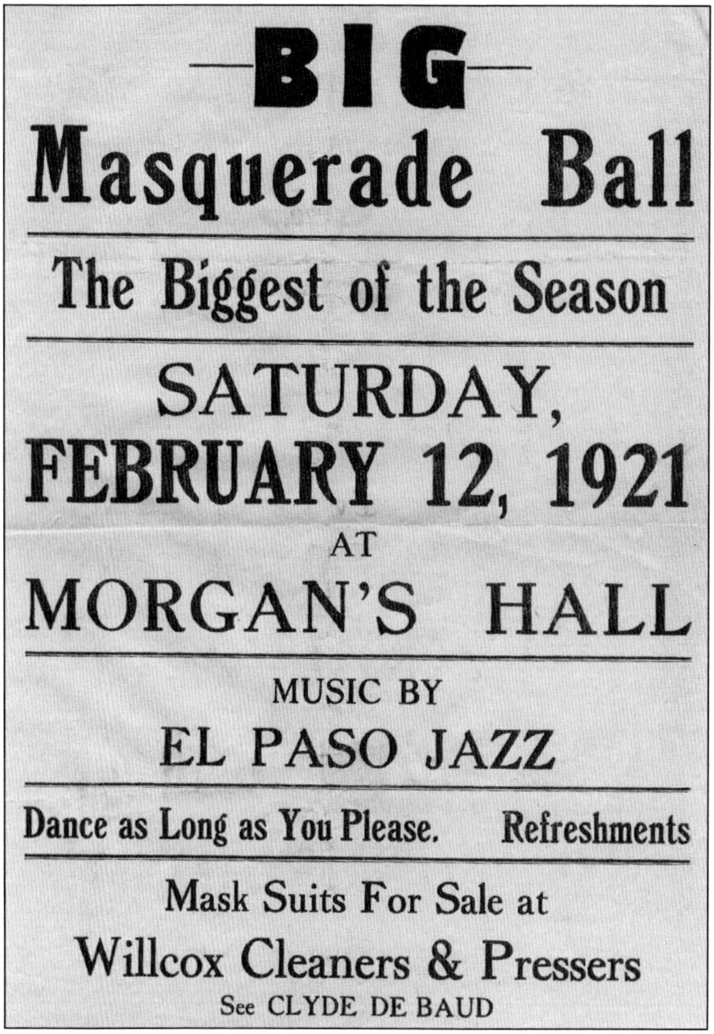

Looking north on Haskell Avenue during the flood of 1923, Morgan's Hall is on the corner of Stewart Street, where Schmelzla's Oil is today. B. G. Motors was located here in the 1950s. All major social events were held here, including graduations and masquerade balls such as the one advertised at left. In 1893, Mrs. Tom Thumb and Company performed, presidential candidate J. B. Weaver arrived on the train and spoke here, and the Home Dramatic Company, made up of local thespians, was newly organized. At that time, it was called Norton's Hall. The sign on the building below is advertising Willcox Bank and Trust. The sign in front is directing shoppers "one block to the right to the Norton-Morgan Department Store." (Jonnie Belle Bethel.)

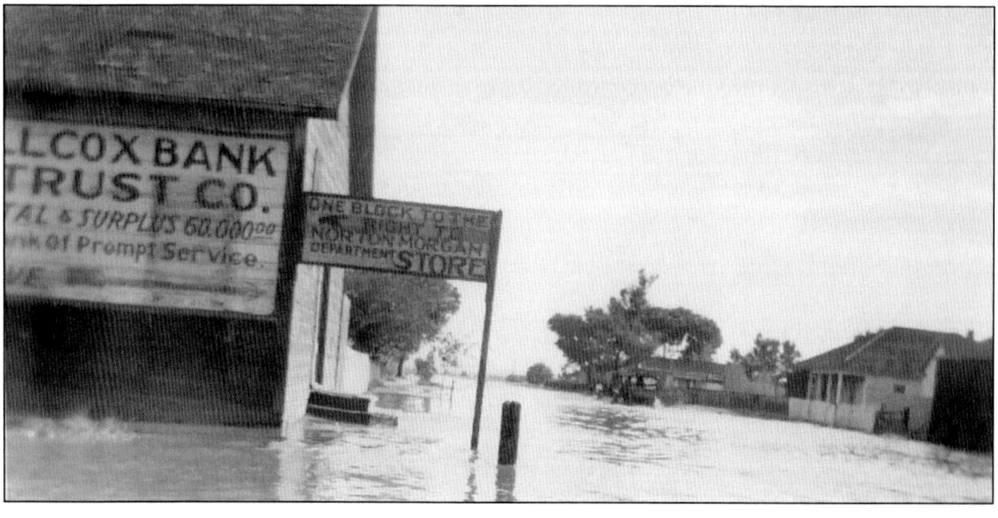

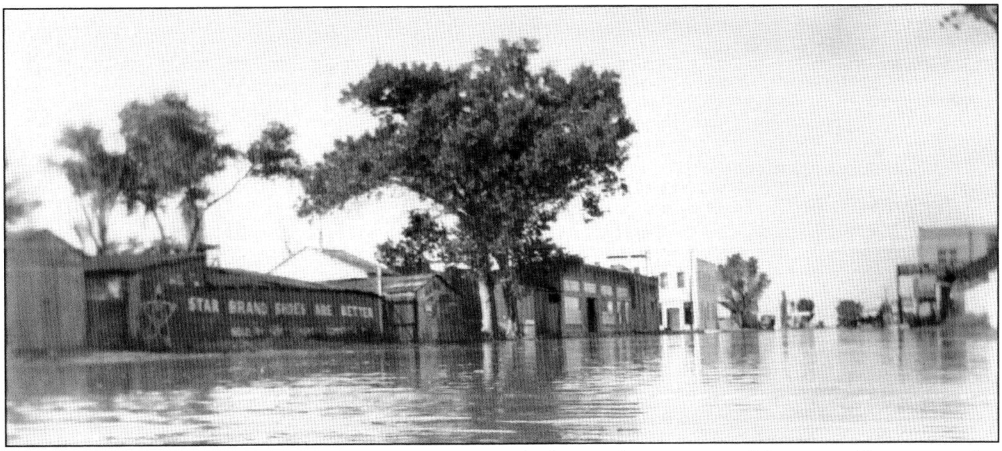

The east side of Haskell Avenue, looking south from the corner of Stewart Street to the Riggs Bank, is shown flooded in 1923. The sign says, "Star Brand Shoes are Better / Sold by Norton-Morgan Commercial." In the 1950s, Harry Parks built his curio shop on this corner. The building to the right of the tree was the Overland Garage, which was razed in March 1941. (Jonnie Belle Bethel.)

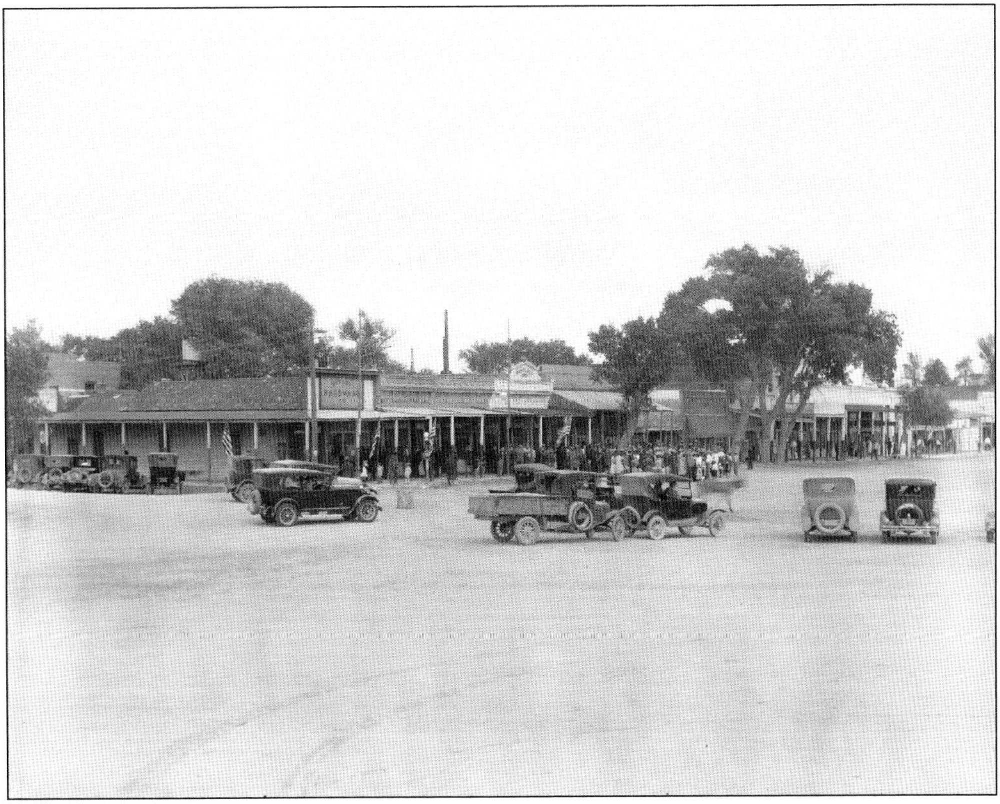

Pictured about 1925, Harley Windsor's Valley Hardware replaced R. G. Lewis Lumber Company on the corner of north Railroad Avenue. The Nicholson's Drug sign can be seen at the top of their store, then a café, and then Willcox Bank and Trust. A huge crowd has gathered for an event sponsored by the Central Copper Company with flags lining the street. (Arizona Historical Society.)

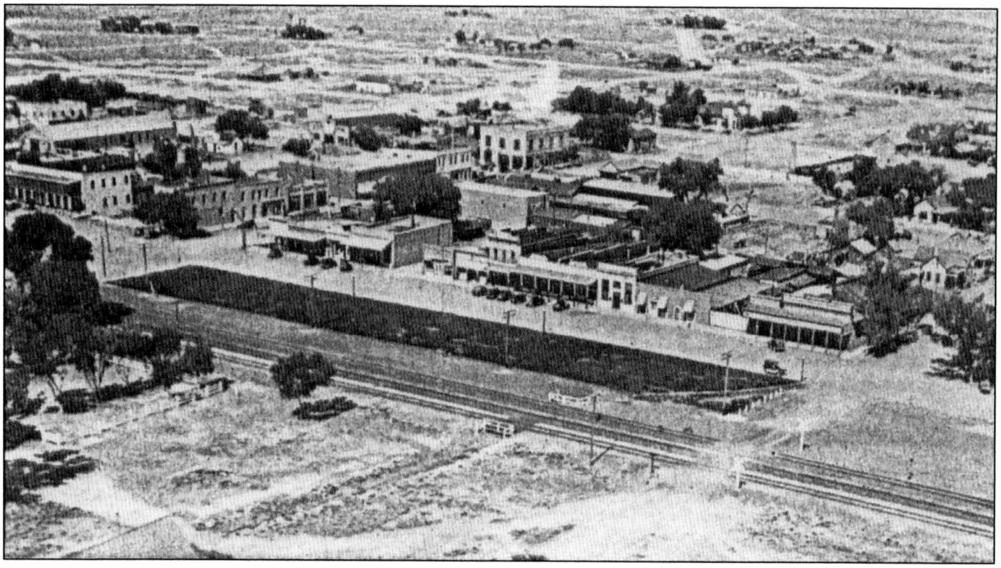

Railroad Park was planted in 1928 to prevent water accumulating after rainstorms, which had been a problem since the town began. Henry Clifford remembers that kids loved to play in this "little bit of heaven" (the only lush grass around) while waiting for the theater to open on Saturdays.

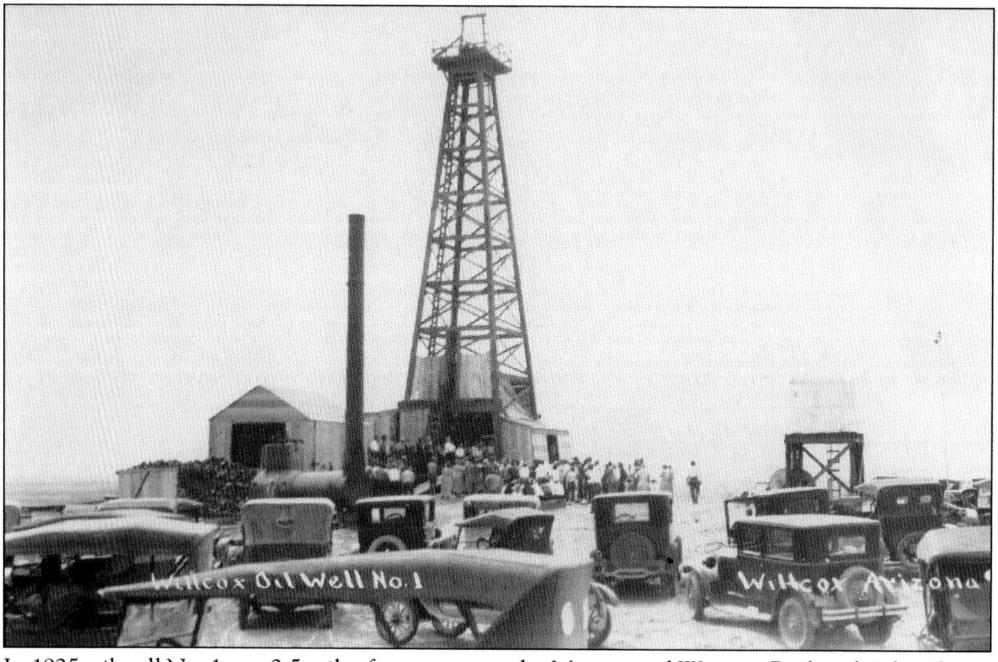

In 1925, oil well No. 1 was 2.5 miles from town on the Mascot and Western Railroad right-of-way. Although there were traces of gas and oil, this well and a second well never produced. Clarke, Holliday, and Associates drilled 66 feet on the Lundquist lots on Railroad Avenue then sold to Geronimo Oil Company, who drilled west of town and encountered a flow of hot artesian water. (Wanda Linam Perry.)

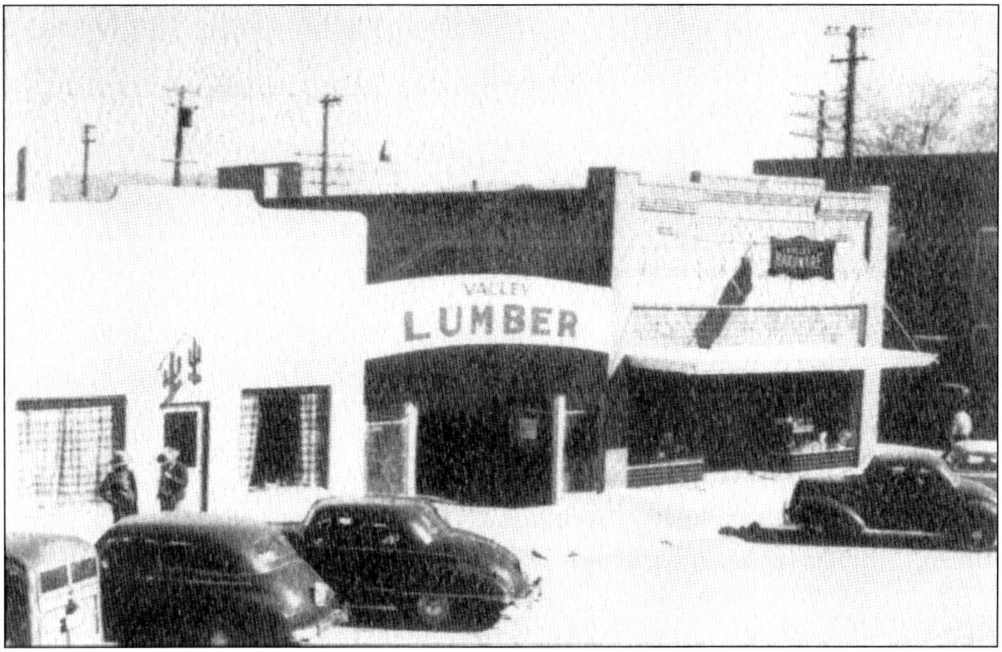

Valley Hardware moved to Maley Street in 1928 with the telephone number 3. Harley Windsor was the owner until his death in 1992. Ned Hogan, whose wife, Elsie, was the city librarian, worked here for many years. In October 1940, Irene Windsor opened the Cactus Gift Shop next door to the lumberyard. The hardware building is now the Chiricahua Regional Museum, and the gift shop is now a beauty shop.

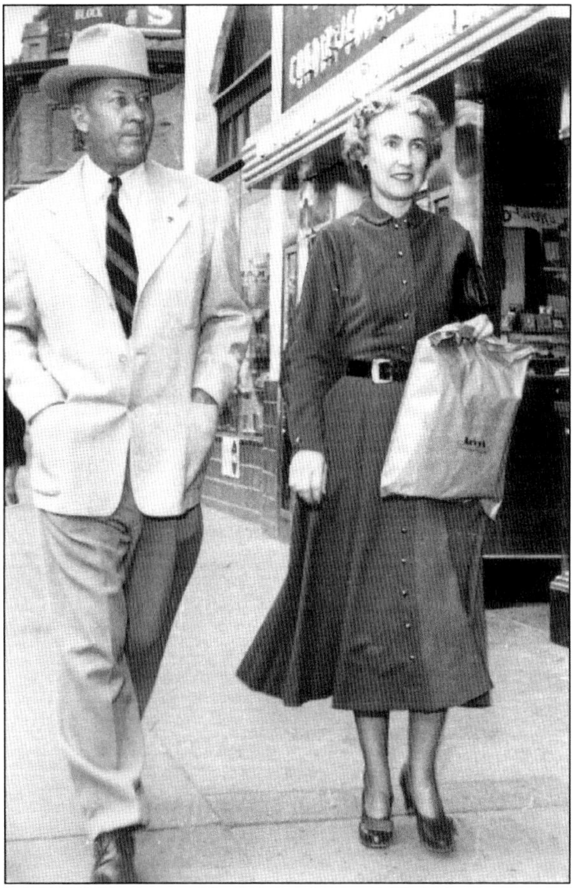

Harley and Irene Windsor are strolling along in the 1950s. The Windsor family came in 1912 by covered wagon, following the railroad tracks in order to find water. Harley's father was the Methodist pastor. Harley married Irene Busenbark in Tombstone in 1924 and bought out his employer, R. G. Lewis, around 1926. He served on the city council in the 1940s and 1950s. (Kay Busenbark Graham.)

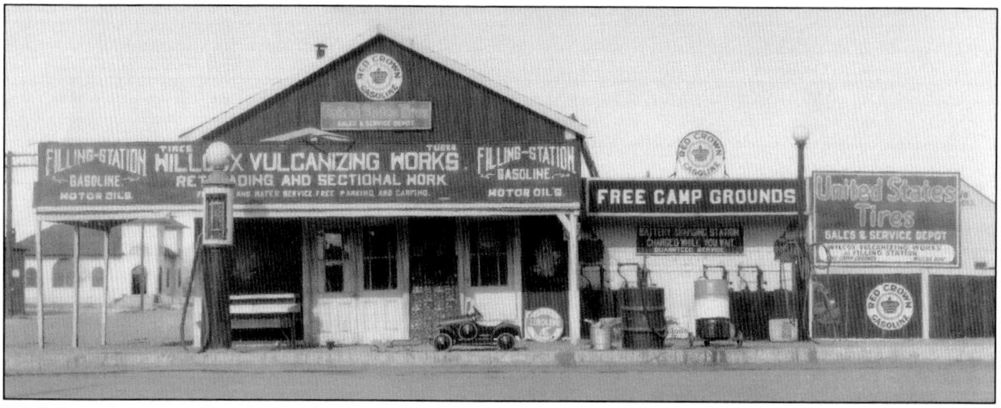

Walter Lohrentz, "that funny little old German," ran this vulcanizing works on Haskell Avenue and Maley Street. To honor the memory of his five-year old son, accidentally killed in 1930, he bought Christmas gifts for every child in town and decorated a beautiful tree for the community for four years. By the time Lohrentz died in 1935, he had become the most beloved man in town. (University of Arizona Special Collections.)

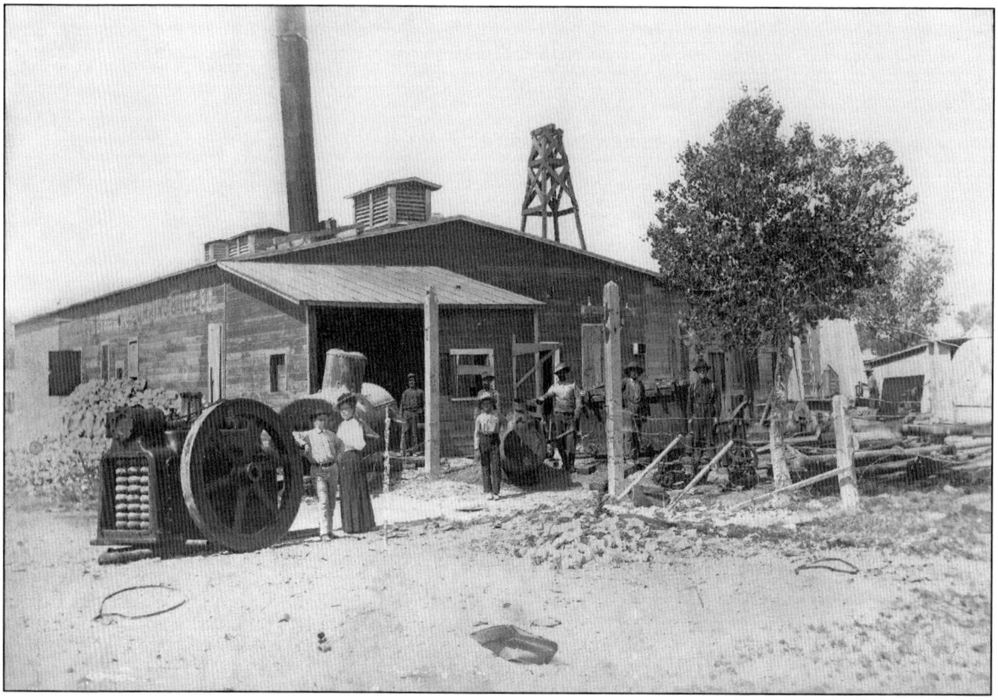

Fred Cadwell and T. D. Swatling's Willcox Lighting, Pumping, and Ice Company began in August 1899. Arc lights were put up near Hauser's Saloon and Norton's warehouse. People were amazed at the businesses lit by electric lights, but as customers failed to pay their bills during the hard times in 1902, the plant closed down. The town was without electricity until 1926. (Arizona Historical Society.)

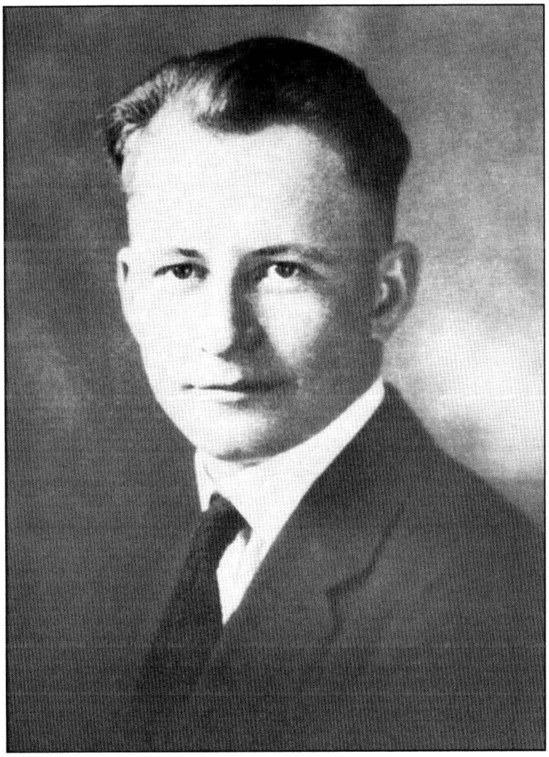

Mark Bliss, Cochise County agricultural agent from 1936 to 1946, launched the Sulphur Springs Valley Electrical Cooperative, bringing electricity to the rural areas. Started in 1938, the office was on Railroad Avenue, then Maley Street. Bliss established Arizona's first FFA chapter in Peoria. In Safford, he grew the first sugar beets and showed farmers how to dramatically improve their cotton yields.

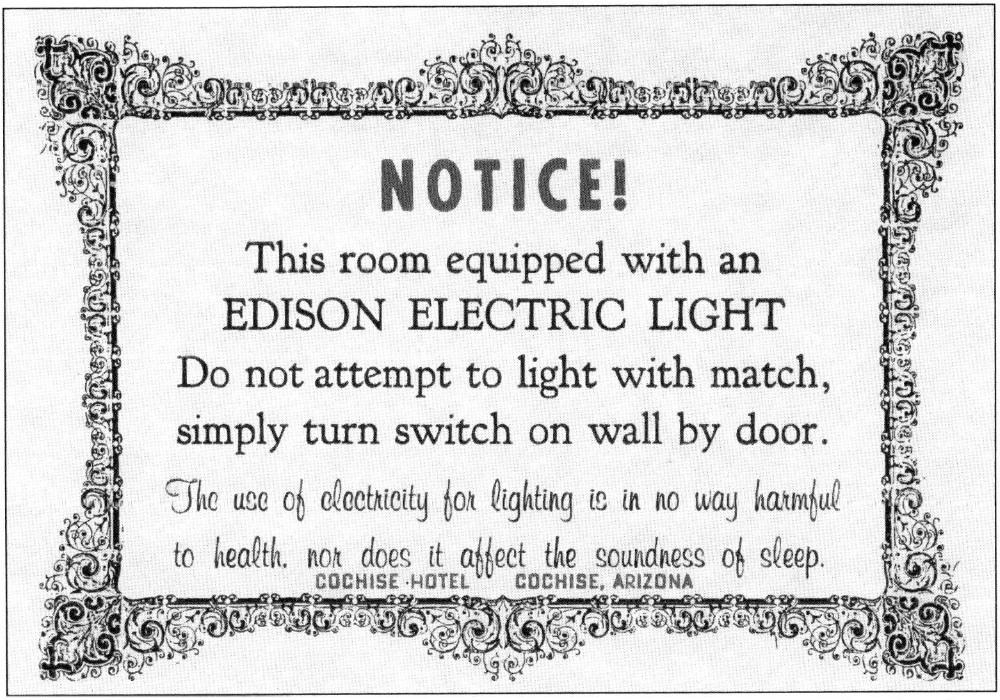

This notice posted at the Cochise Hotel near Willcox, while humorous to people today, shows that as electricity began to be used in the homes and businesses, people had to be educated as to safe usage, and rumors of the dangers of electricity had to be squelched. (Willie Adams.)

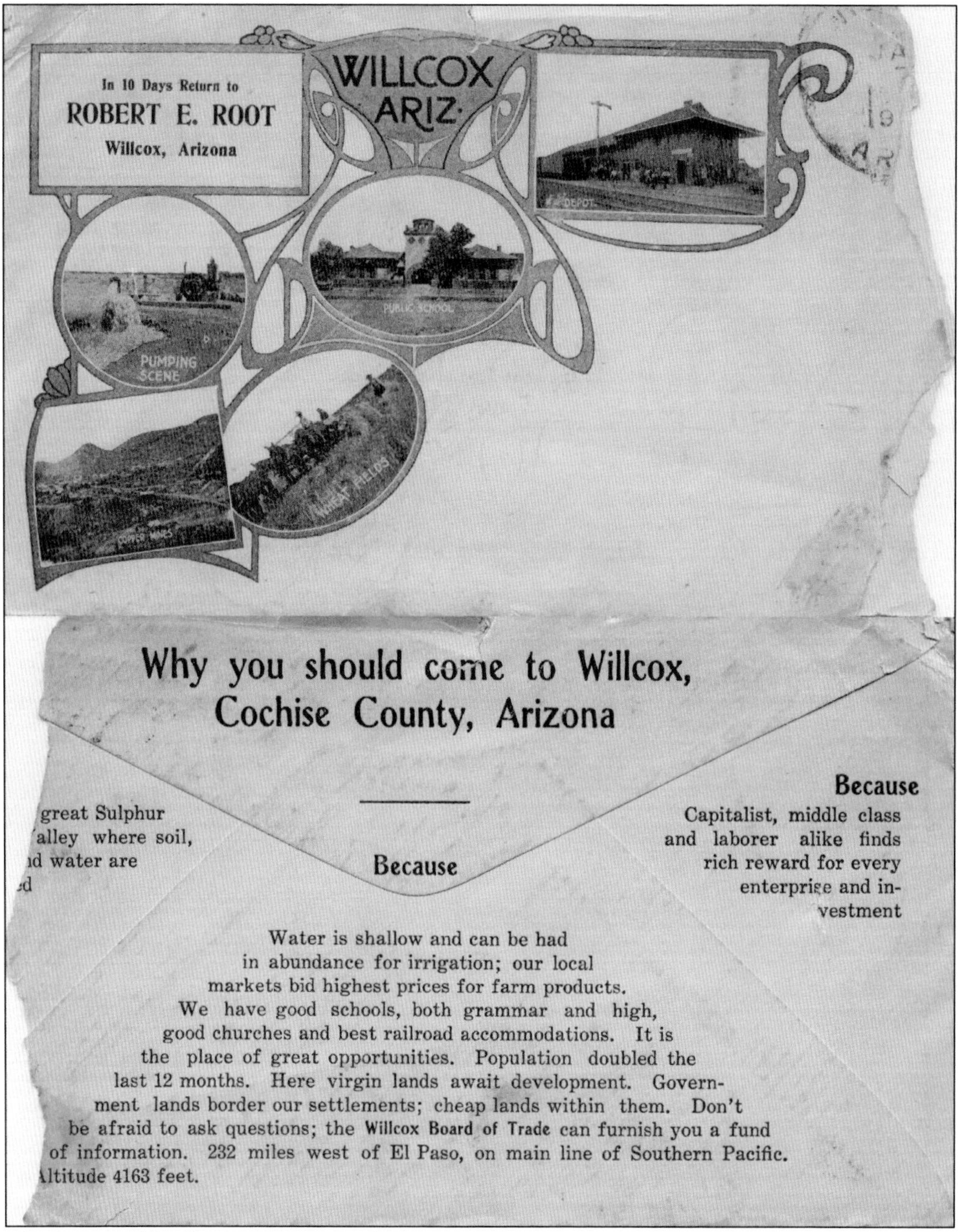

The front and back of an envelope that was mailed by Robert E. Root at the beginning of the 20th century tell the benefits offered in the area to encourage newcomers. Images show pumping for irrigation, plowing the fields, copper mining at the Mascot Mine, transporting by rail, and the importance placed on education by the building of a new school in 1900.

The families of John and Marcia Ann Collins Forsyth and John and Minnie Larkins were among the first to farm in the Kansas Settlement area. John and Marcia's son Byron Forsyth and his new bride, Letha Larkins, are shown on their wedding day in 1924. Charlie Kimsey and Virgil Baker, other pioneer farmers, were related by marriage. (Audrey Thompson.)

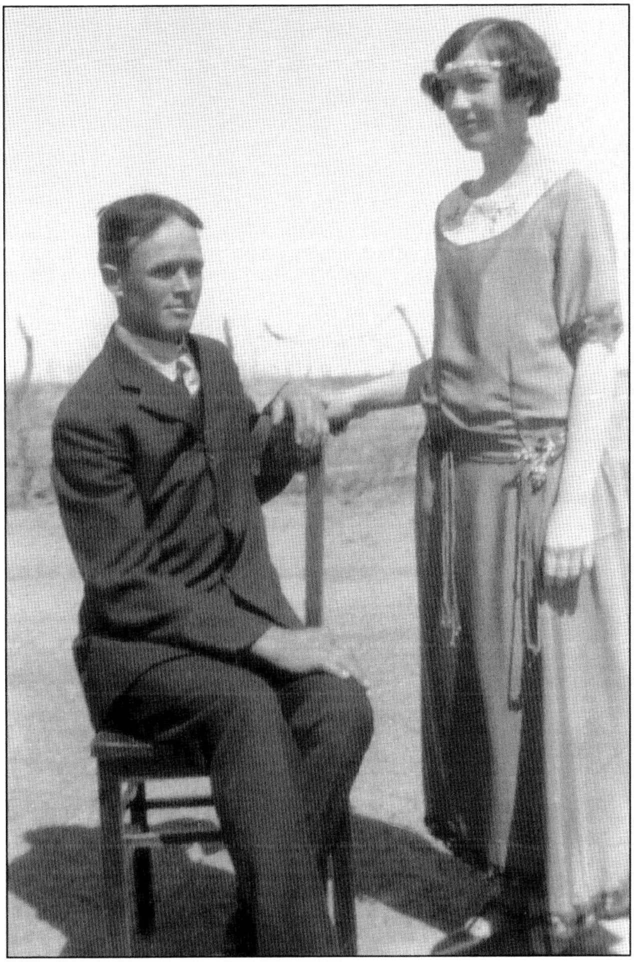

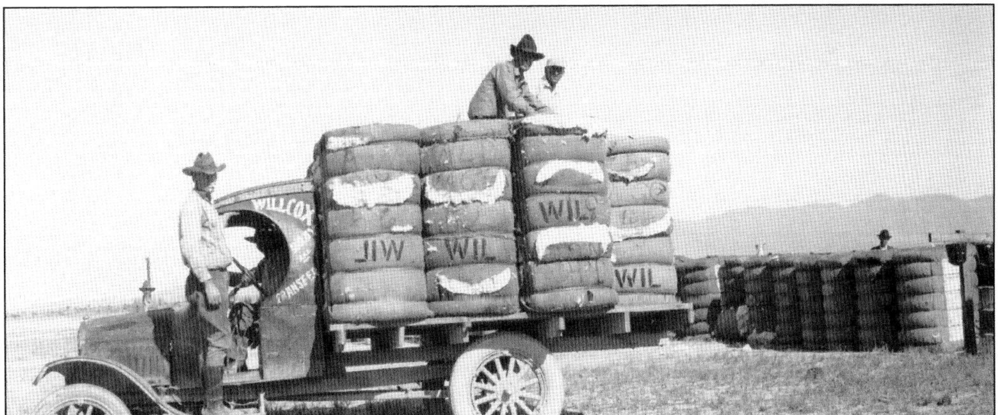

The first, though unsuccessful, attempt to grow cotton in 1920 was followed by J. G. Anderson's acre planted in 1936, yielding a bale and a quarter. By 1945, three farms with 57 acres yielded 31 bales. The first shipment was loaded onto the Willcox Dray and Transfer truck, owned by V. F. Swanner, to be shipped from Willcox by train. (University of Arizona Special Collections.)

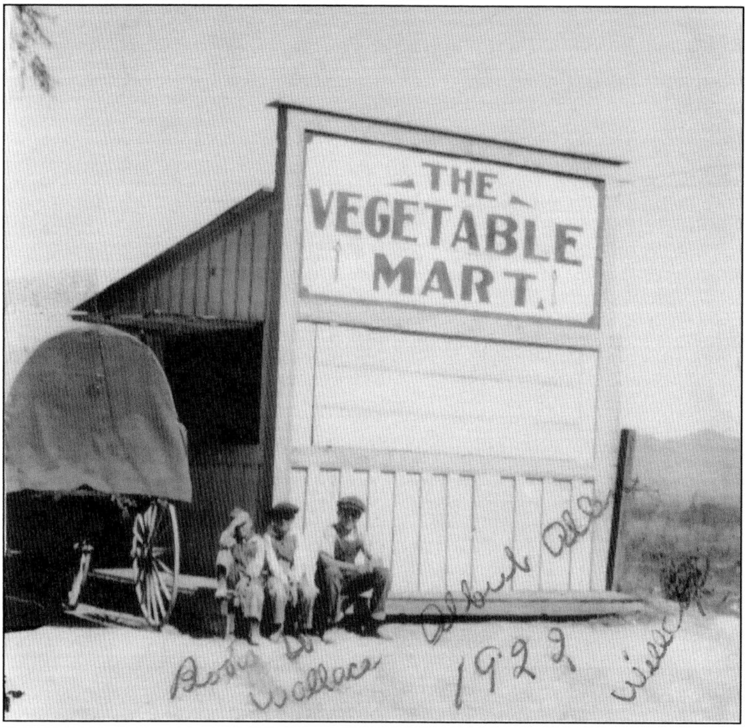

Harry Lundquist and his son Wallace sold fresh vegetables from their garden to local grocers and families. Sitting on the porch of the Vegetable Mart in 1922 are, from left to right, Boots ?, Wallace Lundquist, and Albert Allen. Wallace, a very enterprising young man, also worked at the Sweet Shop and bakery. He married Vera Wooten in 1932, and they had two daughters, Phyllis and Laura. (Lundquist family.)

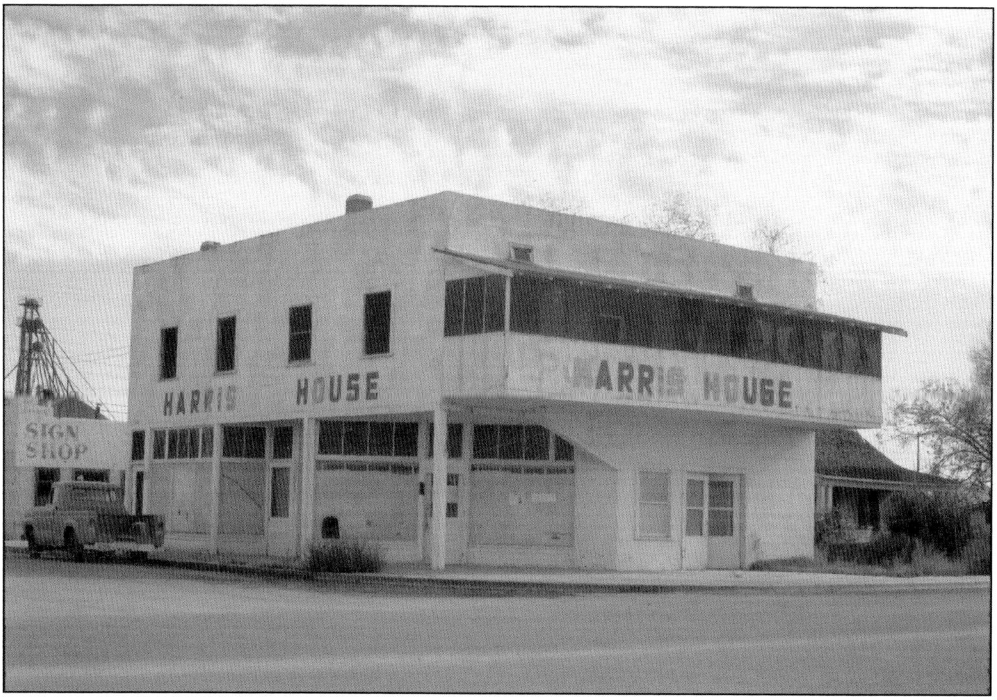

Frank Harris's real estate business started in 1915. He shared the building with Minnie Nordhus's insurance agency. At one time, the building served as J. U. Nanney's Pontiac dealership. Nat Harris had his sign shop in the back, and the second floor was a boardinghouse. The building was torn down about 1971.

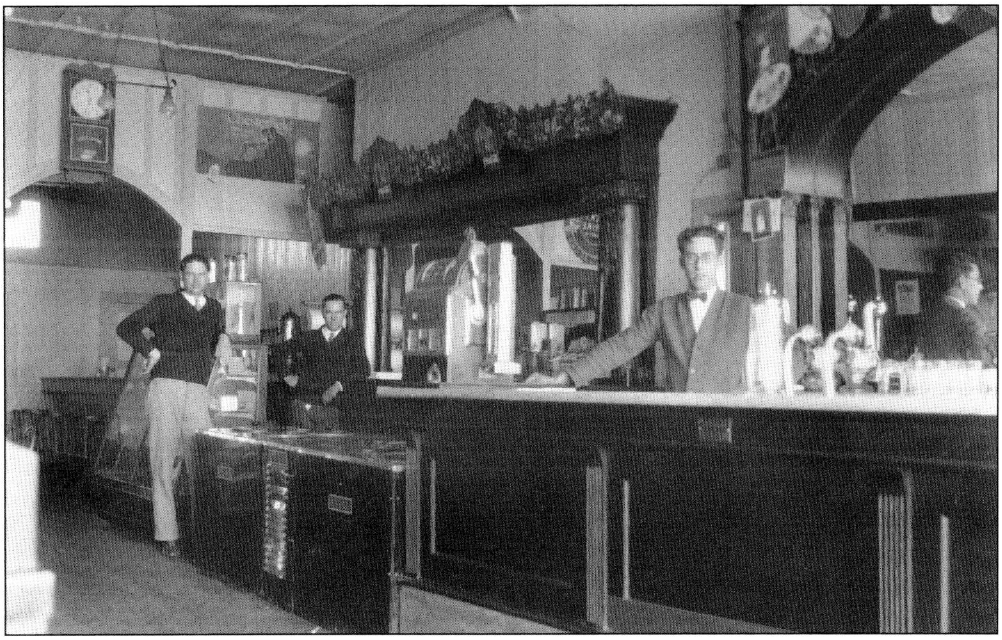

Wallace Lundquist stands behind the counter at right with Roy Goodwin and an unidentified man in the Sweet Shop, a favorite gathering spot. The one-time location of the Elite Saloon, called the King building, was leased by George King for Charley Ho's restaurant in 1889. R. A. Pride and William Speed purchased it for their pool hall in 1915. It burned to the ground along with the Western Bar. (Lundquist family.)

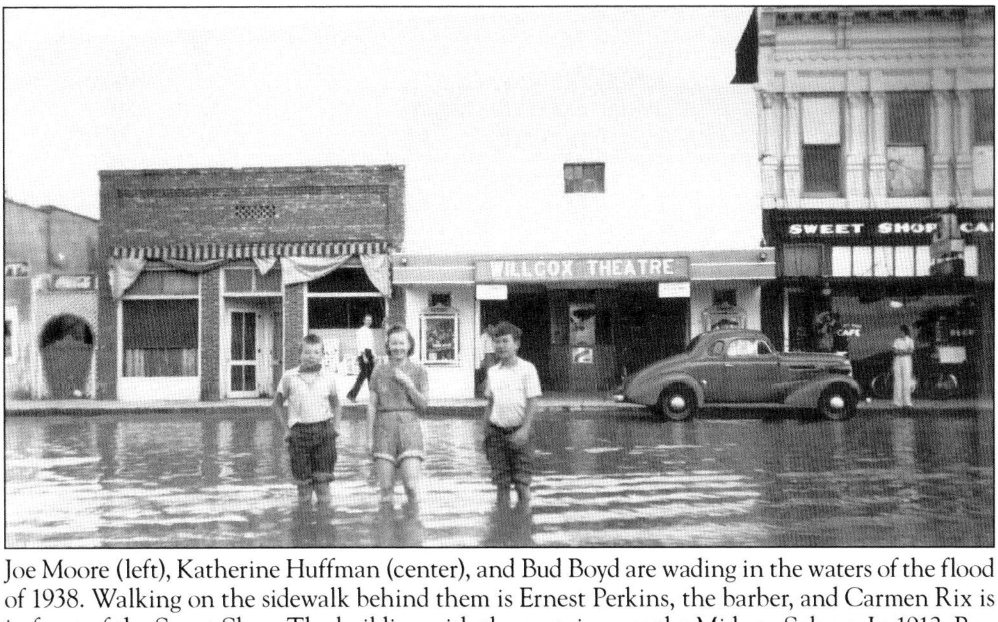

Joe Moore (left), Katherine Huffman (center), and Bud Boyd are wading in the waters of the flood of 1938. Walking on the sidewalk behind them is Ernest Perkins, the barber, and Carmen Rix is in front of the Sweet Shop. The building with the curtains was the Midway Saloon. In 1912, Roy Wiley was shot and killed there by the bartender Mort Bennett. (Lundquist family.)

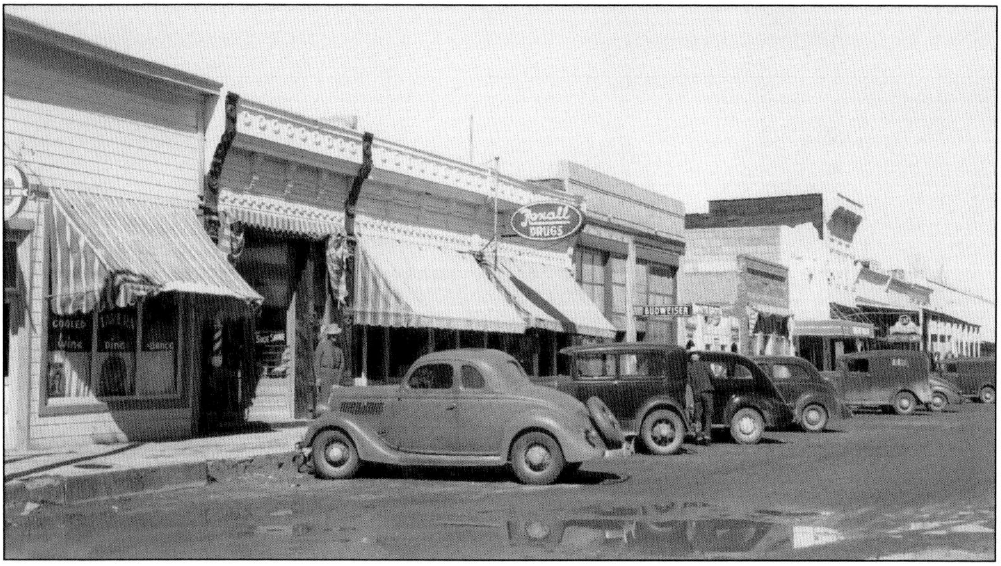

Looking north down Railroad Avenue about 1932 in the above image, one can see the sign in the window of the first building that says, "The Tavern, cooled wine, dine & dance." A barber pole and shoe shine sign is next, then one for Rexall Drugs, and then a Budweiser sign on the Palace Club. The next building has a café sign. The streets were not paved yet, as seen by the reflection of the cars in the mud puddles. Lee Russell took the photograph below around 1936 looking south down Railroad Avenue from the Willcox Bank and Trust building. Almost every building had an awning.

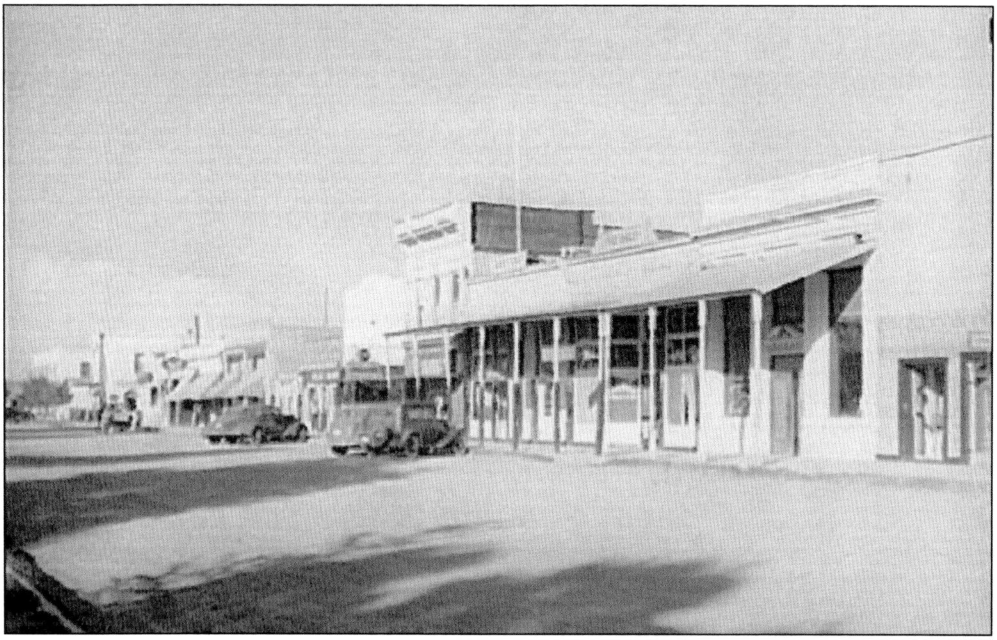

Nine

The 1940s and 1950s

Willcox experienced another boom in building during the 1940s and 1950s. Many new businesses opened. Tourist traffic slowed during the war years due to rationing of tires and gasoline, but it returned to normal after 1945. It was estimated that an average of 3,000 vehicles a day passed through on Highway 86. Willcox also had the advantage of U.S. Highway 666 (now 191) joining Highway 86 eight miles west of town and continuing 12 miles eastward before turning towards Safford, Arizona.

Mining was no longer of significance locally, but cattle ranches still surrounded the area with Willcox still the best place to market the cattle. The number of farms was increasing, and the amount each farm could produce had increased through use of electricity, modern equipment, and education. Willcox remained a trade center, with a huge percentage of retail sales and services being to nonresidents from the surrounding communities. In the 1940s, Dale and Ruth Mellenbruch became editors of the *Arizona Range News*, Porter Fox had the Chevron station, Lynn Camp was manager of the Willcox Commercial, and Thelmer Smith owned Willcox Auto Parts. People shopped for groceries at Plough's, "The Home of Fine Foods," or ate out at the Star Café, owned by George and Mary Grosh. In the 1950s, there was a choice between the Valley Store, Mills Grocery, or Willcox Market. Krucker, Kemper, and Willoughby were the attorneys, and travelers stayed at the Wee Blu Inn Motel.

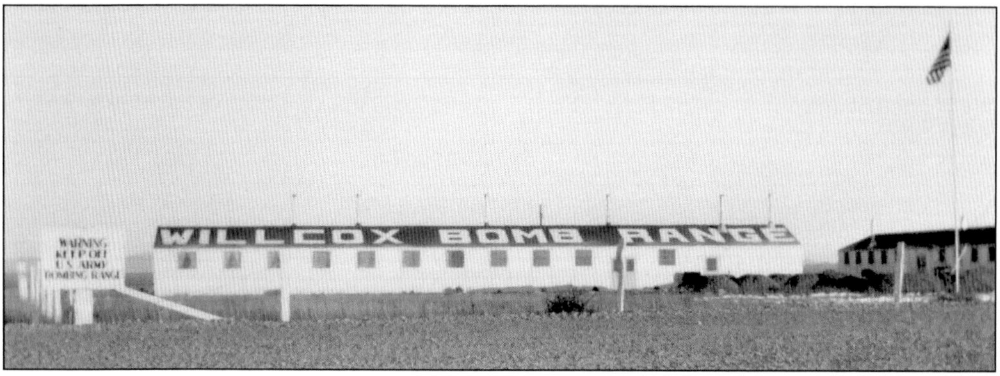

During World War II, the Willcox Playa, or dry lake, was a military bombing range. The base mess hall was behind this barrack along with a radio building and workshop. Planes flew over the Dos Cabezas Mountains and tried to hit targets pulled by remote-controlled trucks. According to Walt Hamilton, the bombs never once hit their target.

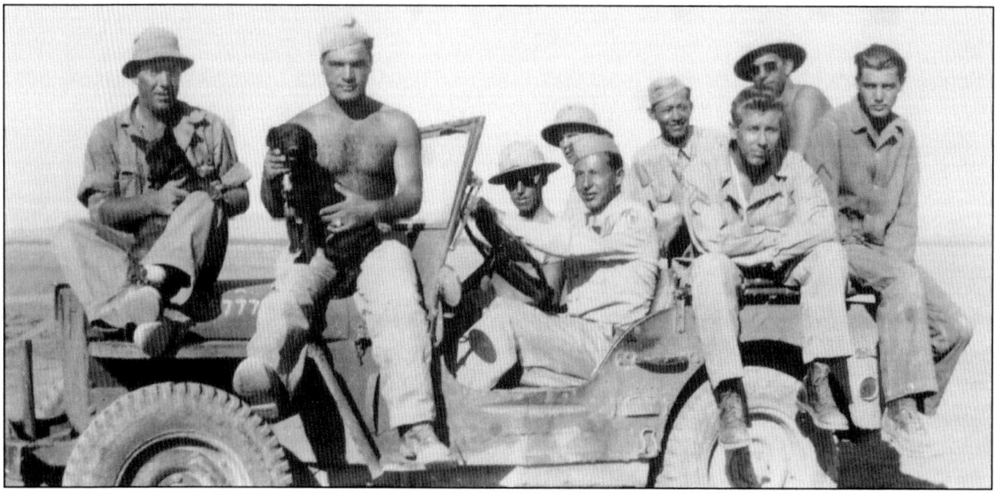

The bombing range crew in 1943 is, from left to right, Horace Mawyer, Jerry Candela, Lynn Nielson, Steve Kotris, Walt Hamilton, unidentified, Howard Clement, unidentified, and Paul Belknap. Their job was to operate the trucks and fill in the holes left by the bombs. Hamilton, Clement, and fellow crewmen Fritz Panchalk and Jesse John married local girls and stayed in Willcox. Hamilton and John went into the auto repair business together.

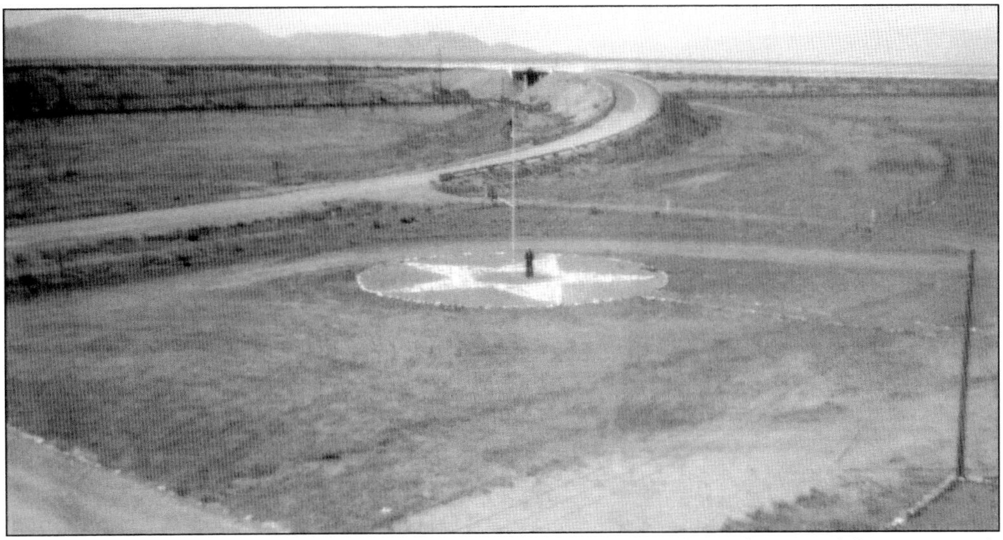

The bombing range front yard and flagpole are pictured as seen from the top of the water tank tower. The Southern Pacific Railroad and Route 666 overpass are in the background. In 1944, a navy seaplane made an emergency landing on the lake after one engine failed. Renamed "The Mirage of the Willcox Dry Lake," the plane was repaired and flown to San Diego.

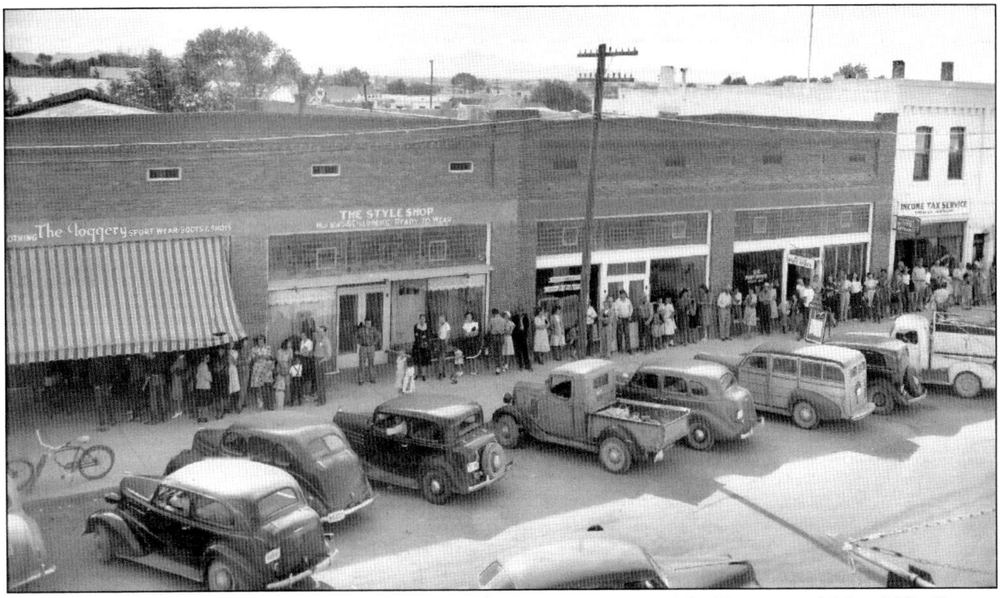

Denim pants were rationed during the war. The Toggery, owned by Bruce and Hazel Huffman, would advertise when a shipment of Lee's and Levi's arrived, and the line of customers waiting to buy jeans would reach all the way down the street. Sulphur Springs Valley Electric Cooperative was next door, then the post office. Theilan Ridge Johnson's tax service and the Maverick Hotel were in the Valley National Bank building.

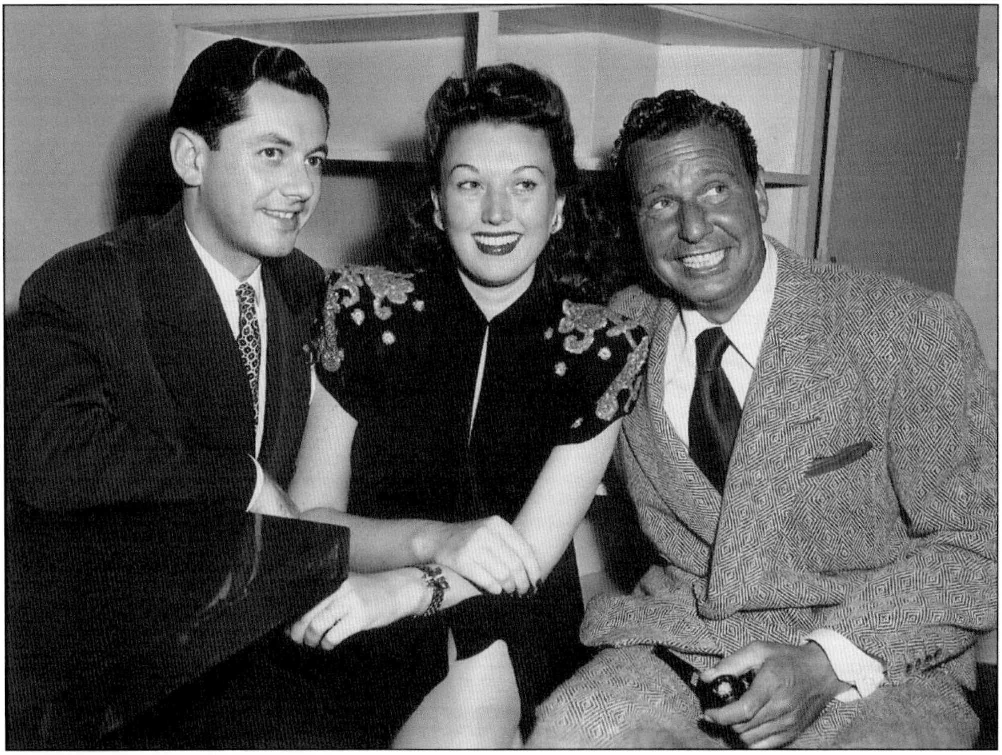

Rex Emrick (left) was owner of the water works and director of the chamber of commerce, and he spent 38 years as organist for the Elks Club. After the war, he sang with Phil Harris (right) and Gorgeous Ginny Simms (center) on her radio talk show in Hollywood. Ginny Simms grew up in Willcox and became a famous singer in Kaye Kyser's orchestra and a movie star. Married three times, she died in 1994.

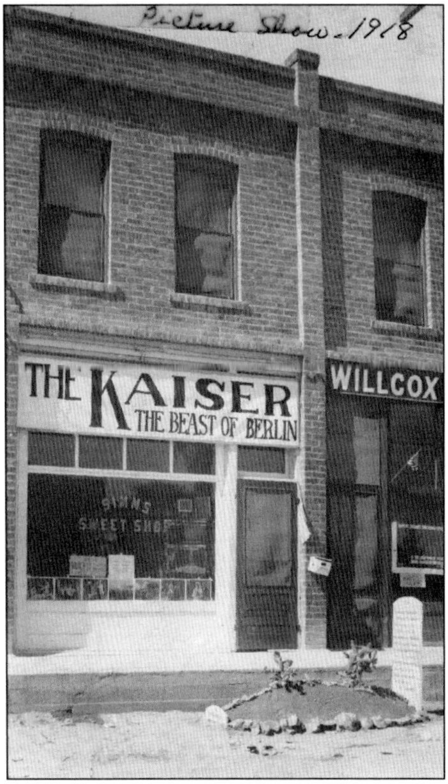

D. D. Simms, the father of Ginny Simms, opened the theater and Simms Sweet Shop on Maley Street in 1918 with sliding doors that could be opened to create a dance floor. An electric piano provided music for the silent films. It was located in the Gersbach (Riggs Bank) Building. Ernest Browning had a Piggly Wiggly store next door. On October 12, 1940, a bowling alley was opened next door to the bank.

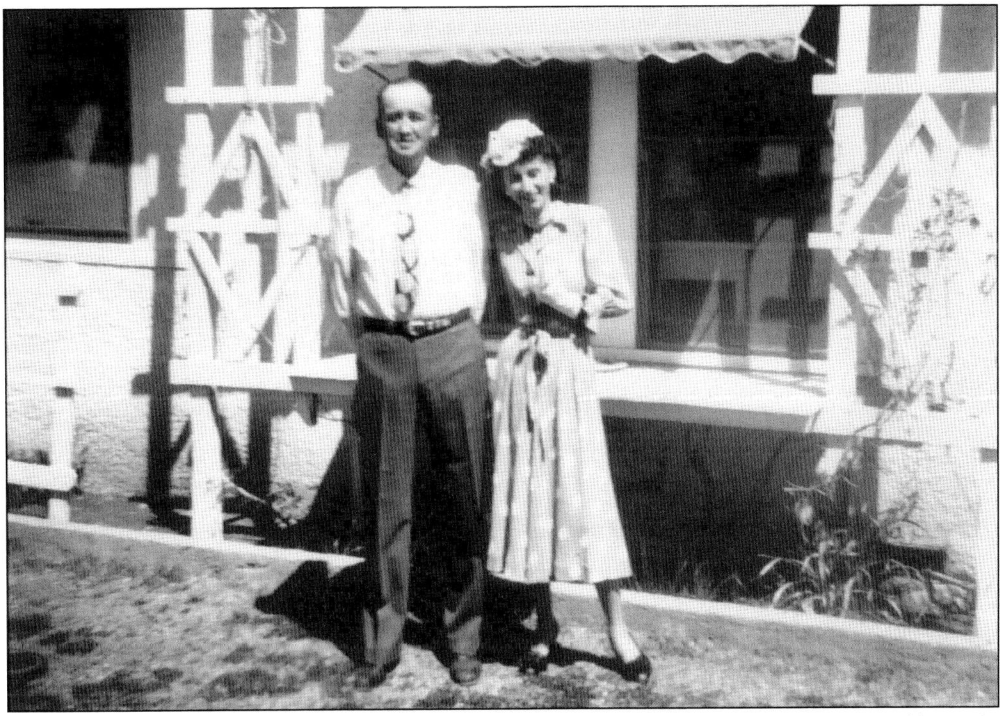

Albert O. Rix and stepdaughter Carmen Detloff are dressed up for Easter Sunday. Rix and his wife, also named Carmen, operated the Willcox Tavern after Chick Williamson. It was located in the old Headquarters Saloon building, which burned in 1948. S. J. Moyer, the owner, constructed a new block building. Renamed Rix's Tavern, the building moved in November 1954 to its present location. Rix's sold the Sweet Shop to the Baumkirchners in 1945. (Jonnie Belle Bethel.)

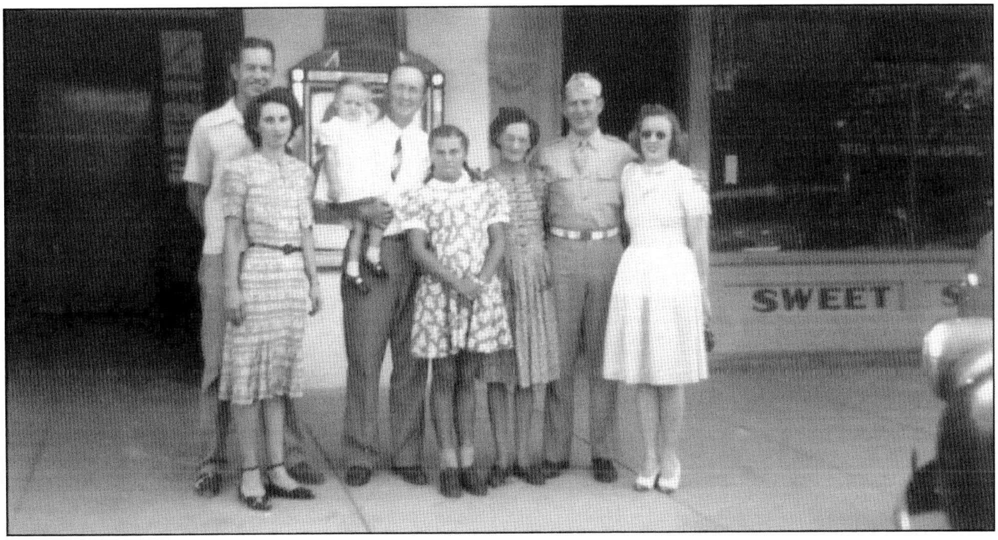

From left to right, Double Detloff, Carmen Detloff, Albert Rix holding Kit Armagnac, Jonnie Belle Detloff, Carmen Rix, and Alex and Katherine Huffman Armagnac gather to send Alex off to war in France. In the 1970s, the Sweet Shop burned in a fire that started in the Western Bar. The theater was saved by a firewall built by A. O. Rix. (Jonnie Belle Bethel.)

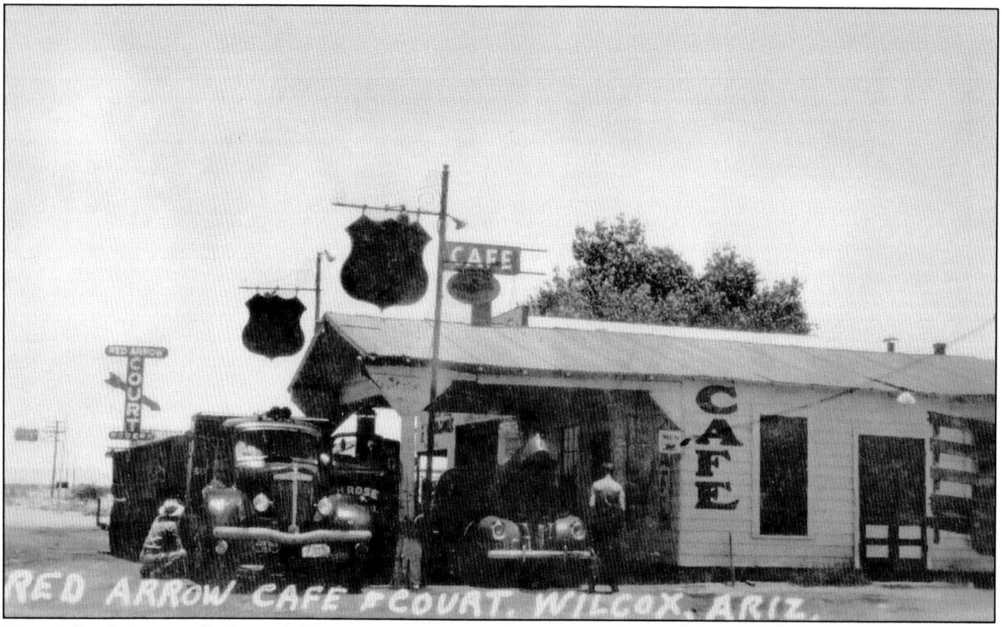

Goar's Red Arrow Café and Court was a service station with little cabins for rent. It was located where Hansen Brothers Pawn Shop is today on Haskell Avenue. Bill Goar hired Lester "Peck" Bethel and his brother George to run it in October 1943. (Betty Allaire.)

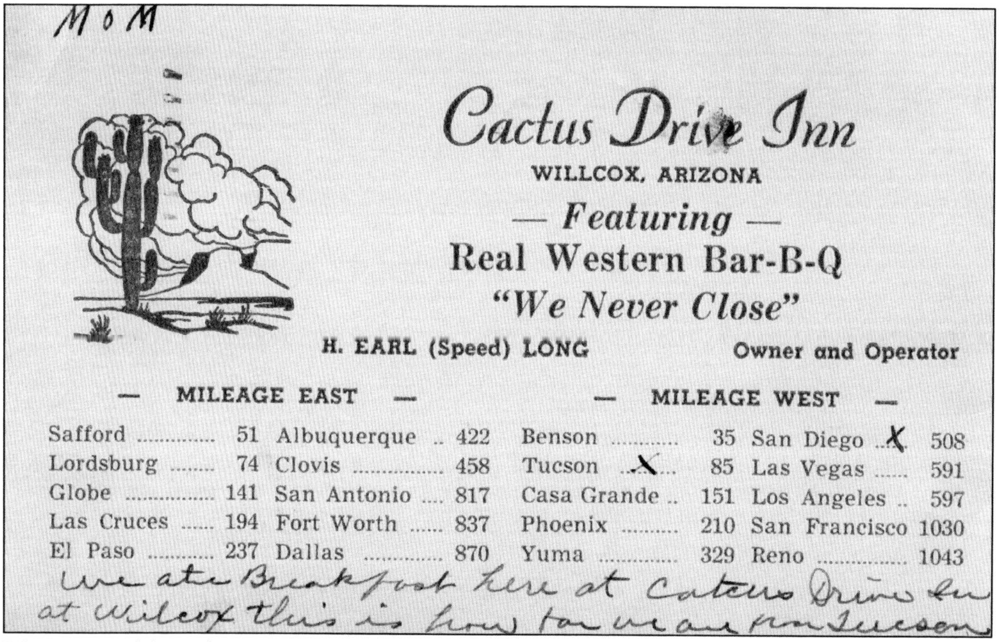

This postcard from the Cactus Drive-In Café was mailed in 1947. It was located on Haskell Avenue across from the current Circle K store. By 1949, ownership had passed from H. Earl (Speed) Long to Bob Rankin. In 1970, the Tip Top Café opened in this location with Jennie and Wade (last name unknown) as proprietors. (Dave Potts.)

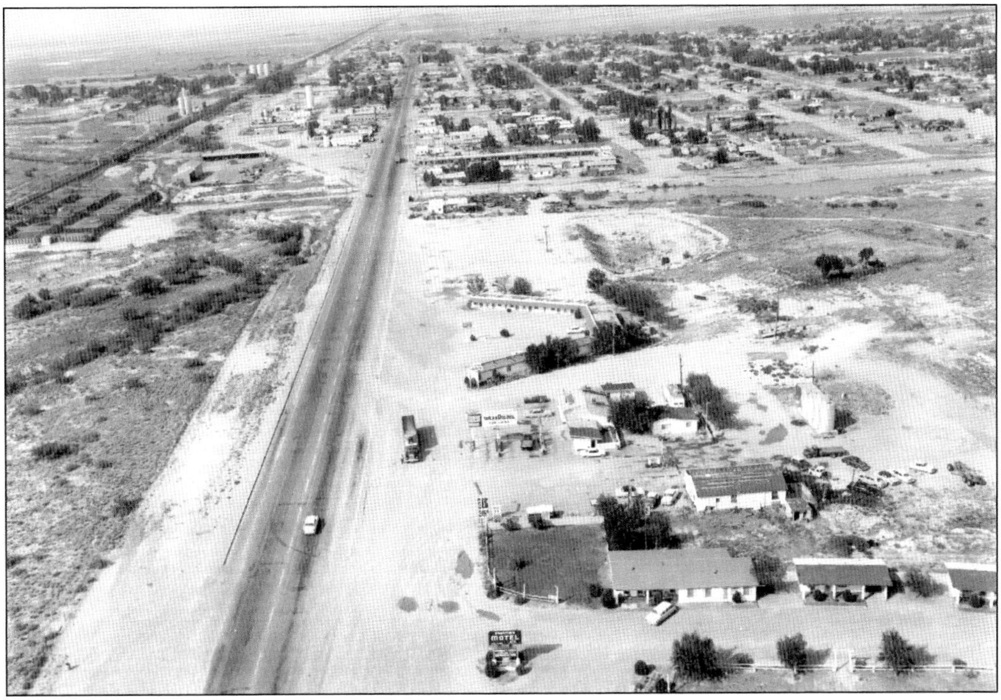

A c. 1950 aerial view shows the Frontier Motel and the Home Café at the end of Chapman's Motel at right. The price of gas was 31.9¢ a gallon. The large building with "Goar" on the roof was the Red Arrow, and the Truck City Café was across the street. Cattle shipping pens are at the far left along with a little white building that held the scales.

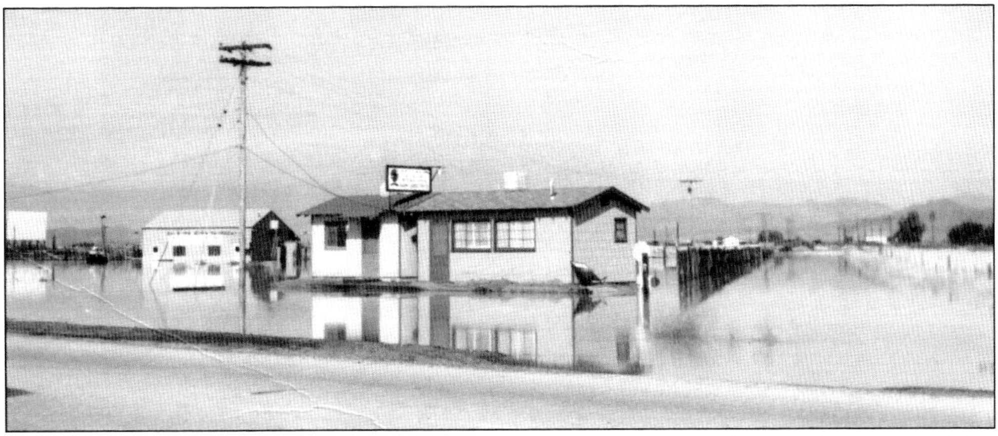

Another flood hit town in the 1950s. The Farm Labor Office, run by Art Gentner, and the livestock auction barn are sitting in water. At the far left, just off Patte Road, is the screen for Long's Drive-in Theater, which was run by Cecil Flint. It closed about 1962 after the screen blew down during a terrible windstorm while *Gone with the Wind* was showing. (Lundquist family.)

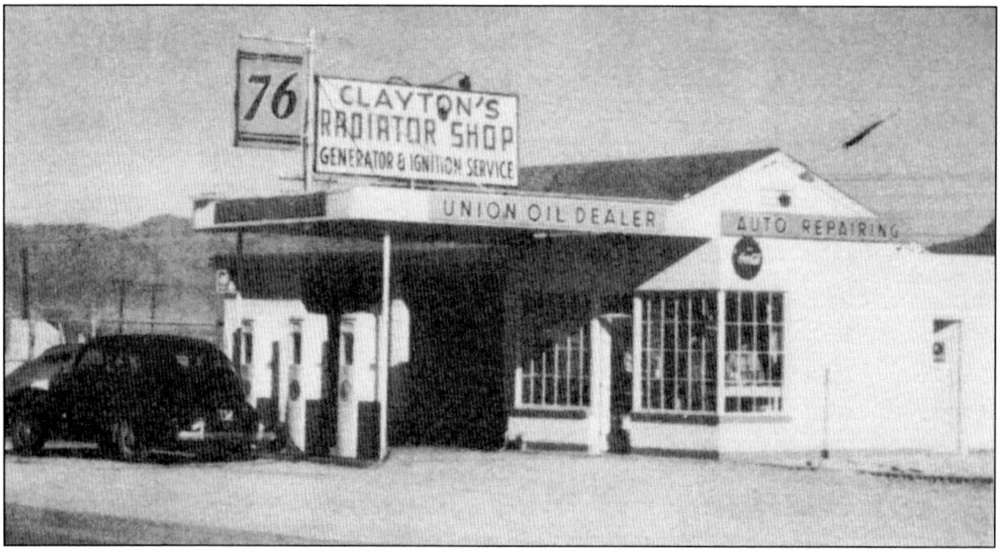

Buck and Maybelle Diehl Clayton owned Clayton's Radiator Shop. It was the 76 gas station, the Union Oil dealership, and an auto repair shop. Clayton ran the business located on south Haskell Avenue from 1948 until 1984. The Claytons' daughter Alice Gwen married Howard Bethel.

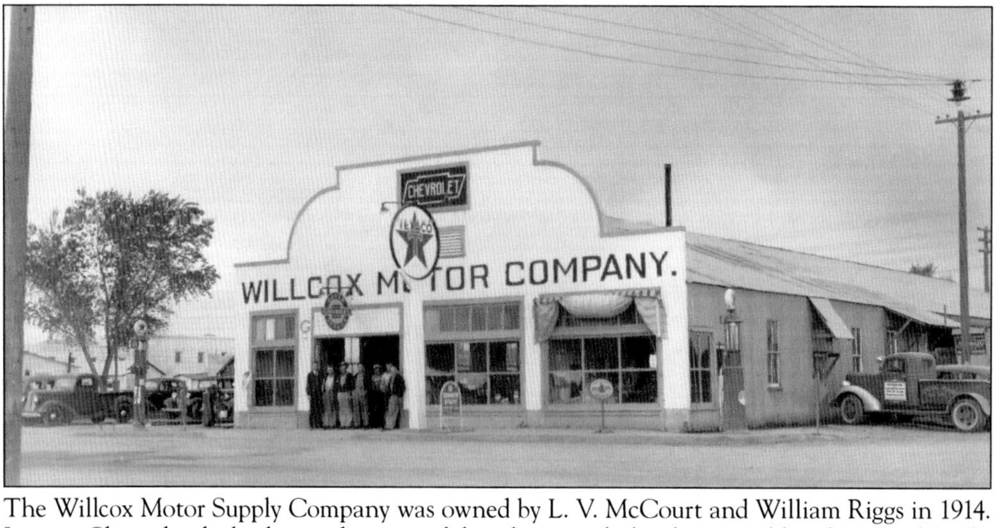

The Willcox Motor Supply Company was owned by L. V. McCourt and William Riggs in 1914. It was a Chevrolet dealership at the time of this photograph, but later it sold and serviced Fords. Located on the corner of Haskell Avenue and Grant Streets, several banks have since occupied this site, including the People's Bank, Union Bank, Arizona Bank, and Compass Bank. (Wanda Linam Perry.)

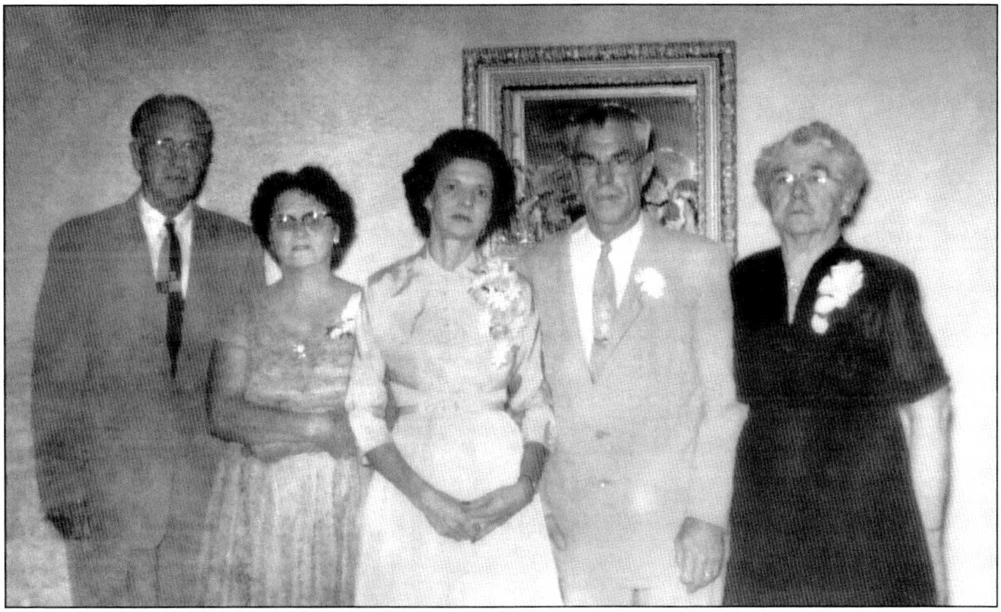

George Coleman (left), president of the Rotary Club in 1941 and elementary school principal for 23 years, stands beside his wife, Gretna. Their daughter Dorothy Phinizy Chaudoin is the new bride of Ben E. Briscoe Jr. on their wedding day, October 9, 1954. His mother, Lula Briscoe, is at right. (Betty Kowalczyk.)

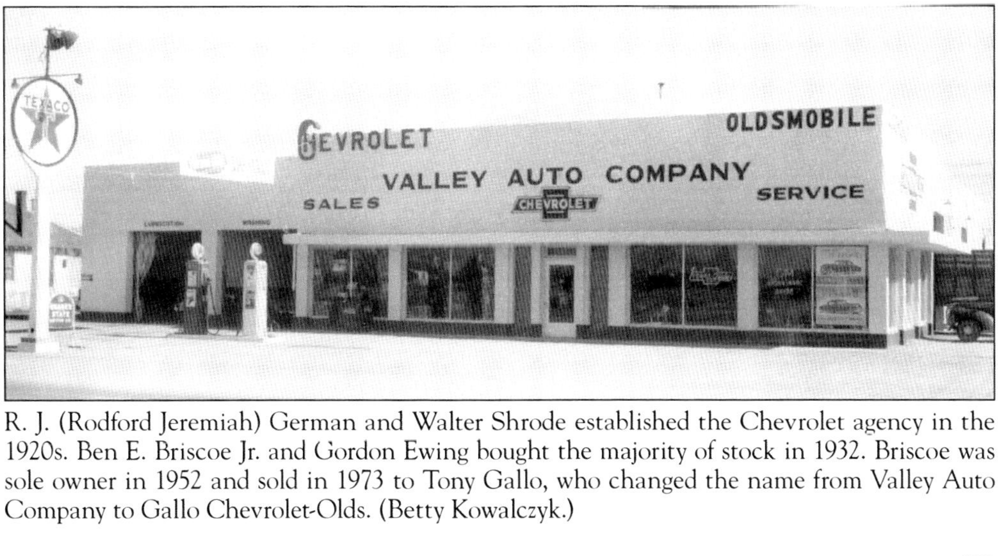

R. J. (Rodford Jeremiah) German and Walter Shrode established the Chevrolet agency in the 1920s. Ben E. Briscoe Jr. and Gordon Ewing bought the majority of stock in 1932. Briscoe was sole owner in 1952 and sold in 1973 to Tony Gallo, who changed the name from Valley Auto Company to Gallo Chevrolet-Olds. (Betty Kowalczyk.)

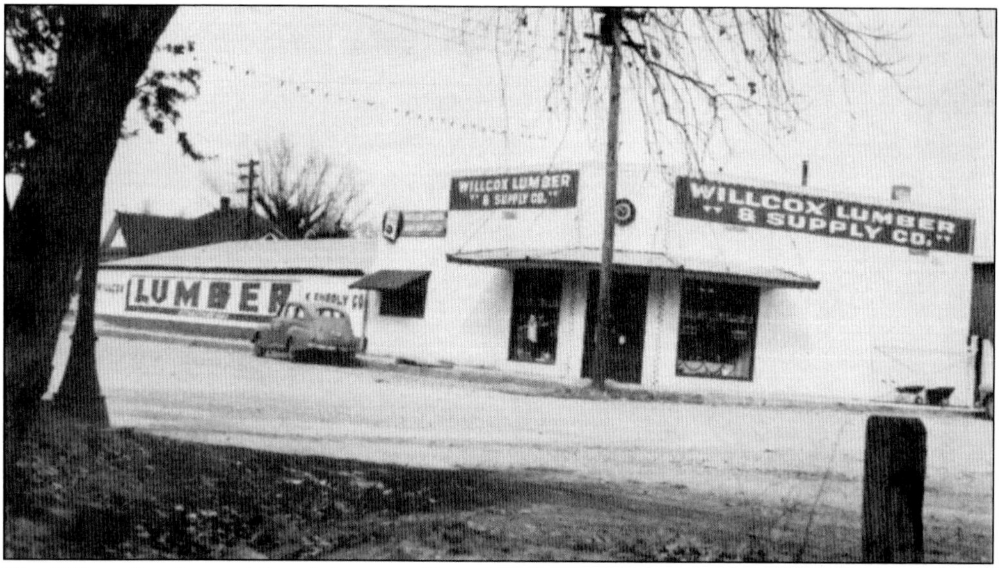

The Willcox Lumber and Supply began as Blinn Lumber Company in 1882. W. F. Nichols purchased it in 1888. Ralph Lewis was the owner when Thomas Fleetham and Harry Saxon purchased it in 1939. Saxon was president; his wife, Anna, was vice president; and Fleetham was secretary/treasurer/manager. Fleetham operated the company until 1981, when he passed it on to his son.

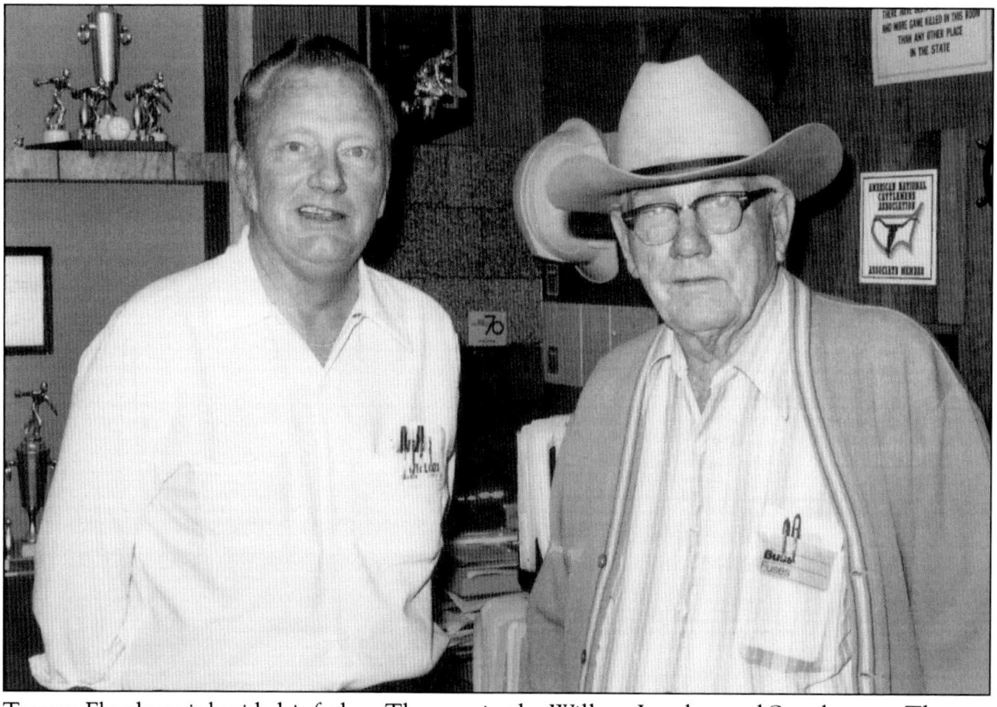

Tommy Fleetham is beside his father, Thomas, in the Willcox Lumber and Supply store. Thomas Edwin Fleetham was born in Pearce, Arizona, to George and Bonella Fleetham. He served on the local school board for 20 years and was mayor of Willcox and president of the chamber of commerce. He married Helen Creech, whose father operated a local garage. Besides their son, Thomas Jr., they also had a daughter named Sharon.

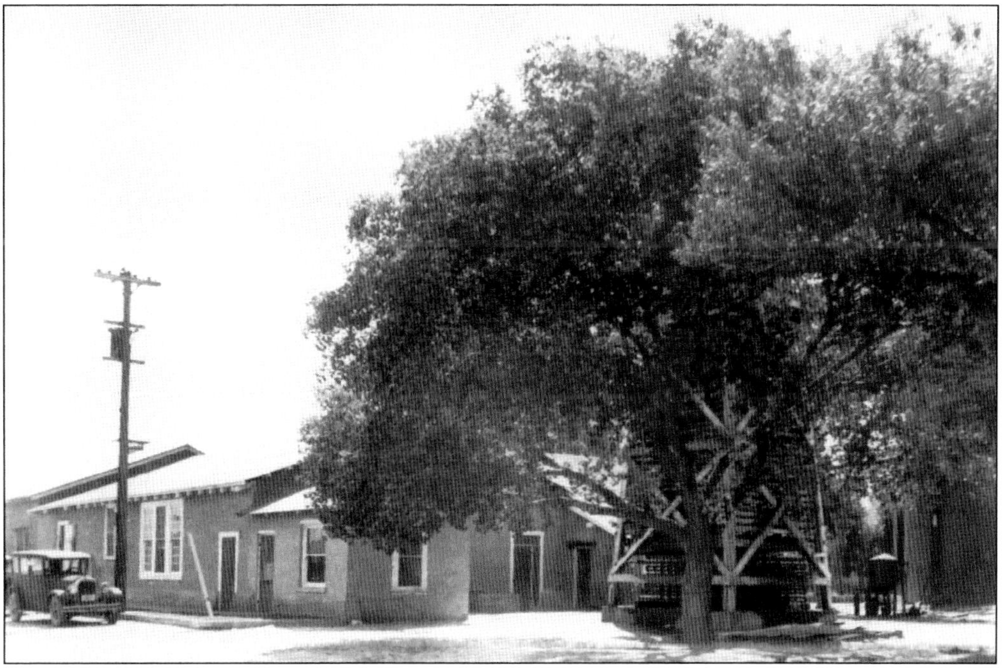

The Willcox Power Company, ice plant, and water works was owned by Ritter and Walker in 1928 and managed by Walter Linam with his office in back. Ownership changed to Arizona Power and Light Company, then Sulphur Springs Valley Electric Cooperative, who sold the water plant in 1947 to John Gung'l and Rex Emrick. The Soil Conservation Service rented the garage portion for an office. (Wanda Linam Perry.)

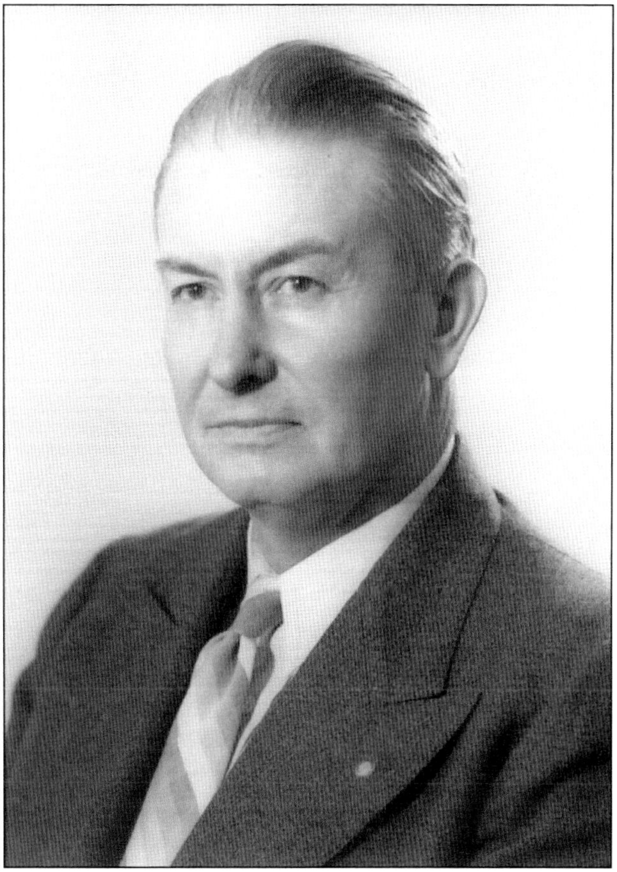

Walter T. Linam's experience in the electrical trade qualified him to help build the new power plant in 1926. During the dust bowl, the power company ran a soup kitchen to feed transients, but demand was so overwhelming that it became too expensive to continue. Linam married Ruth Briscoe in 1929 and served as Worshipful Master of the Masonic lodge. (Willcox Masonic Lodge.)

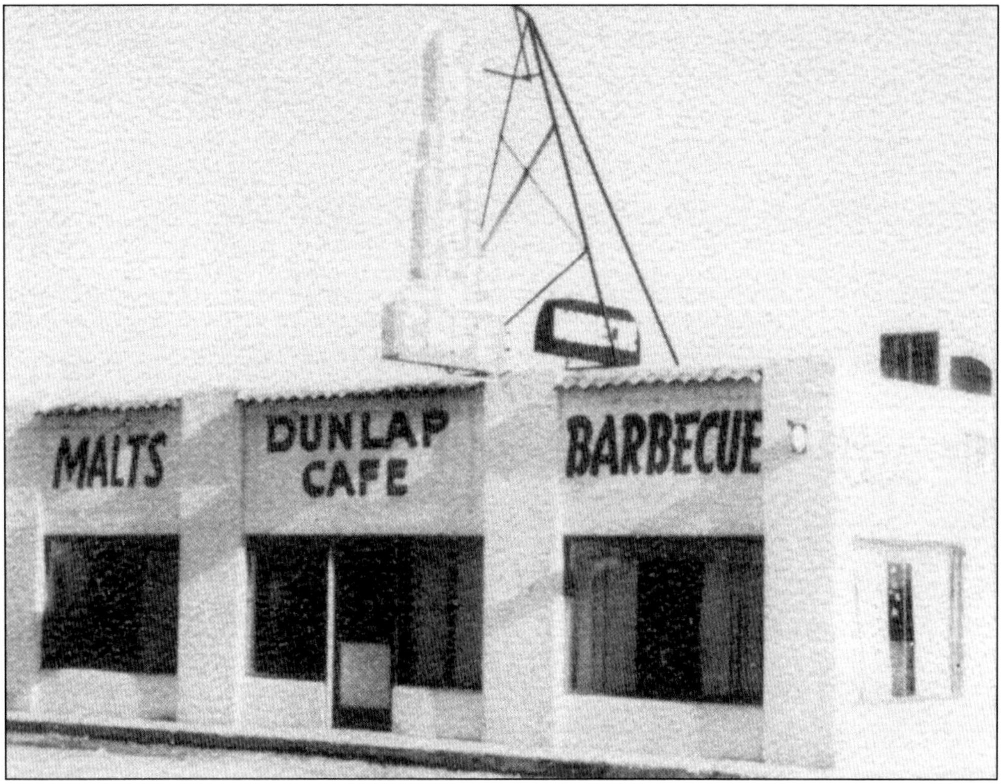

Dunlap's Café was located in front of Dunlap Oil Company on Haskell Avenue at the south entrance to town. Marie Nevins, the manager, was the grandmother of Ted DiBiase, World Wrestling Federation's famous "Million Dollar Man" with the slogan, "Every man has his price." Ted graduated from Willcox High School in 1972. His father was professional wrestler "Iron Mike DiBiase," and his mother, Helen, was a lady wrestler.

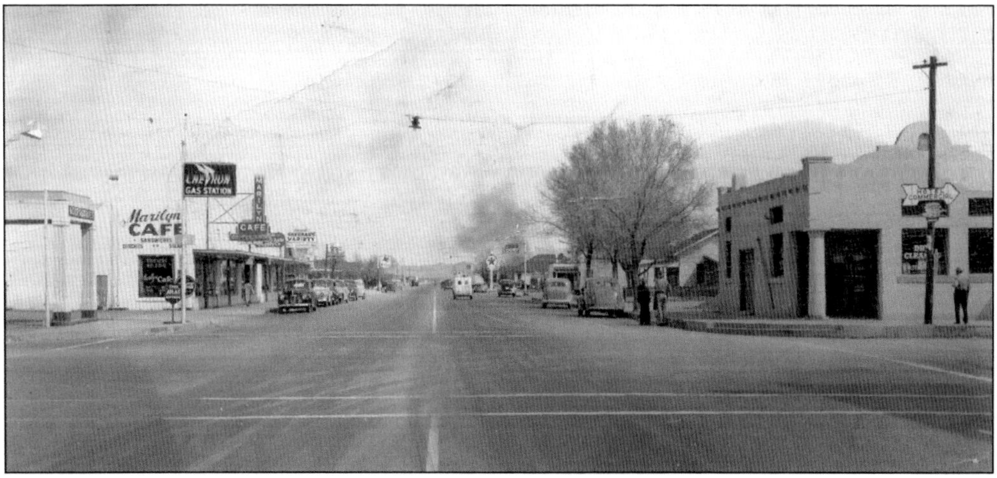

The Marilyn Café, named after the owner's daughter, was located north of Porter Fox's Chevron station on Haskell Avenue. Across the street was the Central Bank Building, which became Frank Tillotson's Cleaners. Shirley Shotton ran her insurance company on that corner for many years. (James and Sandra Thomas.)

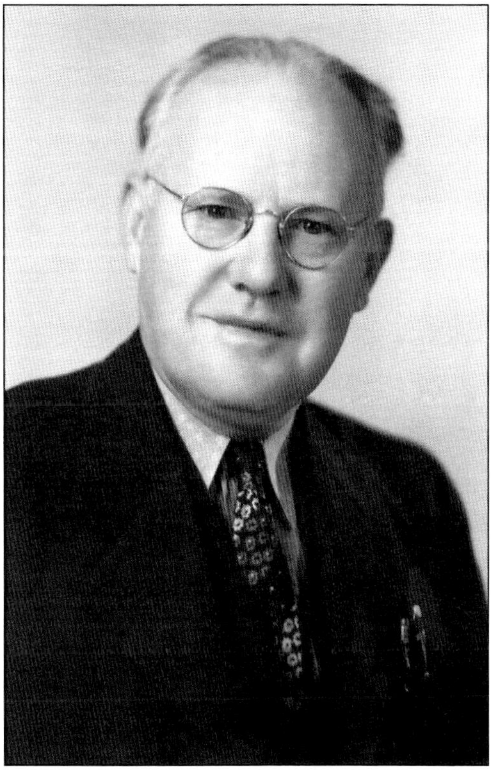

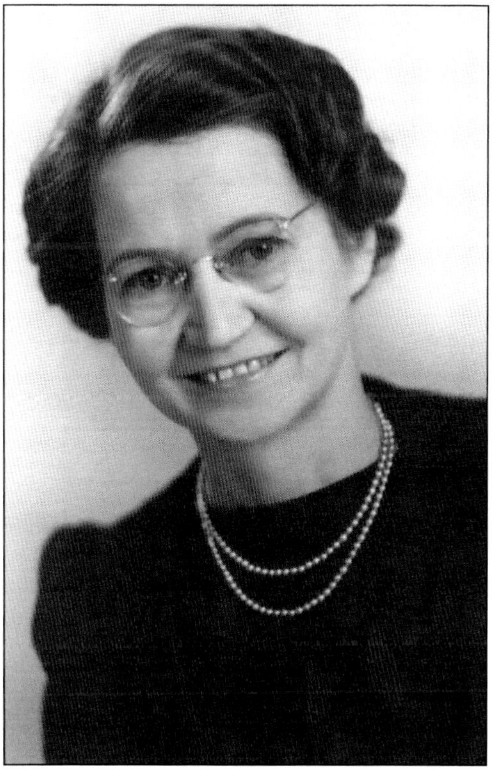

Edward B. McAleb and his wife, Jessie, came to Willcox in 1920. They purchased Frank Rottman's store in 1925 and named it Valley Dry Goods and Grocery. In 1970, they sold the grocery, but they continued to operate the dry goods for several years. Both were active in community affairs. He was a director of the Riggs Bank, elected to the state legislature, president of the Rotary Club, and held offices in the chamber of commerce and Sulphur Springs Valley Electric Cooperative. They had two daughters. Anna Lee married John S. Riggs, and Pauline married Vardon Simmons. (John B. Riggs.)

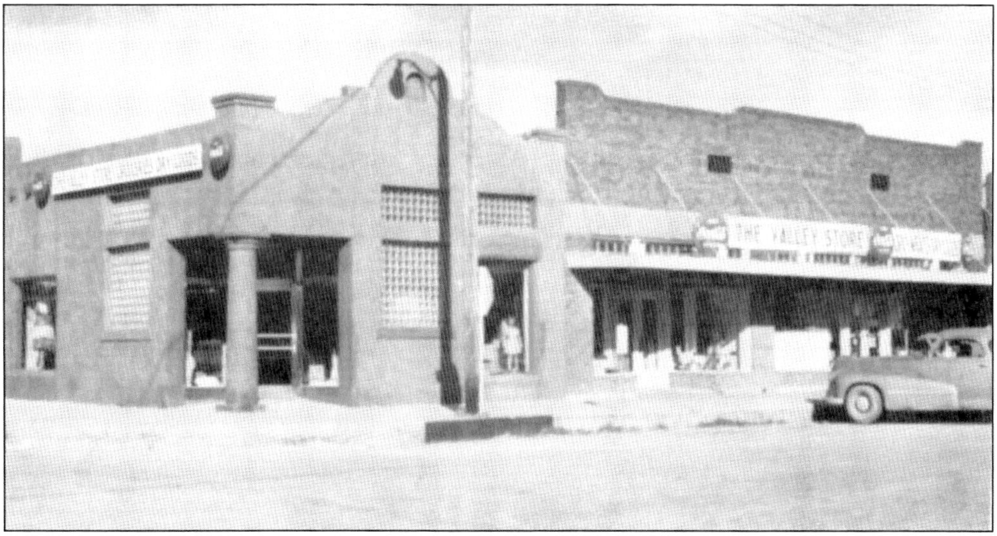

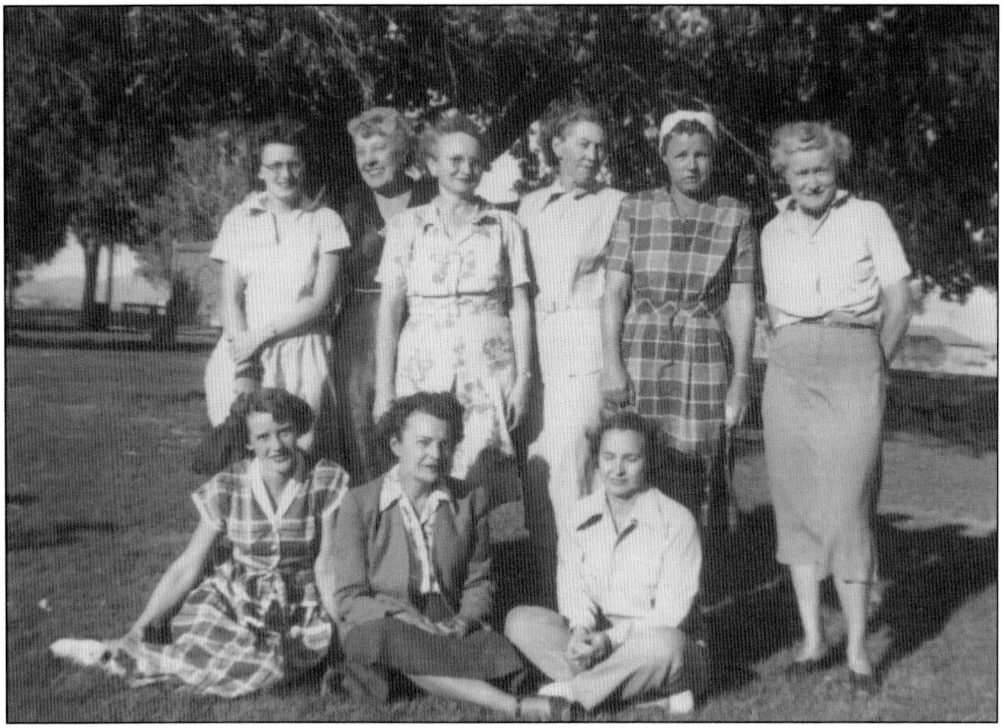

Tenley-Lopez Unit No. 20 won the American Legion's most successful community service project in 1950. For the first time, houses and businesses received a street number. The chamber of commerce had placed street markers at the intersections in 1948. The project committee was, from left to right, Betty Gillette, Emma Stuart, Helen Tschirhart, Ethel Swanner, Elizabeth Ditmars, Erma Ewing, Frances Gordon, Grace Smith, and Betty Lane. Elsie Crookshank is not shown.

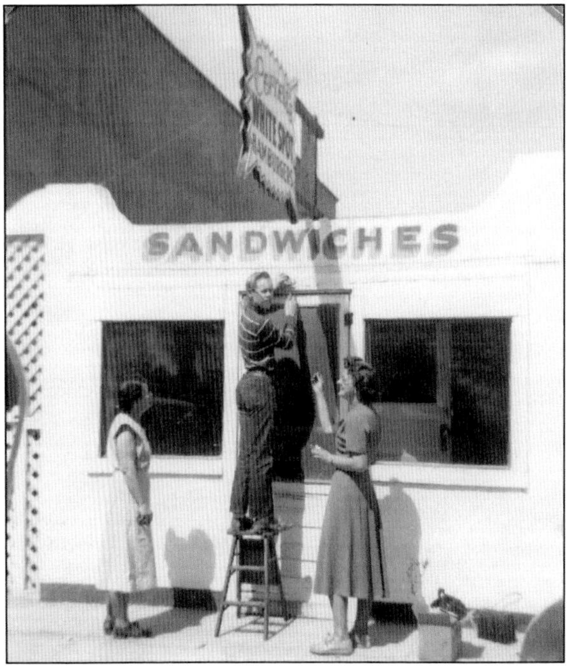

Nora Glenne Cornett (left), who came to Arizona with her husband, Joseph Willard Cornett, in 1927, and Betty Gillette (right) watch as Robert Watson attaches the street number above the door of the White Spot, known for the best hamburgers in town. The White Spot was in this same location on Railroad Avenue from 1940 to 1965. Rodney's is now located there.

The University of Arizona named the Swede Johnson Building after Marvin D. Johnson, son of Wellington and Hazel Johnson. He graduated from Willcox High School in 1946 with a record 17 letters earned for sports. His amazing ability to remember everyone he met helped in his success as vice president of the University of Arizona, as vice president of New Mexico State University, and in public relations for Coors Brewing Company.

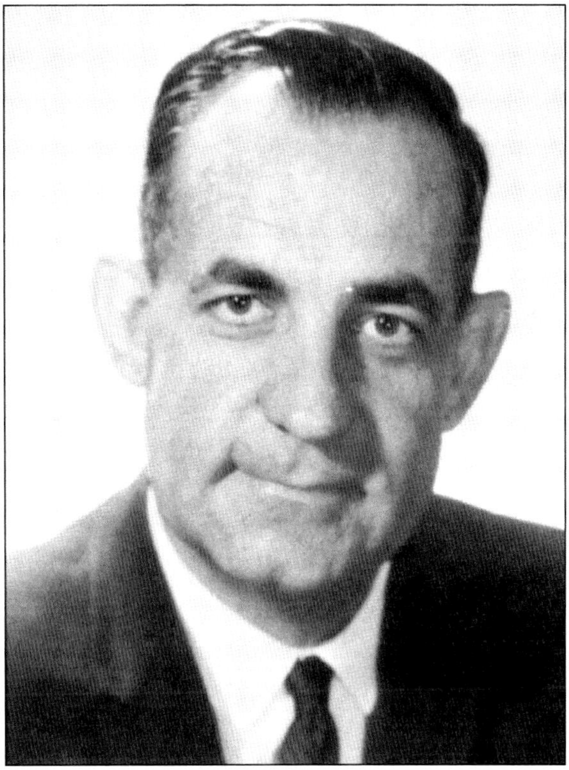

Rex Allen always stopped in at the Toggery to visit his friend Bruce Huffman whenever he was in town. In the 1950s, Rex brought along some friends. From left to right are Tex Williams, Gene Autry, Nudie Cohn (suit designer), Roy Rogers, and Rex Allen. Roy Rogers, when known as Leonard Sly, performed in Willcox with local boy Cactus Mack and the O Bar O Cowboys.

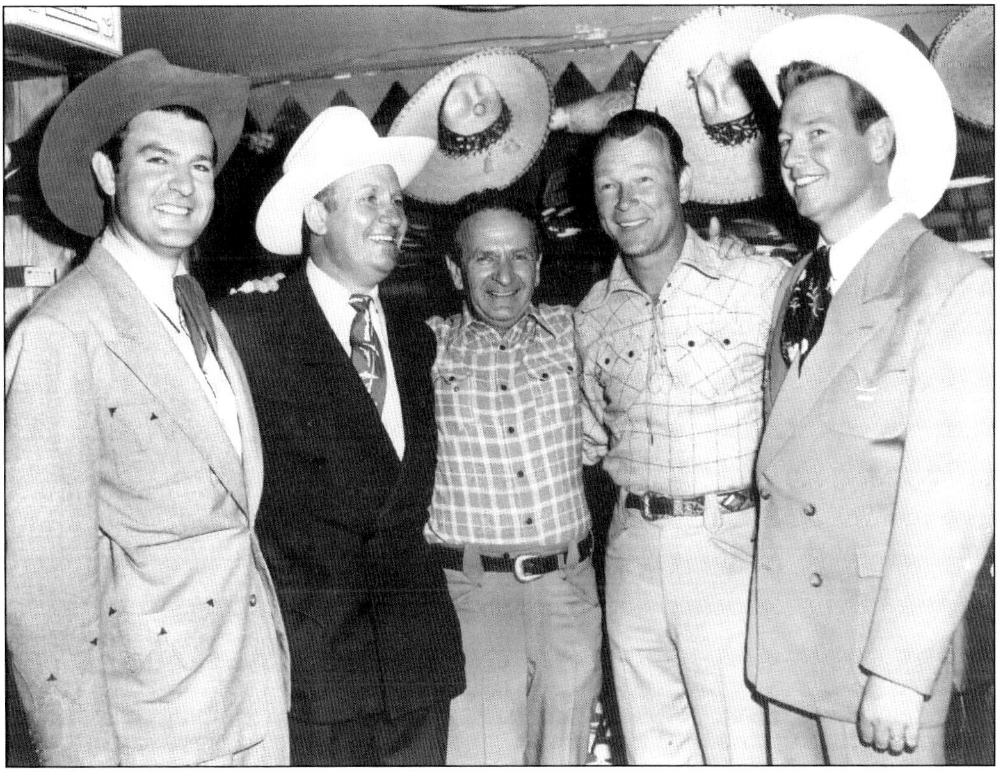

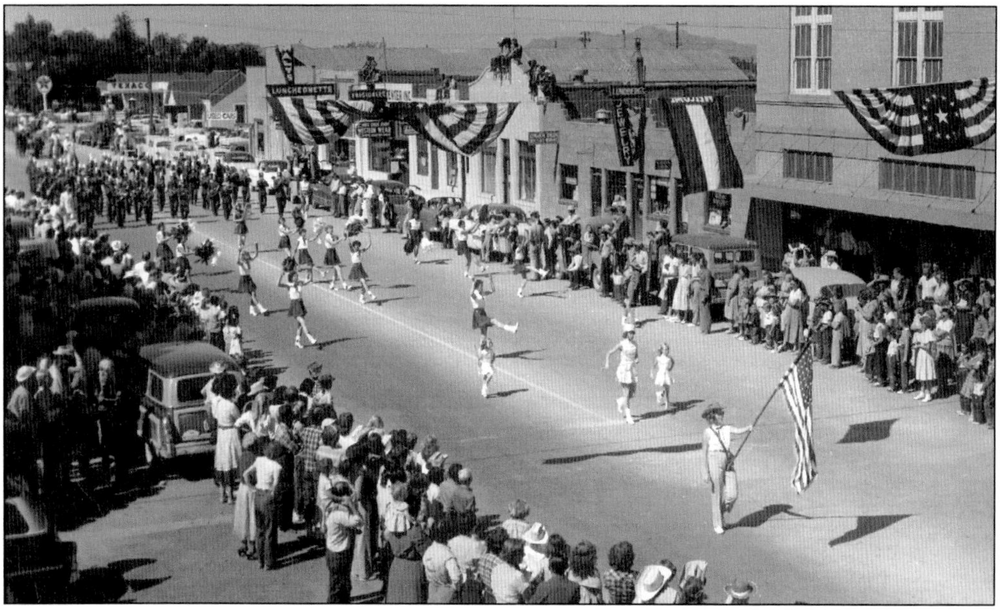

Spectators line Haskell Avenue and the rooftops to enjoy the annual Rex Allen Days parade. It all started in 1952 during an FFA Junior Rodeo when Page Bakarich assigned Bud Flanders to write Rex Allen for donation of a prize for all-around cowboy. He donated a saddle and silver belt buckle and offered to do a free performance during halftime and at a dance that night.

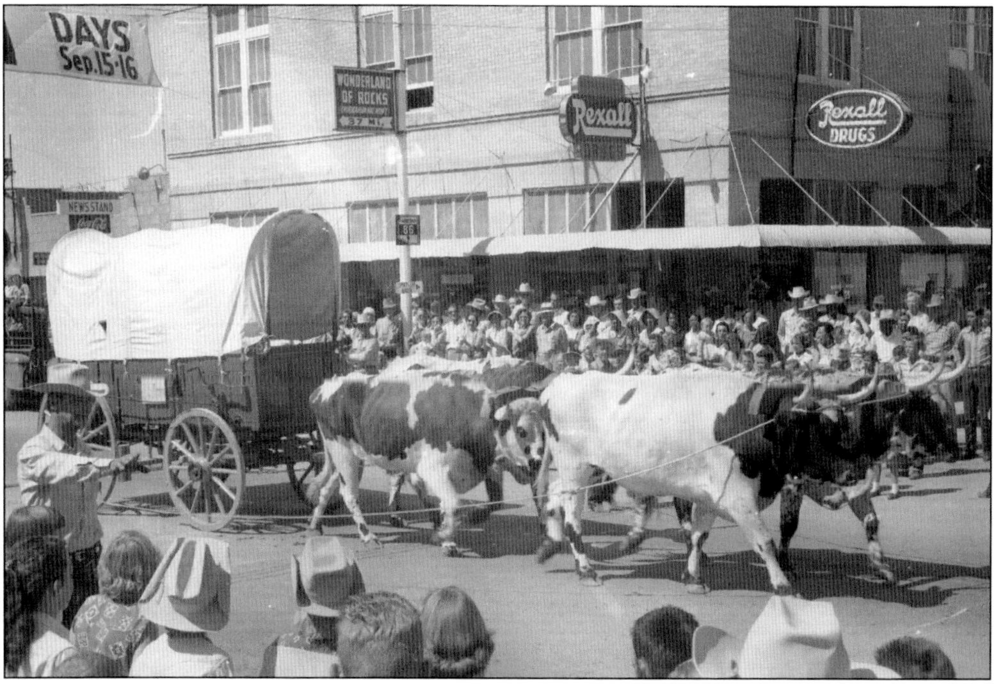

Dee Jernigan's covered wagon, pulled by Texas longhorns, is the one he used when he came from New Mexico to Stockton Pass with his herd in 1934. Lee Jernigan, in a white hat in the center, is helping control the animals with the rope as they proceed down Haskell Avenue during a 1950s Rex Allen Days parade. (Lee and Marte Jernigan.)

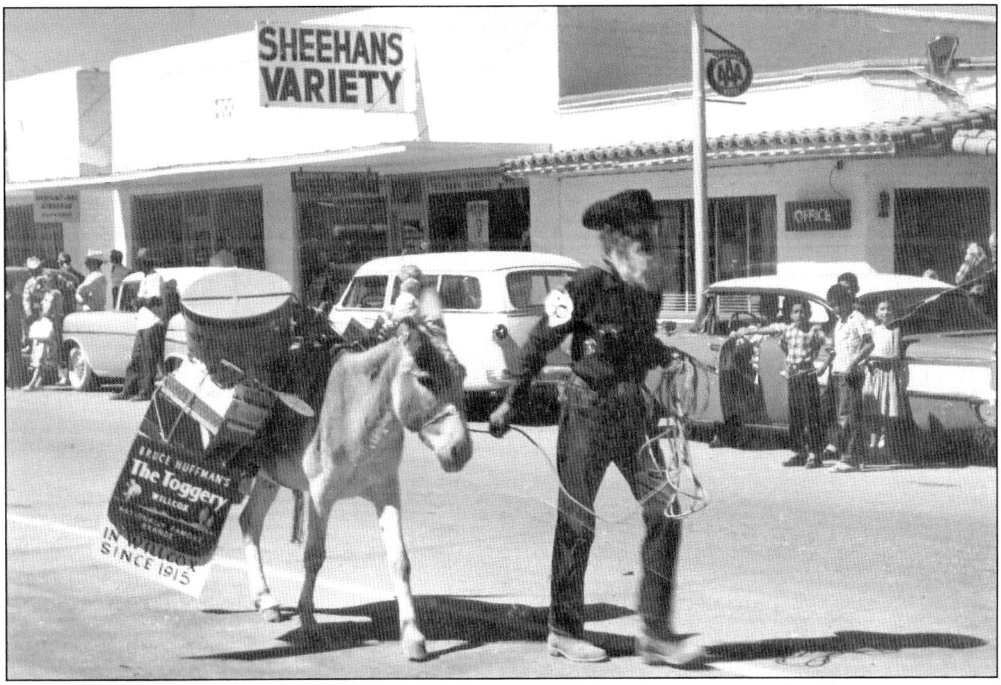

Sheehan's Variety, a five-and-dime store, opened November 30, 1940, in a building constructed by Martin Gentry on north Haskell Avenue. Joseph Sheehan's wife, Louise, was the daughter of A. E. Keeth, justice of the peace and owner of the bakery. Huffman's Toggery always had an entry in the Rex Allen Days parade. This little donkey is loaded with hat and shoe boxes.

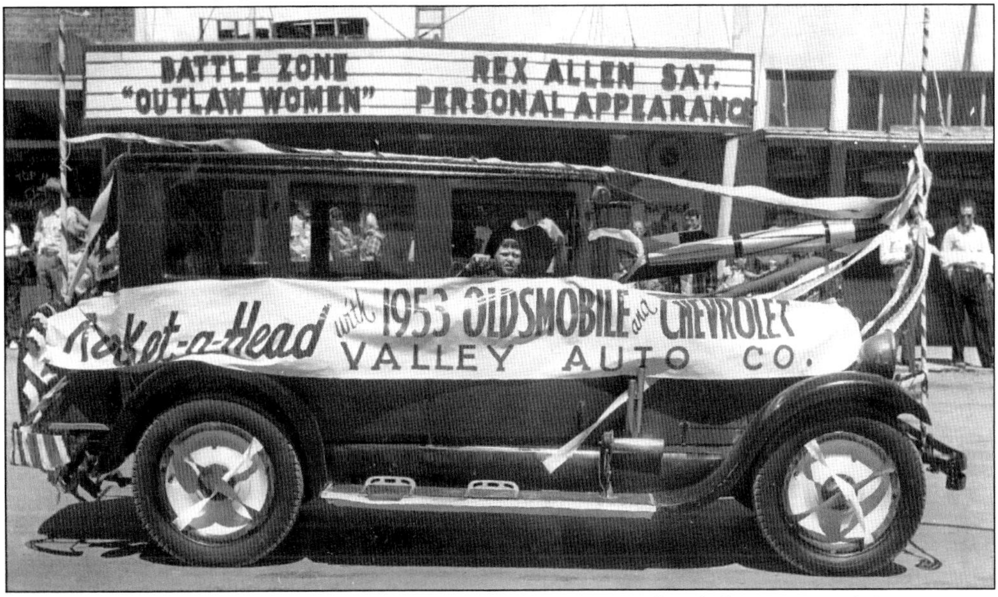

Betty Briscoe peers from a vintage auto with a sign promoting her father's automobile company, which that year featured a Super 88 Chevrolet with a Rocket engine, pedal ease power brakes, Frigidaire air-conditioning, and the autronic eye. During one of Rex Allen's personal appearances at Rex Allen Days, a nine-year-old local girl, Tanya Tucker, performed with him on stage. (Betty Kowalczyk.)

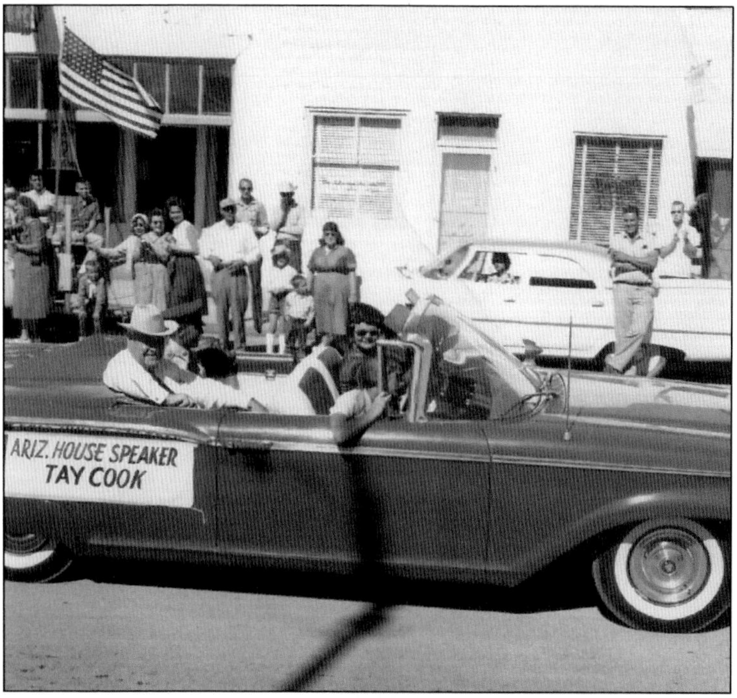

Politicians are a big part of the Rex Allen Days parades. From 1949 to 1966, W. L. "Tay" Cook served 10 terms in the Arizona House of Representatives, including three as Speaker of the House. He was the son of local pioneers James B. and Rebecca Cook, who operated the OT Ranch. He and his brother Mark operated the Cook Cattle Company on the old MOK Ranch.

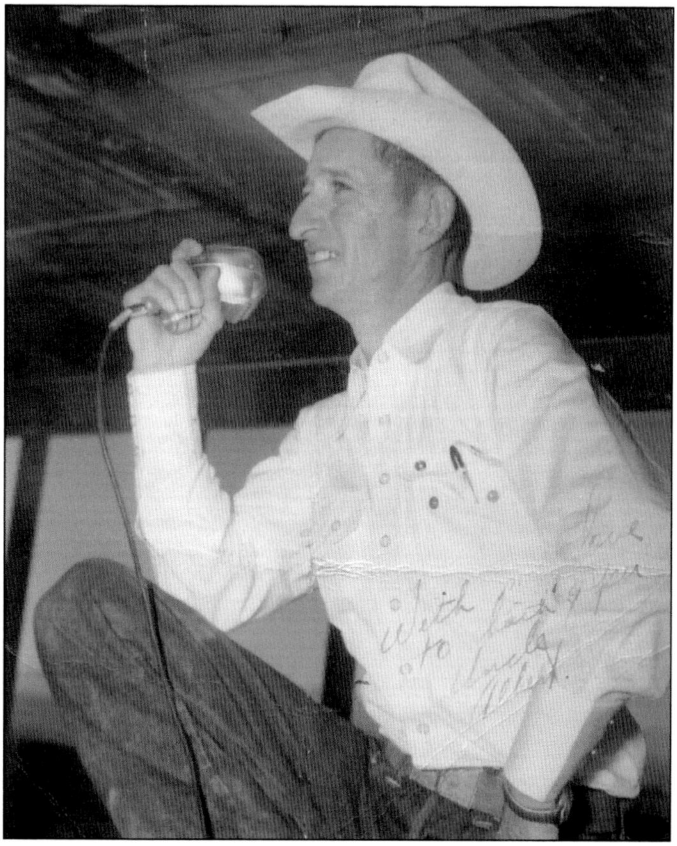

Along with the stage show, dances, and golf tournament, Rex Allen Days always includes a two-day professional rodeo. Albert Armagnac was the rodeo announcer for many years. His family nickname was "Yaqui" because his hair stood up like a Native American's. A longtime dedicated member of the Elks Club, their newsletter the *Yak* was named after him.

Ten

Willcox Today

As Willcox continues to grow, it strives to maintain the small-town atmosphere with friendly western hospitality. Beautiful weather, accessibility to Interstate 10, and the railroad are benefits Willcox can offer to new businesses. A low crime rate and good schools make Willcox an excellent home for young families. As a tourist destination, there are museums that depict Willcox's rich historical heritage, seasonal U-pick farms, and annual events such as Rex Allen Days and the Wings Over Willcox birding festival. As gateway to the "golden circle of Cochise," Willcox Visitors Center, operated by the Willcox Chamber of Commerce and Agriculture (www.willcoxchamber.com), provides information and access to interesting destinations throughout the county such as Cochise Stronghold and the Wonderland of Rocks.

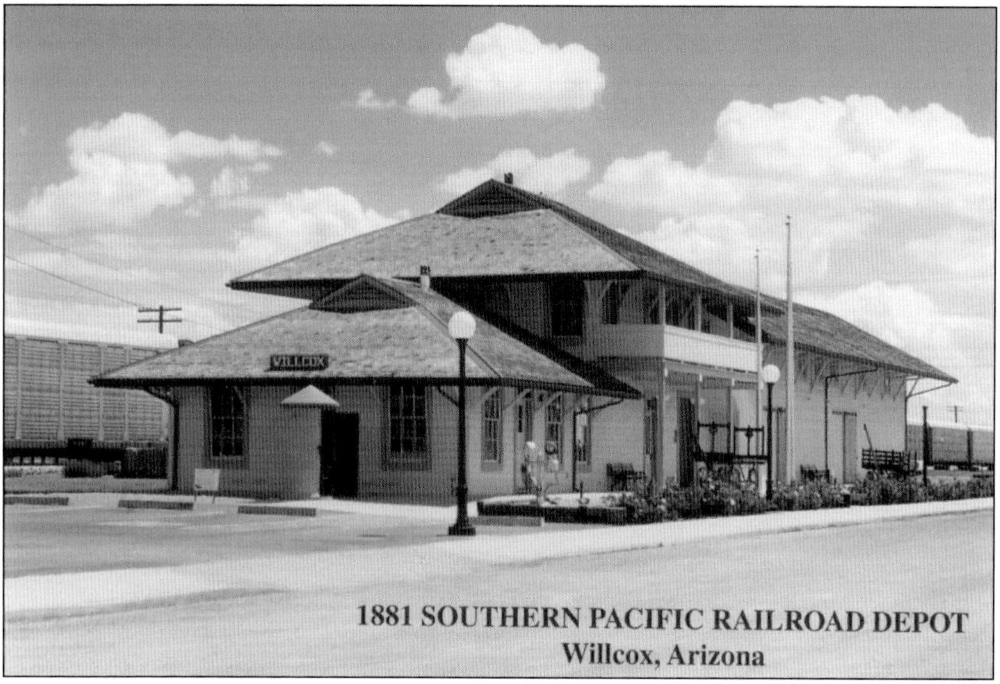

City hall is located in the 1881 Southern Pacific Railroad Depot. Frances Bliss photographed the site on the day of the renovation dedication, September 16, 1998. Southern Pacific agreed to a special one-time stop in Willcox as 28 people, in 1880s period costume, rode the train from Benson to Willcox. Frances and her husband, Robert M. Bliss, donated a significant portion of the money needed for the restoration.

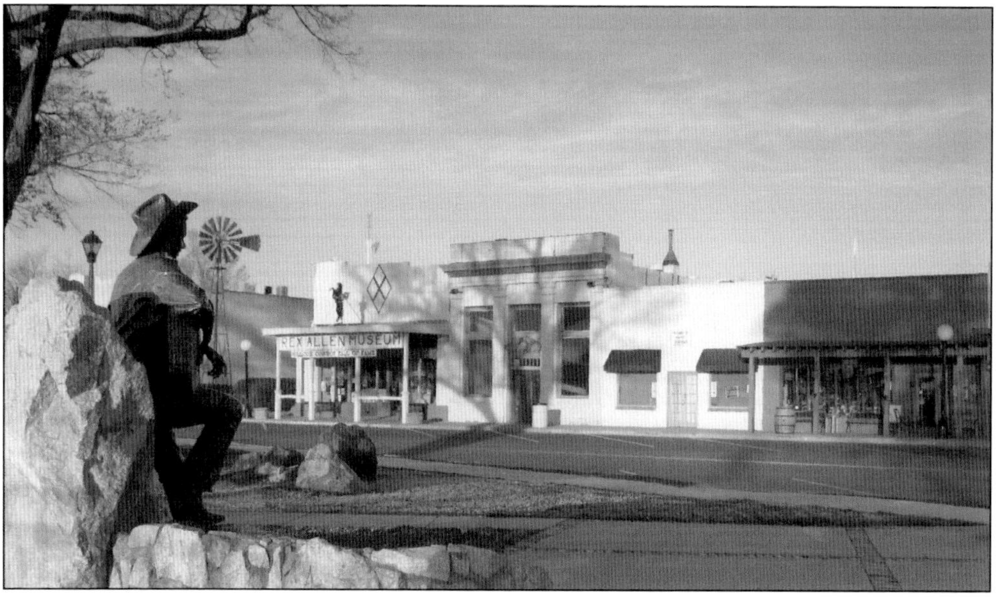

Railroad Avenue, with its original buildings, brings Willcox's history to life. Tourists enjoy the Rex Allen Arizona Cowboy Museum and Cowboy Hall of Fame (left) and the new Friends of Marty Robbins Museum. The bronze statue of Rex Allen by artist Buck McCain stands over the walkway of local cattle brands in the newly redesigned Railroad Park. (Peta-Anne Tenney.)

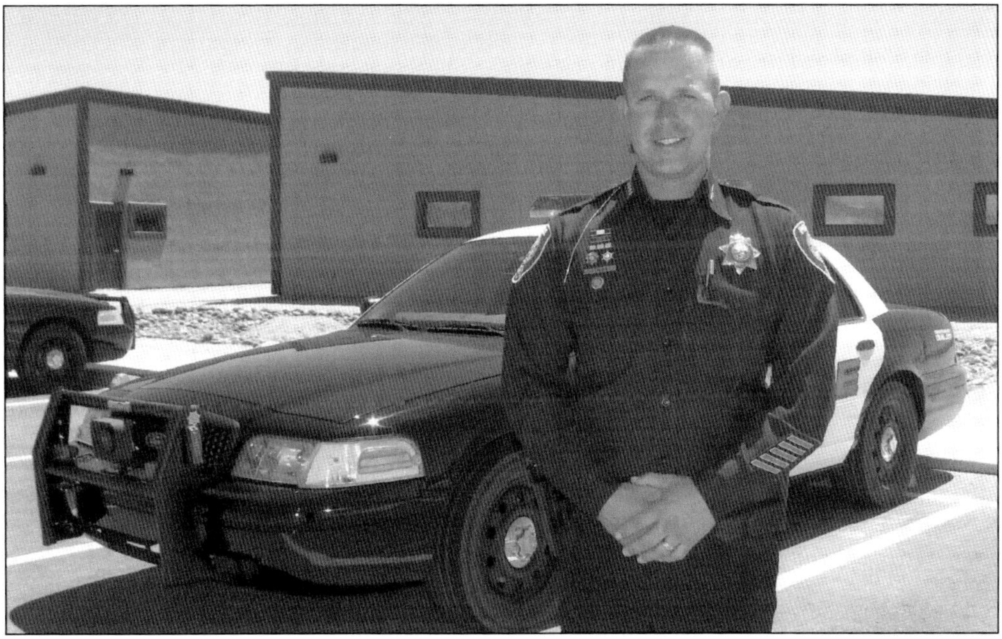

The Justice Center has recently been constructed on Rex Allen Drive and is still receiving its finishing touches. It is the new location of the Department of Public Safety, Development Services, and council chambers. Jake Weaver, the chief of police, graduated from Willcox High School. (Peta-Anne Tenney.)

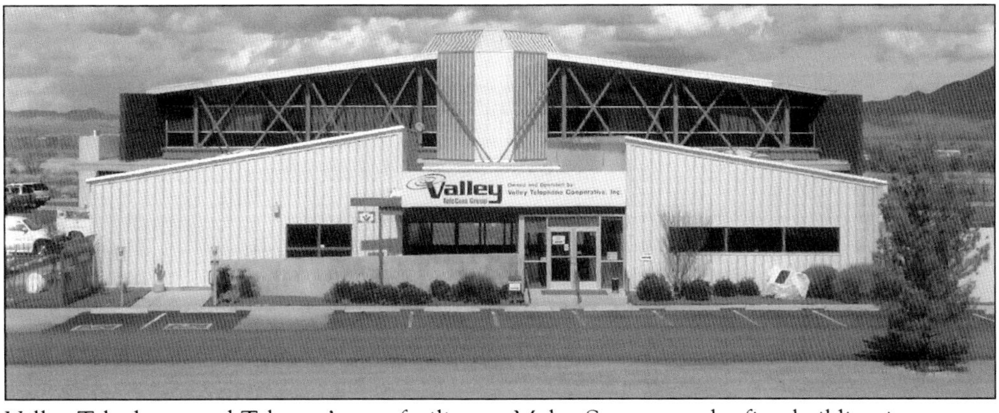

Valley Telephone and Telecom's new facility on Maley Street was the first building in town to have an elevator. Valley Telephone Cooperative was organized in 1962 to provide telephone service to outlying areas not covered by Mountain Bell. Under general manager Lyle Donovan in 1975, subscribers were being upgraded from party lines to private lines. The cooperative now ranks near the top in number of area employees.

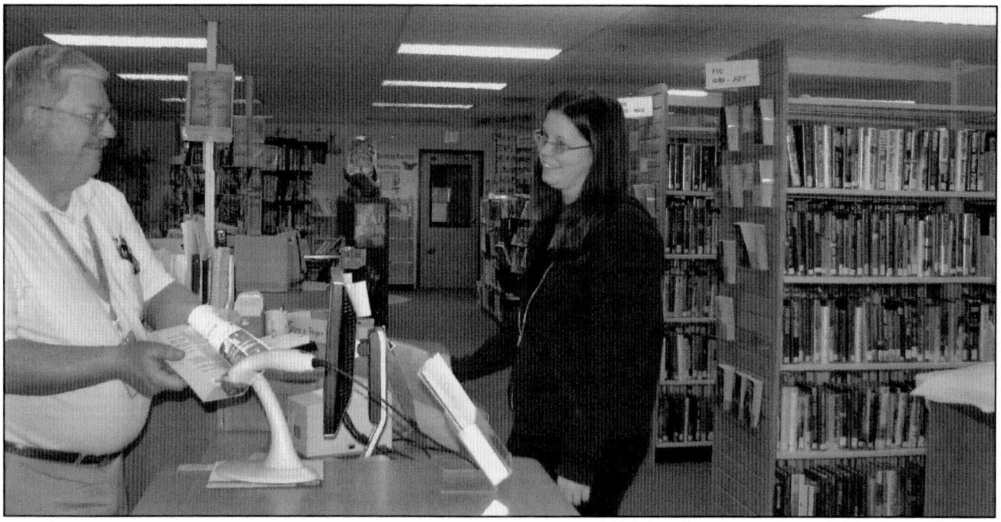

Willcox is especially proud of the Elsie S. Hogan Community Library and the services it provides to those of all ages. The library moved to this new building in 1998. This year, the library will be redesigned and expanded into the rooms the court previously occupied. The teen program publishes its own magazine, called *Tag*. Pictured are Tom Miner, librarian, and Donna Boehm, staff.

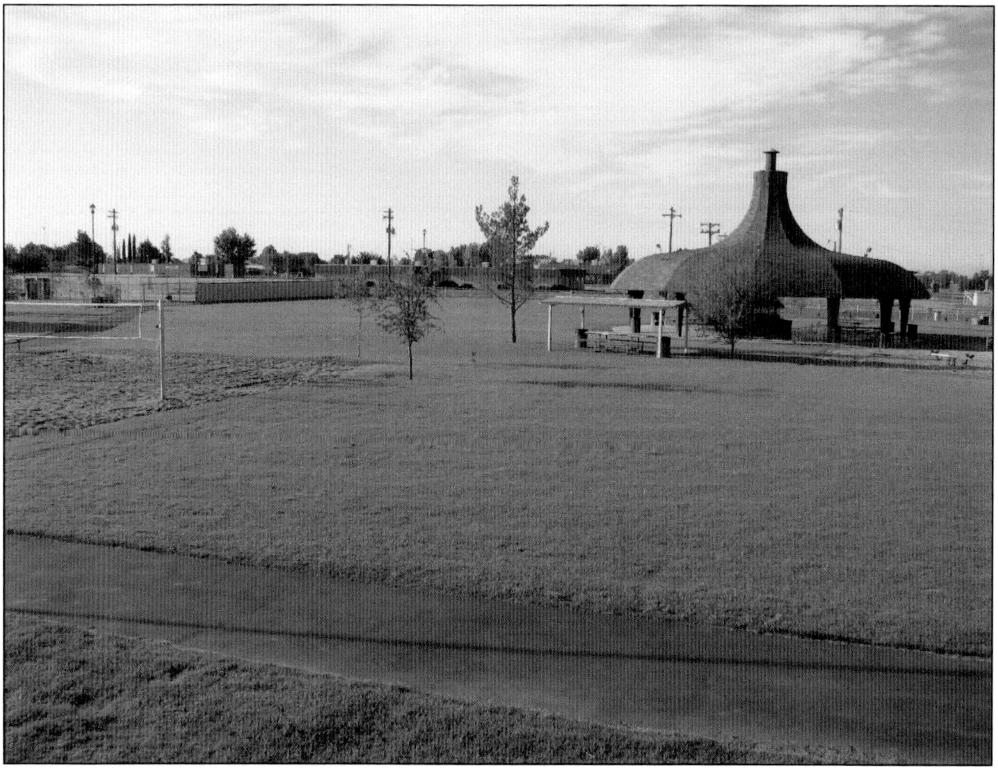

Keillor Park was named after Mayor Matt Keillor. Newly redesigned with the help of the Parks and Recreation Commission, it includes an Olympic-size swimming pool, baseball and soccer fields, a tennis court, bicycle and jogging paths, picnic facilities, and a playground. (Peta-Anne Tenney.)

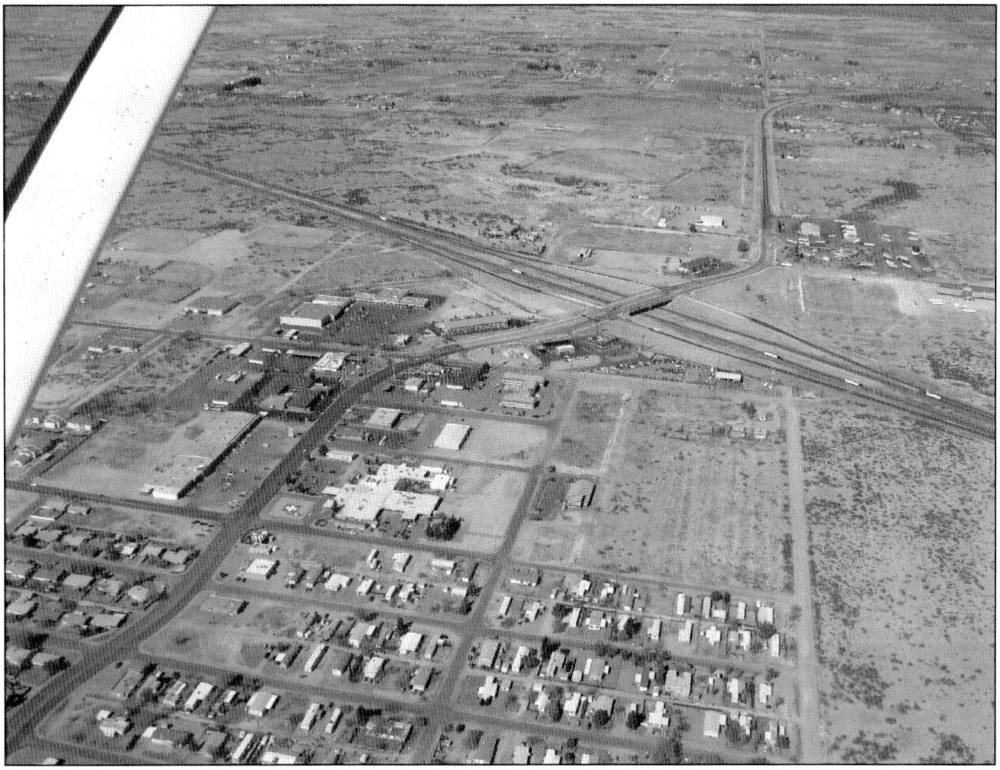

An aerial overview of the exit 340 overpass on Interstate 10 shows the amazing development of this business district. Five motels and T. A. and DOC's Truck Stops all offer every kind of accommodation and meets all the needs of travelers. Two shopping centers, the hospital and several clinics, and restaurants and fast food businesses are also located in this area. (Peta-Anne Tenney.)

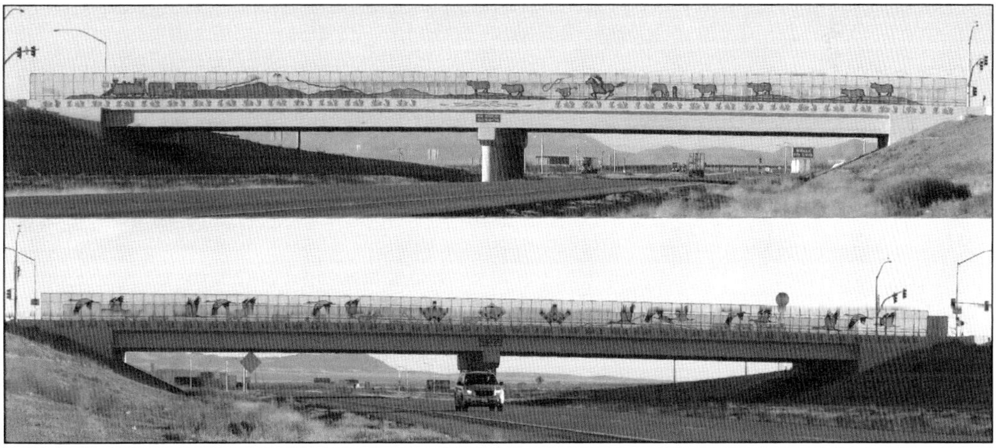

The unique two-sided designed overpass at the 340 Milepost on Interstate 10 was created with the help of a committee of local Willcox citizens. Heading east, sandhill cranes fly over the traffic with Chiricahua Apache Gan dancer headdresses in the middle. Heading west, a railroad train chugs along in front of the Dos Cabezas Mountains as cattle roam and a cowboy ropes a steer. (Peta-Anne Tenney.)

About Sulphur Springs Valley Historical Society

Founded in 1974 to preserve the heritage of Willcox and the surrounding area, the Sulphur Springs Valley Historical Society was successful in getting the original business buildings and homes on the National Register of Historic Places and creating a historic district. They began to document the history of these buildings and applied for grants and raised funds to help in their preservation. After renovating the 1880s Schwertner family home and the Southern Pacific Railroad Depot, the society opened the Chiricahua Regional Museum and Research Center in 1999. Located at 127 East Maley Street, the museum features the history of the Chiricahua Apache people, plus ranching, mining, and the history of Willcox and the surrounding towns. The research center archives include books, photographs, newspapers dating from 1894, family histories, displays from the Toggery store, and the Judge Edward R. Monk family collection.

Operated completely by volunteers with funding by donations and memberships, the museum is open Monday through Saturday. The research library is open Wednesdays and Thursdays and by appointment. For more information, call the museum at (520) 384-3971.

About the Authors

Kathy Klump, a third-generation Arizonan, was selected as an Arizona Culture Keeper in 2008. She is president of the Sulphur Springs Valley Historical Society and librarian for the Chiricahua Regional Museum and Research Center. She cofounded the Friends of Elsie S. Hogan Community Library. Her husband is a cattle rancher whose family came to the Willcox area in 1904. They are the parents of six children.

Australian-born Peta-Anne Tenney has lived in Willcox since 1985. In Australia, she was known nationwide for her equine photography. She and her husband, Todd, started the Paint Horse Association of Australia and published the *Australian Western Horsemen* magazine. She was inducted into the Australian Paint Horse Hall of Fame in 2008. She and Todd have two sons.

BIBLIOGRAPHY

Bailey, Lynn R., and Don Chaput. *Cochise County Stalwarts: A Who's Who of the Territorial Years.* Tucson, AZ: Westernlore Press, 2000.

Bliss, Bob. *Sufferin' Springs Valley: Early Southeast Arizona as I Lived It.* Scottsdale, AZ: self-published, 1980.

O'Neal, Bill. *The Arizona Rangers.* Austin, TX: Eakin Press, 1987.

Roberts, Clyde S., ed. *Willcox, Hub of Northern Cochise County, the View to 1975.* Willcox, AZ: *Arizona Range News*, 1975.

Schultz, Vernon B. *Southwestern Town: The Story of Willcox, Arizona.* Tucson, AZ: University of Arizona, 1964.

Theobald, John and Lillian. *Arizona Territory Post Offices and Postmasters.* Phoenix, AZ: Arizona Historical Foundation, 1961.

———. *Wells Fargo in Arizona Territory.* Tempe, AZ: Arizona Historical Foundation, 1978.

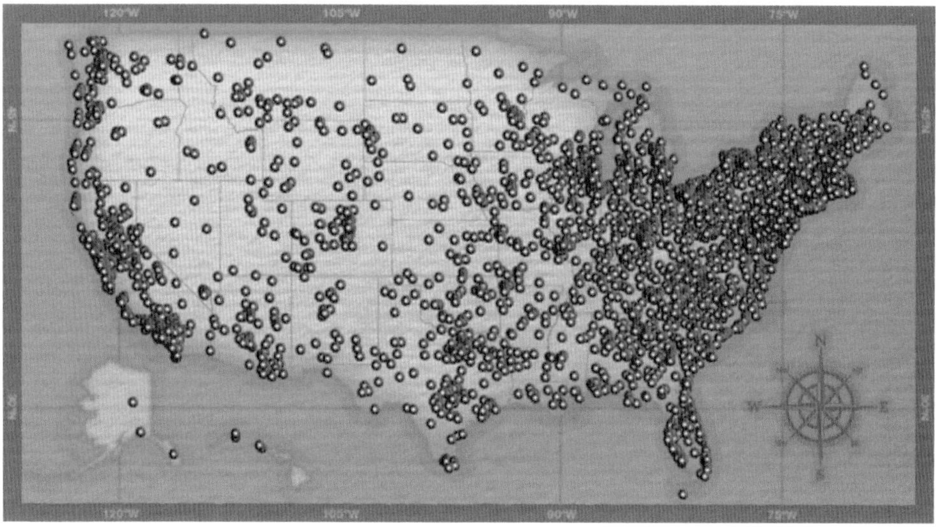